UNIVERSITY OF WESTMINSTER

KU-249-876

Changing Fashion

ONE WEEK LOAN

26 0171816 4

W 746.92 LYN

Dress, Body, Culture

Series Editor: **Joanne B. Eicher,** *Regents' Professor, University of Minnesota*

Advisory Board:
Ruth Barnes, *Ashmolean Museum, University of Oxford*
James Hall, *University of Illinois at Chicago*
Ted Polhemus, *Curator, 'Street Style' Exhibition, Victoria and Albert Museum*
Griselda Pollock, *University of Leeds*
Valerie Steele, *The Museum at the Fashion Institute of Technology*
Lou Taylor, *University of Brighton*
John Wright, *University of Minnesota*

Books in this provocative series seek to articulate the connections between culture and dress which is defined here in its broadest possible sense as any modification or supplement to the body. Interdisciplinary in approach, the series highlights the dialogue between identity and dress, cosmetics, coiffure and body alternations as manifested in practices as varied as plastic surgery, tattooing, and ritual scarification. The series aims, in particular, to analyze the meaning of dress in relation to popular culture and gender issues and will include works grounded in anthropology, sociology, history, art history, literature and folklore.

ISSN: 1360-466X

Recently published titles in the series

Brian J. McVeigh, *Wearing Ideology: The Uniformity of Self-Presentation in Japan*
Shaun Cole, *Don We Now Our Gay Apparel: Gay Men's Dress in the Twentieth Century*
Kate Ince, *Orlan: Millennial Female*
Nicola White and Ian Griffiths, *The Fashion Business: Theory, Practice, Image*
Ali Guy, Eileen Green and Maura Banim, *Through the Wardrobe: Women's Relationships with their Clothes*
Linda B. Arthur, *Undressing Religion: Commitment and Conversion from a Cross-Cultural Perspective*
William J.F. Keenan, *Dressed to Impress: Looking the Part*
Joanne Entwistle and Elizabeth Wilson, *Body Dressing*
Leigh Summers, *Bound to Please: A History of the Victorian Corset*
Paul Hodkinson, *Goth: Identity, Style and Subculture*
Michael Carter, *Fashion Classics from Carlyle to Barthes*
Sandra Niessen, Ann Marie Leshkowich and Carla Jones, *Re-Orienting Fashion: The Globalization of Asian Dress*
Kim K. P. Johnson, Susan J. Torntore and Joanne B. Eicher, *Fashion Foundations: Early Writings on Fashion and Dress*
Helen Bradley Foster and Donald Clay Johnson, *Wedding Dress Across Cultures*
Eugenia Paulicelli, *Fashion under Fascism: Beyond the Black Shirt*
Charlotte Suthrell, *Unzipping Gender: Sex, Cross-Dressing and Culture*
Yuniya Kawamura, *The Japanese Revolution in Paris Fashion*
Ruth Barcan, *Nudity: A Cultural Anatomy*
Samantha Holland, *Alternative Femininities: Body, Age and Identity*
Alexandra Palmer and Hazel Clark, *Old Clothes, New Looks: Second Hand Fashion*
Yuniya Kawamura, *Fashion-ology: An Introduction to Fashion Studies*
Regina A. Root, *The Latin American Fashion Reader*
Linda Welters and Patricia A. Cunningham, *Twentieth-Century American Fashion*
Jennifer Craik, *Uniforms Exposed: From Conformity to Transgression*
Alison L. Goodrum, *The National Fabric: Fashion, Britishness, Globalization*

Changing Fashion

A Critical Introduction to Trend Analysis and Meaning

Annette Lynch
and Mitchell D. Strauss

Oxford • New York

W 746.92 LYN

English edition
First published in 2007 by
Berg
Editorial offices:
First Floor, Angel Court, 81 St Clements Street, Oxford OX4 1AW, UK
175 Fifth Avenue, New York, NY 10010, USA

© Annette Lynch and Mitchell D. Strauss 2007

All rights reserved.
No part of this publication may be reproduced in any form
or by any means without the written permission of
Berg.

Berg is the imprint of Oxford International Publishers Ltd.

Library of Congress Cataloging-in-Publication Data
Lynch, Annette (Annette Ferne)
   Changing fashion : a critical introduction to trend analysis and meaning /
Annette Lynch and Mitchell D. Strauss.
      p. cm.
   Includes bibliographical references and index.
   ISBN-13: 978-1-84520-389-4 (cloth : alk. paper)
   ISBN-10: 1-84520-389-5 (cloth : alk. paper)
   ISBN-13: 978-1-84520-390-0 (pbk. : alk. paper)
   ISBN-10: 1-84520-390-9 (pbk. : alk. paper)   1. Fashion—United States—
History. 2. Fashion design—United States—History.   3. Popular culture—United
States—History. I. Strauss, Mitchell D. II. Title.

   TT504.4.L95 2007
   746.9'20973—dc22   2007020055

British Library Cataloguing-in-Publication Data
A catalogue record for this book is available from the British Library.

ISBN-13 978 1 84520 389 4 (Cloth)
        978 1 84520 390 0 (Paper)

Typeset by Avocet Typeset, Chilton, Aylesbury, Bucks
Printed in Great Britain by the MPG Books Group, Bodmin and King's Lynn.

www.bergpublishers.com

We wish to dedicate this book with love and affection to our children, who bring meaning to our lives. They are Jessica Lynn, Mary Katherine, Sally Catherine, Madeleine Louise, Benjamin Guy, and Parker Van Dyke.

Contents

Acknowledgements

We would like to acknowledge Joanne B. Eicher for editorial support and guidance in the writing of this manuscript. The support of Tristan Palmer and Hannah Shakespeare at Berg Publishers also helped us to move this volume from concept to finished draft. The book was further enhanced by the comments we received as a part of the blind review process. The breadth and quality of the fashion change case study material throughout the chapters is due to a large extent from contributions of fashion editorial writers at the New York Times, most notably Guy Trebay and Rob Walker. Finally, we would like to thank the College of Social and Behavior Sciences at the University of Northern Iowa for financial assistance in obtaining research sources and assisting with cover art costs.

1

Fashion Change in the New Millennium: An Introduction

Raised as a Roman Catholic, Madonna adopted the Hebrew name Esther . . . Madonna's interest in Kabbalah has been covered intensely by the media. She gained a surge in sales of Kabbalah red string bracelets, a red string or stone-studded bracelet used to ward of evil. She reportedly refused to work on Friday night and Saturday, the Jewish Sabbath. Awareness of the Kabbalah Center has grown considerably.

The cabala red string is one way she demonstrates it in public. It is considered a talisman to ward away negative influences. In some circles, it appears not to have an effect.

Madonna has been criticized for turning a serious, multi-thousand year old religious study into entertainment. But she claims she has chosen her new faith and is serious about its study. The Jewish Kabbalah has been practiced mainly by male rabbis in secret for centuries. Even the average Jew is unfamiliar with this mystical study of the religion. Madonna helped bring Kabbala into mainstream awareness.

Music Entertainment Magazine, September 2004

Fashion in the new millennium is brash, and doesn't stop to ask permission. The domain of fashion's influence ignores taboos, traditions and the lines of sacred space. Our lives, our intellect, our religion, our creativity, our sexuality are all the vocabulary of fashion and are open for renegotiation and representation. Yet we view fashion as suspect, insubstantial, the stuff of dreams not reality. We want it, yet we don't. We may not choose to wear it, but we still watch it, and we pay attention. We are seduced in spite of ourselves. It is out of these uneasy relationships that fashion change emerges, and understanding it becomes a route for understanding human life in the twenty-first century. We open this book exploring eight key contemporary themes that make fashion change hit with such impact in the new millennium.

1 Surfing the Web . . . the World at our Fingertips. Fashion depends for its power on communication. Fashion change can only occur if information is shared, the more information, the more dramatic the impact of fashion on human behavior. One of the most significant reasons for the democratization of fashion in the twenty-first century focuses on the rapid modes of communication now available. In order to best understand the power of current fashion communication technology, a review of the past may be helpful.

Fashionable clothing behavior emerged in Italy during the birth of the first major European cities of Milan, Florence, and Venice in the 1400s. Some of the first fashion trends included body revealing styles such as a shortened men's doublet, and a low neck gown for women (Steele, 1988). The fashion capital focused on the court of Burgundy in the fifteenth century, then following power and influence, moved to Spain, a country newly wealthy from New World monies. Fashion leadership moved to France during the era of Louis XIV, culminating in the domination of French fashion during the eighteenth century (Russell, 1983).

Fashionable dress was used in this early period to differentiate class and access to power, with changes most commonly marked in fabrications and trims, rather than overt style changes. Information about fashion trends was first communicated through personal contact with the aristocracy, with in some cases fashion being dictated by the ruling court. Fashion changes were initially slowed by Louis XIV, who strictly controlled court styles during his reign. With the aging of Louis XIV, and the proliferation of tailors, dress-makers, and milliners headquartered in Paris, control eased giving rise to more rapid fashion change (Russell, 1983).

Access to fashion information greatly increased in 1715 with the reign of Louis XV. The tight rules controlling social life during the previous century were loosened significantly, and a more socially open, modern, urban culture developed in which classes began to intermix and mingle. Fashion, in its more modern guise, emerged during this time period as lower and middle classes were exposed to the fashion of the wealthy through integrated social events, and second-hand clothing markets featuring fashions of the newly deceased. Fashion dolls wearing the newest fashion looks were used to send trend information to dressmakers throughout the world, with some fashion journalism emerging at the end of the century (Steele, 1988).

French fashion trends moved into the United States in the nineteenth century with the emergence of what Banner (1983) referred to as commercial beauty culture. With the invention of the lock-stitch sewing machine in the 1840s, American entrepreneurial spirit ignited with the growth of the garment industry being characterized by Von Drehle as 'sudden and wild, like an economic tornado' (2003: 39). Early American fashion entrepreneurs included immigrants skilled in the needle trades, department store owners, dressmakers, magazine publishers, and cosmeticians, all of whom help to disseminate fashion information to a wide range of classes and regions across the United States. With this democratization of fashion information, diverse classes and ethnicities began to affect fashion behavior, as well as the dominant upper class.

With dissemination of fashion information through written sources, beginning with the publication of *Godey's Lady's Book* in 1830, trends could be followed by individuals with initiative, despite uneven access to resources. This democratic trend intensified with the beginning of mass media exposure through television in the 1950s. The proliferation of fashion magazines and fashion editorials, combined with the dramatic increase in televised fashion information from such sources as MTV in the 1980s, made European and New York runways accessible in everyone's living room – making fashion a key ingredient of popular culture.

The opening up of the Internet and World Wide Web, with its imaging capabilities, global access, and quick response time further increased the level of fashion information made available to everyone. With the development of web-based trend services such as WGSN, students designing in small isolated colleges as well as established designers can get into the streets of Tokyo, London, and St Petersburg to check out the latest street fashions. So today, you no longer have to travel to observe international trends.

2 **The Era of Negotiable Identity.** The once abstract notion of post-modern identity has become a popular culture staple, with such performers as Madonna continually reinventing herself for the next tour. Madonna can move from a Jewish identity in Israel (see opening chapter quote) to a privileged 'to the Manor born' British identity (*Vogue,* August 2005), to performing an on-stage Christian crucifixion – with the 2006 release of the movie *The DaVinci Code*; all within a two-year period. The now seemingly quaint idea that we are born and grow up within cultural traditions that we accept then pass down to our own children is laid by the wayside – along with Madonna's Roman Catholic childhood – and all of us get to pick and choose what we want to be and who we want to become. In an article on the fluidity of ethnicity and race in America, Jack Hitt (2005) pointed out the systematic acceptance of this identity shift with the change in the 2000 census allowing Americans to declare multiple race and identity boxes at the same time.

The prevalence of a trend toward negotiable identity, while certainly strongly evident in the United States, also appeared in cultures one might assume to be more resistant to change. For example, Nassem Khan's study of British-Asian women's dress of the 1990s indicated the transformation of the sari within this immigrant population: 'Walk along any street in a so-called "Asian area" and you can see the range of allegiances now represented: saris and home-made *shalwar,* designer "suits" and jeans. Mobility and choice are far greater than only ten years or so ago' (1992: 73–4).

The increased access to information made possible by the web also impacts our perceived identity choices. As we surf the web we are exposed to cultural identities throughout the world, so the Gothic Lolita trend from the streets of

3

Japan can take root in America and develop via teenage girls communicating fashion information and value choices through websites and chat rooms (Holson, 2005). Even the most isolated teenager living in a rural area can connect with a community via the web, and the opportunities to enact shared sub-cultural values and community through fashion abound.

3   **Nothing is Sacred, Everything is Marketable.** The combination of increased access to consumer research data and the erosion of relatively fixed notions of identity and stable value systems have turned the world into a marketing playground. With everyone turned into a consumer category, everything from politics, to religion, to gender identity is marketed to us to try on and see how it fits. Traditional Lutheran churches are marketing nontraditional 'Awesome God' services to what they refer to as the 'unchurched,' Madonna is selling fashionable Kabbalah red string bracelets, marketed as expressive of sacred Jewish religious meaning, and politicians from the right *and* left are crafting marketing campaigns to appeal to the religious right – according to Frank Rich (2006) in an editorial comparing Washington politics to the marketing of the film *The DaVinci Code*.

4   **Andy Warhol's 15 minutes of Fame becomes 'Real'.** The ability of the ordinary person to catapult to instant fame has been dramatically increased in the new millennium due to the convergence of reality-based television programming; internet access to a large audience through personal websites, and social networking sites such as Facebook and Myspace; and the instant imaging capabilities of cell phones and digital cameras. As a result of the combination of these recent cultural and technical developments a digital image of a 'real' college coed flashing her breasts on the beach during spring break becomes a marketing opportunity for 'Girls Gone Wild' soft pornography film producer Joe Francis, and the route to unsolicited instant fame for the young college student (Levy, 2005, also see case study in Chapter 5).

Style writer Alex Williams argues that the availability of inexpensive portable digital cameras and the proliferation of opportunities to broadcast a posed self-portrait to a mass audience using web accounts like Facebook and Myspace has created a cultural fascination with projected identity which he calls 'a new kind of folk art of the digital age' (2006: 1). Fashion products are often central to the posed identities, which are then studied by others as they construct their own cyber personalities. The ability to join groups based on interests and backgrounds with people to experiment with identity and bond with others with similar backgrounds and interests intensifies the experimentation with identity, and use of fashion to express mood, values, and social and/or cultural identity.

5   **The World Feels Crowded, Identities in Conflict.** The world that seemed so large and limitless in earlier centuries is beginning to feel cramped and finite. The scarcity of oil is an apt metaphor that captures the growing sense of limitation beginning to haunt the twenty-first century. Immigration and land-sharing issues have erupted throughout the world, with uneasy temporary solutions being forged for illegal Mexican workers in the United States, Algerian immigrants in France, and Palestinians living on Israeli-controlled land. Jobs for the educated classes are being tightly guarded and just as vehemently pursued as access to education and Internet communication have opened up high-technology opportunities to those living in countries once dismissed as backward, particularly India and China (Freidman, 2005).

Dress and fashionable behavior are visible symbols of conflicts over land, resources, jobs, and national identity. Within a five-year period in France headscarves, which emerged as a trend to symbolize Muslim identity among once Westernized Algerian women, were uniformly banned from French public schools (Sciolino, 2003), and in response subsequently showed up on fashion runways. Within the United States, traditional-style men's leather bomber jackets emblazoned with the Mexican flag made by USA leather show up for sale on Internet websites, at the same time as illegal immigrant issues sizzle on the American stage. In Israel a fashionable and modern Palestinian girl baffles her parents and close friends as they discover that she has dressed in a traditional veil, strapped on explosives, and sacrificed herself as a suicide bomber at a local supermarket (Greenburg, 2002). In all these cases dress becomes the visible emblem of identity announcing difference, and articulating conflict.

6   **Urbanization.** The story is the same: the rural states in the United States differ mostly in name, sometimes in agricultural specialty, but all have a common problem – no cities to attract young people, and a dramatically lowering population. Richard Rubin described North Dakota, an American state in the rural Midwest as 'Vast. Open. Windy. Stark. Mostly flat. All but treeless. Above all, profoundly underpopulated, so much so that you might, at times, suspect it is actually unpopulated. It is not. But it is heading there' (2006). While the national population more than doubled between 1930 and 2004, the population in North Dakota dropped from 680,845 to 634,366. Rubin further commented that 'Of the 25 counties nationwide that lost the largest portions of their populations in the 1990s, 12 were in North Dakota' (2006). Vermont, a rural east coast state, has a similar problem with young people leaving the state at a 'precipitous clip' with 'three-quarters of its public schools having lost children since 2000' (Belluck, 2006). The trend toward urbanization sweeping the United States is worldwide, with the share of the world's population living in urban areas standing at 50 percent today,

5

compared to 30 percent in 1950, and 3 percent in 1800 (*Atlantic Monthly*, October 2005).

Innovation and economic activity are similarly concentrated in urban areas. Nobel prize-winning economist Robert Lucas argued that 'Ideas flow more freely, are honed more sharply, and can be put into practice more quickly when large numbers of innovators, implementers, and financial backers are in constant contact with one another' (*Atlantic Monthly*, October 2005). A small list of cities including London, New York, Paris, Tokyo, Hong Kong, Singapore, Chicago, Los Angeles, and San Francisco have been identified as participating in a global technology system led by a creative educated class of about 150 million people, who are highly mobile and interconnected (*Atlantic Monthly*, October 2005). This concentration of people, talent, technology, and innovation in international cities increases the rate of fashion change and creates global not national trends.

7 Starbucks in China, International Franchises to International Looks. Road trips across America used to treat the taste buds to a range of regional cuisine from independently owned small cafes and restaurants. Franchises now dominate the interstates, with food critics offering advice on what fast food to buy on cross-country road trips (Bruni, 2006). While certainly international travel still affords the luxury of local cuisine, McDonalds and Starbucks Coffee are also easy to find in most European and Asian cities. The attempt to homogenize taste, spotlighted by Starbucks' recently published corporate goal of 'altering China's Taste in Caffeine' – from tea to coffee – is symptomatic of creating a form of global identity, highly influenced by American norms (Bradshear, 2005).

The creation of homogeneous cultural features like Starbucks throughout the world speaks to the growing lack of cultural boundaries between key financial innovative centers – with the highly mobile educated class moving comfortably in and out of international borders without experiencing cultural shock or relocation anxiety. This concept of an international 'look' has the potential to affect fashion trends with less visible differentiation between appearance styles throughout the world within the major urban centers. As these are also the centers of innovation, the look of these cities will affect style throughout the rest of the world as well.

8 The Growing Divide Between the Haves and Have-nots. Economist Paul Krugman, writing on the changing face of wealth in the United States, pointed out that the America of the 1950s and 1960s was dominated by a strong middle-class, and relatively egalitarian distribution of the wealth (2002). Certainly ethnicity and gender divided the nation, with ethnic minorities and women still haunted by poverty, but the sharp lines between the haves and have-nots that characterized the late 1800s and early twentieth century had dramatically softened by mid century. Krugman goes on to argue that in the 1980s and 1990s the egalitarian spirit that supported the strong middle-class leadership characterizing the mid twentieth century was eroded by a permissive embrace of capitalism, without regard for ensuring that profits were equally shared among rank-and-file members of organizations. The CEO elite emerged, often linked to historically wealthy families, resulting in 2002 with '1 percent of families [in the United States] receiving about 16 percent of total pretax income, and having about 14 percent of after-tax income' (2002: 67).

This trend toward concentration of wealth is happening internationally as well. Economists writing on the distribution of innovation and wealth throughout the world stated that the 'growing divide between rich and poor countries is the fundamental feature of the world economy' (*Atlantic Monthly*, October 2005). Also reported in *Atlantic Monthly*, within developing countries like China income disparity is intensifying as the educated and talented are drawn to urban areas located a long distance from the poor undeveloped rural areas, with salaries in urban areas nearly three times the rates in the rest of the country.

The impact of the increasing divide between those of power and influence and those isolated by poverty on fashionable behavior is to first of all focus attention once again on fashion as a status marker, and how fashion spreads as a result of copying those of greater power and influence. The trend also points toward the emergence of increasing amounts of high end product marking income-based status, as well as rebellion looks that challenge the authority of a status-based system. Finally, on an international level, it points toward the continuing influence of affluent nations on fashion-trend development, with countries of lower power and influence always in the imitating mode. As an example we cite the case of Korean musician Rain, whose American premiere performance was given scathing reviews, with the music critic Jon Pareles quipping that 'seeing him onstage was like watching old MTV videos dubbed in Korean', and dismissing his music as an outdated 'nostalgia act' based on copying video performances of Michael Jackson and Justin Timberlake. As a summary statement the review directly linked the lack of individual character of Rain's music to the 'globalization that pumps American products through worldwide media channels' – and not surprisingly noted that Rain was 'mimicking Mr. Jackson's costumes' as well (Pareles, 2006).

Historical Overview of Fashion-change Theory

Fashion-change theory looks different in the twenty-first century than in earlier time periods, but in order to understand its contemporary manifestation, it might be helpful to have a broad overview of the history of the subject matter. As articulated by Marilyn DeLong in her entry on fashion theory in the *Encyclopedia of Clothing and Fashion*, 'Fashion involves, change, novelty, and the context of time, place and wearer.' Theoretical explanations for the fashion change began to first emerge out of the core social science disciplines of anthropology, psychology, and sociology; and the field of economics. Discipline-based explanations for fashion change were influenced by the historical school of thought, or theoretical paradigm dominating the discipline at the point of development.

Many of the underpinnings of psychological explanations for fashion change covered in Chapter 2 rest on Freud's original division of the personality into three components: the super ego, ego and id. In Freud's model of personality, subconscious motivation emanates out of the id, a concept that became the inspiring force behind a wealth of psychological explanations as to why people were attracted and interested in both wearing and seeing new fashions. Many of the early psychological theories that contributed to understanding fashion change focused on the ability of fashion to satisfy two sets of contradictory motivations. Firstly, fashion both conceals the body, satisfying the desire for modesty; and reveals the body, satisfying the desire for sexual display (König, 1973 and Steele, 1985). Secondly, dressing to conform to fashion norms of a group satisfies the need to belong, but fashion also satisfies the need to feel special, unique, and apart as an individual. Fashion changes, according to these theories, in order to continue to create sexual interest and as a means of continually feeding the need for individual expression as well as group membership. Consumer behavior, motivation-based models such as the widely applied VALS[tm] approach draw from Maslow's hierarchy of needs model (1943), with its focus on understanding differing levels of both conscious and subconscious psychological needs.

Anthropology, the disciplinary focus of Chapter 3, emerged in the late nineteenth century during the time period of colonization of Africa, and was first dominated by Darwin's concept of evolution. From this vantage point, changes in fashion were first interpreted in Darwinian terms with the rapid changes in European and American women's dress compared to non-Western adornment, and tied to a drive to attract a sexual partner. More simple Euro-American men's styles were interpreted as more evolved, thus indicative of higher-level thinking and a higher position along the chart of human development. As the discipline moved toward functionalism, anthropologists began to focus less on why dress changed, and more on analyzing the social functions of dress in marking membership and social value (see Radcliffe-Brown in Johnson, Torntore and Eicher, 2003). With the beginnings of cultural relativism, and focus on cultural meaning in the twentieth century, anthropological theory began to explain dress changes as indicative of cultural transformation and cultural conflict (see Geertz, 1973 and Turner, 1988) – themes that resonate in the twenty-first century. While Chapter 3 provides some background on early anthropological theory, the focus of the chapter is on cultural approaches as a means of understanding how fashion changes help to create meaning in the new millennium.

Sociological theories covered in Chapter 4 focus on fundamental collective behavior, and the role of ever-changing fashion in marking group membership and more importantly status and power. Central to the sociological approach is the attempt to trace the flow of fashion, with attention paid to the power dynamics driving the collective behavior. Early theories utilized social class as the primary mode of status division, with fashion trickling down from the upper class to those below driven by both emulation of the lower classes, chase; and continued need for differentiation among the upper classes, flight (Simmel, 1904). New fashions in this model are chosen by the upper class as they continually attempt to assert their elevated status, through dress and appearance. More contemporary models are still power-based but the flow of fashion has been shown to come up from the streets as well as down from the wealthy (McCracken, 1985). Identity-based theories, emerging in the late twentieth century, focus on collective responses to socially ambivalent identities – with fashions emerging at points of cultural conflict and stress (Davis, 1985).

Style-based, fashion-change theories emerged in the later half of the twentieth century as scholars, most notably Anne Hollander (1975, 1995) and Valerie Steele (1985, 1988) applied art-historical methods of charting style changes to fashionable dress. Chapter 5 explores a range of art-historical approaches focused on design-based variations and aesthetic relationships between the body and cloth. Theories within this section of the book focus on the influence of innovative design techniques, emerging new technology, images of dress and appearance, and past stylistic patterns on emerging new design. An example of a style-based fashion trend recently reported by style writer Cathy Horyn is the innovative bias-cut technique introduced by Galliano that has now become an industry standard. Lauding Galliano's ability to handle cloth, Horyn writes: 'He is one of the few designers working today who actually knows how to cut cloth. If your daughter is wearing a bias-cut prom dress this spring, it is largely because years ago Mr. Galliano pushed manufacturers to try the technique on an industrial scale' (2006: S1).

In the 1990s, the multi-disciplinary field of performance studies, discussed in Chapter 6, began to yield insight into fashion change in the twenty-first century. Scholars began to argue that both stage and street performances were formulating new identities and fashion changes. Everyday performances discussed in Chapter 6 include those we are exposed to daily as a form of popular culture, those focused on capturing the spirit of the times, and finally performances within sub-cultures that have a broader transformational impact. Staged performances, including formal audiences, covered in the second section of this chapter, include runway shows, theatre, film, and music. This approach focuses on the transformative power of fashion to rearticulate identity, and redefine the parameters of cultural categories such as gender, class, and ethnicity.

As an example, Joshua Zeitz, in his book on flappers, gives great credit to the public appearances of Zelda Fitzgerald, as well as F. Scott Fitzgerald's fictional depiction of her antics in formulating and marketing the modern flapper look. The newspaper accounts of the couple's escapades were followed with rapt attention by readers throughout the country:

> The Fitzgeralds basked in publicity. They arrived at parties with Zelda cheering from the roof of a taxicab and Scott perched on its hood . . . On slow news weeks, Zelda wasn't above diving into a park fountain fully clothed, and Scott was perfectly willing to stand on his head in a hotel lobby to impress nearby reporters and cameramen. Zelda arrived at people's homes for parties and casually shucked her clothing to take long hot baths. (Zeitz, 2006: 57)

The role of F. Scott in translating their lives into fiction increased the impact of this couple on formulating the modern flapper identity, with F. Scott later commenting that 'I sometimes wonder whether the flapper made me or I made her' (Zeitz, 2006: 47), acknowledging the integration of his life and fiction in creation of the iconic image of the flapper.

Cyclical theories of fashion change covered in Chapter 7 of this book emanated for the most part out of the discipline of economics, and focused on the rate of fashion flow and the duration of a fashion trend from introduction to termination. Economists differentiated between what are referred to as short term, several months to two years; and long-term cycles, sometimes as long as a century (Sproles, 1981). Theories underlying the cyclical approach to fashion-trend analysis include evolutionary and style-based models for long-term cycles, status-based models for short-term cycles, and gender-role-based interpretations, focused on linking cycles to cultural roles. With the growing gap between affluence and poverty, both in the United States and world-wide, status-based cyclical theories are particularly relevant in the new millennium. Dress historians have helped to influence the application of fashion-change theories and have been impacted by theories of dress change from other disciplines. Chapter 8 provides a review of a range of examples of late twentieth and early twenty-first-century dress history approaches. Finally, the concluding chapter synthesizes the different theories coming from different disciplines, and concludes by pointing out the connecting strands from the theories presented throughout the book.

Introduction to the Structure of the Book

Individual chapters are devoted to each of the discipline-based, fashion-change, theoretical approaches briefly reviewed in this introduction. Chapters are structured similarly, with the first part of each chapter focused on reviewing historical and contemporary writings on fashion change relevant to analyzing and forecasting fashion change in the new millennium. All chapters are selective rather than exhaustive in their coverage of fashion theory. Many theories of fashion focus on why it exists, not why it changes. This book is purposefully limited to exploring fashion-change theories. The chapters also devote more space and depth to theories that resonate in the new millennium. In some cases historical theories are bound to the period in which they developed; in these cases they are either treated summarily or have not been included in the chapter. Extended historical case studies are used in many chapters to guide you through the application of the different theories to specific styles of dress and circumstances. The second half of each chapter begins with a brief discussion of using the summarized theories to analyze and predict new millennium fashion, followed by concise restatements of the theories. The chapters conclude with case study examples which apply the theories in the twenty-first century.

Fashion and the Self

2

'All clothing is erotic.'

Valerie Steele (1985)

The comprehensive term dress (Eicher and Roach Higgins, 1992) includes not only clothing, but also body modifications and other non-clothing items added to the body as a part of completing self-presentation. Our entire visual presentation of self can be viewed as intrinsically erotic, with dress considered our 'social skin,' or the public patina that exposes our sexuality and our inner self to the outside world (Turner, 1980). The integral relationship of the psychology of self to fashion change begins with understanding the role of dress and appearance in the development of self-consciousness along with the need for external recognition from others.

The self is more than what appears on the surface. It is a slowly developed sense of who and what we are both externally and internally, with the process beginning in early childhood and continuing to develop throughout the life span. It is of interest to us in the fashion field because the clothes we wear are believed to be fundamentally integrated with our sense of self. As Bliss suggested, one of the primary motives for wearing clothes is to address a 'fundamental feeling of incompleteness ... [and] dissatisfaction with the self as it is' (1916: 221).

G. Stanley Hall (1898) wrote one of the initial expositions on early development of the self and included in his analysis the integral nature of dress and fashion to the development of self. Sense of self begins, according to Hall, with notice of one's physical extremities. Study of infants indicated that the earliest sense of self began with notice of external body features such as hands and fingers around about twelve months of age. This was followed later by notice of feet, toes, ears, nose, hair, etc. as the child aged between the first and second years. Between the ages three and five years, attention shifted to skin and internal physical elements such as bones, stomach and respiration. Hall pointed to dress and adornment as the next key development of a child's consciousness. Hats, buckles, stockings, trousers, and gloves soon all played an important role in the creation of self-consciousness. At this point in development, Hall believed fashion comes to play as he noted that children were especially passionate about people noticing something new or novel about their attire. Admiration of their clothing by others became particularly important to children in early childhood. So we see, according to Hall, that the self develops step by step from the sense of our bodies and eventually includes that which covers our bodies. In sum, that which covers our bodies becomes part of who we think we are with personal excitement built around the notion of apparel newness or novelty. This all suggests that fashion may well be propelled by the very nature of who we believe ourselves to be! As Hall stated, it all begins in childhood when the 'great pleasure in wearing new and beautiful objects of attire . . . is to secure thereby the attention and interest of others' (Hall, 1898: 366).

As a number of twentieth-century psychologists discovered, most notably Sigmund Freud, the human self is a complex mix of both conscious and unconscious thoughts and motivations, which we will see in this chapter have an impact on fashion behavior. Because of psychology's complexity the field is subdivided into several disciplinary branches; however, they tend to overlap with each other when fashion behavior is considered. The following discussion of fashion and psychology will to the extent possible be given from within the context of the following pertinent branches of psychology. Subdivisions of psychology that will be drawn from in this analysis of psychological fashion-change theories include:

1. The psychology of motivation, which focuses on the conscious and unconscious forces that drive people's behavior.
2. The psychology of emotion, which is the study of the relationship among thoughts, physiological changes, and an outward expression or behavior.
3. The psychology of perception, which focuses on how humans and animals use their senses and associated nervous system to perceive and comprehend their environment.
4. The psychology of personality, which attempts to account for the types, characteristics, and traits of individuals and how their behavior is influenced by those factors.

Our discussion will begin with fashion changes most directly linked to theories of motivation.

Fashion Change Motivated by Novelty

René König (1973) entwined the threads of several different psychology sub-disciplines in *A La Mode*, his classic analysis of fashion, but his core argument rested on the psychology of motivation. He argued that fashion behavior, which was grounded in motivations such as curiosity, inquisitiveness, and receptivity to things new, was a fundamental form of human psychological functioning. He noted that humans, as well as other species of animals, were consistently motivated by novelty and newness. Thus, it is a constitutionally hard-wired human behavior to be attracted to the novel, to adopt it, and also to move on eventually to something even newer after only a brief period of stability.

Drawing from studies of perception, König pointed out that among all senses, such as the tactile, or the auditory, sight was the primary sense utilized by humans. Thus it is no suprise that humans respond with such avidity to the visual sensations created by a new fashion look. He then connected the visual draw of fashion to motivational psychology by contending that fashion-oriented behavior was embedded in human sexuality. The drive to see and be seen, according to König, was an instinctual sexual behavior necessary to attract a partner and propagate the species. Thus, 'the power that drives man to examine anything new . . . is rooted in the greatest depths of his existence' (König: 78). In sum, we learn from König that the human propensity to seek new forms of dress is part and parcel of fundamental human psychology. It is no wonder then, from a psychological perspective, that fashion behavior is so common among humans.

Fashion Change Motivated by Modesty and Display

Young (1956) theorized there were three general underlying psychological motivations for the wearing of dress, with two of them directly related to fashion. According to Young the most basic motivation for wearing clothing was for bodily protection; however, because this behavior simply satisfies a physical need it is not related to fashion theory. The second psychological motivation for wearing clothes pertained to modesty. Modesty is a social and moral construction that defines how we appropriately present ourselves, in terms of a combination of body exposure and covering. The final general theory of clothing motivation spoke to dress as a mechanism for vanity-driven display, which is correlated with expression of sexuality and the erotic nature of dress. What we consider erotic versus modest are deeply intertwined and varies over time with the dictates of fashion, thus the final two motivations work in tandem with each other to move fashion forward. Pertinent to our prior discussions, the consistently changing forms of display seen over time with fashion suggest that motivation for dress as a novel form of display often drives fashion behavior.

Flügel (1930) argued that part of the fuel feeding fashion change was the psychological conflict between the human motivation to cover the body, and the motivation for display, which created ambivalence within the self regarding dress styles. He argued that 'dress attempts to balance two contradictory aims: it emphasizes our attractions and at the same time supports our modesty' (quoted in König, 1973: 36). Flügel also claimed that underpinning the psychological conflicts of modesty versus adornment was the 'common root of the sex urge' (quoted in König, 1973: 36), which is a major recurring theme in the psychological examination of dress and fashion. Steele (1985) referred to this same theme as the 'lust-shame theory' of the origin and purpose of dress. Fashion changes emerge out of this conflict as the self continually reinvents itself, in an endless attempt to resolve the two conflicting motivations.

Libido: Fashion Change as Driven by Desire

Our understanding of the sex urge and how it underpins fashion behavior can be linked to the seminal work of Sigmund Freud, the founder of psychoanalysis. Freud is recognized as one of the giants in psychological theory with contributions to foundational work in areas such as awareness, personality structure, and psychosexual stages of human development. He was in the forefront of theorists who advocated the huge influence of unconscious motivations on conscious behavior. Though his work has been criticized over the years, Steele (1985) still found his theories substantial and relevant to our understanding of fashion behavior. Consequently, from a dress standpoint, it is important to possess some basic understanding of Freudian personality structure because it comes into play in our response to fashion.

Personality, according to Freud, is divided into three substructures: the ego, the super ego, and the id. The ego is the rational, conscious, problem-solving part of the personality. We respond to the real world with the power of reason that is housed in the ego. The ego also negotiates the competing demands between the super ego and the id. In counterbalance to the id, the super ego is our conscience, the storehouse of values and morals, and in terms of dress moves the self toward modesty and decorum. The id, on the other hand, is detached from practical reality and works strictly at the unconscious level powered by a storehouse of psychological energy referred to by Freud as the libido. As a purely pleasure-seeking aspect of the personality, the id is both constructive and destructive, where the urges emanating from the id/libido move the self toward sexual and other forms of sensual pleasure, including viewing and wearing fashionable apparel. Also according to Freud, within our inner psychological selves are also constructed a number of defense mechanisms that are used to protect ourselves.

Why this is all important is because, according to Freud, dress can symbolize sexuality when a psychological defense mechanism called displacement comes into play. Displacement is the shifting of actions from a desired target to a substitute target when there is some reason why the first target is not permitted or not available (Changing minds, 2006). This chain of events can be explained as follows: In Freudian terms there is a major conflict between the super ego's sense of modesty offered to us by the covering of dress versus the id/libido-driven sexual desire to attract attention to our bodies and their respective erogenous zones. Thus we have psychological tension and anxiety created between these competing motivations. Since our bodies are covered with apparel, the need to be sexually noticed is displaced, as a psychological defense, onto our clothing which consequently reduces tension and anxiety. In sum, our clothes serve a dual and contradictory purpose of covering for modesty sake, but also attracting the view of others for the purpose of sexual attraction. The confusion created by these two conflicting motivations is said to cause ambivalence, or simply put, mixed feelings with the meaning and purpose of our apparel.

Among Freud's extensive writings, there was very little that directly addressed the subconscious sexual meaning of dress, though his work involving symbolism and dreams made reference to some of the potential symbolic elements of dress pertinent to sexuality, such as fur representing pubic hair (Steele, 1985). J.C. Flügel (1950) expanded on Freud's notions of dress and symbolism speaking of decorative elements such men's hats and ties serving as an image of the phallus. More modern scholars have stressed that displacing our sexuality or any other part of our self-image to our clothes is a central tenet of the relationship between dress and our inner psychological selves. Steele (1985) stressed the importance of dress and the wearer's self-image, with fashion revealing the inner facets of the individual. In fact, she stated that it is apparel which gives the person more individuality than our bodies offer alone. People, according to Steele, project an ideal self to the viewing world through the dressed self that they present to the viewing world.

According to Freud, libido-driven 'looking' is a core element of the sex drive (Steele, 1985), with the dressed body playing the tantalizing role of representing sexuality to the viewer and the wearer alike. Central to an understanding of male and female sex drive are fundamental differences in male and female sexuality, and the impact of these differences in the pleasure men and women get from the adorned female body. Ellis and Symons (1990) found that 'men are more likely to view *others* as the objects of their sexual desires, whereas women are more likely to view *themselves* as the objects of sexual desire' (p. 529). The result of this difference in construction of male and female sexuality is that men and women play complementary roles in the contemporary fashion system, with women most often the object of male gaze resulting in the high relative expenditures on women's versus men's fashion items in today's US and European markets. While both men and women experience libido-driven pleasure as a result of the use of dress to represent female sexuality, the sources of the pleasure are very different. Both are however fundamentally based on the sexual objectification of women's bodies, and the use of dress and appearance to accentuate and mark sensuality.

The pleasure women experience is indirect, and based on imagining themselves as objects of male gaze. Bartkey (1990), in an essay exploring the relationship of femininity, narcissism, and Marx's theory of alienation, argued that sexual objectification of women's bodies alienates women from their own sexuality, in a similar sense as workers, according to Marx, were alienated from their own humanity through capitalist production methods. Using the seminal work of Simone de Beauvoir, Bartkey articulated the process of objectification, charting the separation of a young girl from her own body at adolescence, a time period when she learns to step out of herself and begins seeing her body as a separate object of male gaze and desire. Feminine narcissism, the pampering of the physical body and resulting pleasure that results from seeing yourself as a reflection of male gaze, becomes, according to Bartkey, a form of 'repressed satisfaction' (Bartkey, 1990: 42). This repressed satisfaction is what pulls women into the media beauty culture, a culture that gives women pleasure as they use dress and other beauty methods to better prepare themselves for male gaze and desire.

Bartkey's arguments are supported by Johnston (1997) who cited the socialization of women as a problem in the construction of a healthy sexual identity:

> As she learns to view her body as an object to be viewed, adorned, controlled, and changed, a dichotomy develops between her mind and her body. As she is surveyed, she learns to survey everything she does and everything she is because how she appears to others is culturally linked to what is thought to be success in her life. Her own sense of self is supplanted by a sense of being viewed, evaluated, and appreciated as herself by another. (p. 67)

In terms of direct impact of this socialization and sexual objectification, Johnston goes on later to state:

> She learns to 'be desired' is much more important than to 'feel desire.' As a client succinctly stated, 'I never knew if I wanted men or not, but I sure knew that I wanted them to want me.' (1997: 71)

Fredrickson and Roberts (1997) and Calogero (2004) used what they label objectification theory, to argue that women self-objectify, imagining themselves as they will be seen by men.

Men also experience pleasure as a result of the sexual objectification of women's bodies, and the related use of fashion to mark and accentuate sexuality. The fundamental tie between cultural construction of American masculinity and sexual objectification of women's bodies has been identified by multiple researchers. Brooks (1997) and Litewka (1974) identified primary elements of male sexuality including sexual objectification of women, voyeurism, and a tendency toward fixation on certain portions of female anatomy, including the breasts. As suggested earlier, what motivates men to gaze upon women, according to Freud, is a sexually-driven curiosity or the libido to look. The engine that maintains men's curiosity in women's attire is fashion itself, or the constantly changing look in the appearance of dress, such as color, silhouette, or ornamentation.

Explanations for why women's fashions change using Freud's theory of displacement focus on the tendency of men to fixate on certain portions of women's bodies at different time periods. Flügel, interpreting Freud, argued that fashion and curiosity are intertwined with our notion of erogenous zones, which are the locations of the human body that can sexually arouse others or they themselves can be aroused by others (as cited in Steele, 1985: 25). There are primary erogenous zones, most notably the genitals, and secondary zones such as breasts or the derrière. In addition, there are also erogenous areas that are created through cultural construction, for example, feet, legs, or the waist. Flügel argued that curiosity stimulated shifts in the location of culturally constructed erogenous areas over time, leading to fashion change. In the case of women's fashions, Flügel's argument held that male interest or curiosity about a specific female erogenous zone changed with time and that astute designers followed the path of erotic appeal and illuminated the new zone of sexual interest with new fashionable apparel designs. This whole phenomenon is referred to as the moving erogenous zone theory of fashion change.

More recently fashion theorists such as Steele (1985) have dismissed the moving erogenous zone theory as too simplistic. She argued that the interaction of concealment and display within psycho/sexual motivation is too glibly explained by the theory and that a more complex analysis is warranted. Bringing her own interpretation to bear, Steele reminds us how central clothes are to our identity. She argued that outside of our body, clothing is the most immediate element of our personal appearance. Further, our clothes are laden with various strata of meaning; however, at the most basic level the core communication is sexual because of the immediate connection of our apparel to our physical selves.

Drawing again from Freud, Steele suggested that human curiosity itself was primarily motivated by erotic motivations lodged in the subconscious libido. She tied her argument together by then suggesting clothing incited sexual curiosity through the simple process of concealment, which created curiosity. Responding simultaneously to the innate human need for novelty and sexually-driven curiosity, the fashion business moved the erotic focus around the garment over the course of time, which stimulated sales. Finally, and most importantly, Steele concluded that sexually-driven curiosity need not be aroused only by the exposure of erogenous elements of the body. Instead, basic fashion changes in dress features such as color, drape, or trim can also elicit curiosity; nevertheless, this behavior is still caused by the underlying unconscious libido-driven erotic response.

Buy Your Dreams: Consumer Behavior Applications of Freudian Theory

In New York City in the 1920s, Edward Bernays, a nephew of Sigmund Freud, along with his colleague Bruce Barton, began to apply the psychoanalytic principles established by his uncle to consumer behavior (Curtis, 2002; Zeitz, 2006). By appealing to the unconscious, underlying, psychological motivations of people, Bernays was the architect of advertising that initiated the development of mass consumer culture in the United States. As a result of Bernays's efforts (Curtis, 2002), the consumer culture in the United States shifted from one based on needs to one based on consumer desires.

The shift in the 1920s from needs-based purchasing behavior to desire-based consumer models was in part made possible by the era of mass production and the resulting emergence of inexpensive and plentiful products:

> 'Sell them their dreams,' urged an advertising professional. 'Sell them what they longed for and hoped for and almost despaired of having. Sell them hats by splashing sunlight across them. Sell them dreams—dreams of country clubs and proms and visions of what might happen if only. After all, people don't buy things to have them . . . They buy hope—hope of what your merchandise might do for them.' (Zeitz, 2006: 66)

One of Bernays's first major advertising campaigns, dubious as it may seem today, was to persuade women to smoke cigarettes, which was considered taboo prior to his advertising manipulations. Playing to the underlying male phallic power symbolism of the cigarette, Bernays convinced women through his campaign that smoking represented acquisition of male power status. Adopted first by women seeking suffrage, the cigarette was marketed as a 'freedom torch.' With women feeling more powerful by adopting the practice, smoking soon thereafter became socially acceptable for women.

Bernays's work (Curtis, 2002), created a tectonic shift in the way in which consumer purchases were considered. Appealing to desires, and unrecognized longings, consumption became viewed as a palliative, with the express purpose of making people feel better about themselves. For example, apparel purchases were marketed to post- World War II women for the purpose of improving self-image. A common strategy was to convince women that their apparel choices could be used to better express themselves. Playing on the notion of dress psychology, clothes were purveyed to women as an opportunity to reveal their inner selves. Adopting new fashions, in this model becomes an advertising-induced way to feel better about yourself, and purchase some form of the American dream.

To this day, American consumers are largely motivated by the id-driven pleasure principle to make purchases. For example, year after year in class discussions, Textile and Apparel majors at the University of Northern Iowa (UNI) report that apparel purchases are, to a great extent, made to improve their own mood and self-image. Not doing well on a class project, scoring too low on an examination, or breaking up with a significant other, has driven UNI students to the shopping mall to make a palliative or 'feel-better' purchase. Of course, all this expression of the id drives the fashion business to consistently present a panoply of new products to their consumers.

Fashion as an Expression of the Desire to Conform

A second application of Freud's psychoanalytic approach to consumer behavior, which focused on a desire for conformity, emerged during the immediate post-World War II time frame. Ernst Dichter, another disciple of Freud, along with Freud's daughter Anna, developed the notion that mass consumption was essential for the stability and group mental health of United States citizens (Curtis, 2002). Based on the Freudian belief that people were haunted by irrational, perhaps dangerous subconscious id-resident proclivities, they prescribed strict conformance to the rules of society as the means of keeping the pleasure-driven id in check. Sigmund Freud himself pointed to the depredations of Nazi Germany as an example of people responding too freely to their darkest subconscious psychological drives.

Anna Freud's and Dichter's recommendations underpinned the United States National Mental Health Act of 1946, which led to a massive experiment in motivating the consuming aspect of the population (Curtis, 2002). Based on a Freudian-inspired theory that products have the power to satisfy inner human desires, the consumer researchers argued that one method of imposing social conformance to a common identity was to encourage group purchasing of mass-consumption items. Freud's and Dichter's social experiment was based on the assumption that buying products similar to others within the same social milieu would reduce anxiety and improve self-image, thus keeping the individual pleasure-driving id under control, resulting in a more secure person.

Manufacturing industries in the United States responded by mass-producing and marketing common consumer items, including Levittown-like neighborhoods, automobiles, and home appliances. And what better product than mass-produced fashion apparel could suit the purpose of creating a mass-consumption identity? Industry in the United States, including textiles and apparel, flourished during the post-World War II period through the production of mass-produced items. Product variety was minimized to maximize manufacturing effectiveness and profitability. Predicting fashion change using this model thus became centered on detecting and following patterns of conformity, driven by the psychological need to fit in and feel secure. It was a particularly apt model in post-World War II America, an era characterized by the desire to conform.

Market Segmentation: Fashion Change Directed Toward Distinct Consumer Groups

According to Curtis (2002), a dramatic shift in consumer behavior occurred during the 1960s, which had a major impact on industry/consumer relationships. With the coming of age of the Baby Boomers and their collision with the war in Vietnam, distrust in perceived governmental manipulation and social conventions such as mass consumption led to new expressions of individualism. People remained consumers, but their motivations and desires changed. Consumption moved away from conformance to mass culture toward purchases to expressions of individuality, self-enactment and self-revelation (Dichter, 1985).

Manufacturing industries, traditionally producing a narrow palette of products, had to respond to the evolving marketplace, where consumers now sought variety and individuality in their products, including apparel, for the purpose of self-expression. Despite the new focus on self, people still behaved in patterned and predictable ways. Combining psychological theory and advanced marketing techniques, corporations eventually began to view the consuming population not as homogeneous, but rather consisting of distinguishable clusters of individuals with similar tastes and predictable proclivities in their purchases. Psychologists, particularly Abraham Maslow, began to view the population as dividable into subsets based largely on needs, motivations, and levels of self-development.

Abraham Maslow authored one of the fundamental psychological theories of human motivation, which serves as an important foundation for market segmentation strategies used today. The understanding that 'man is a perpetually wanting animal,' (1943: 370) served as the basis of Maslow's theory. Full of never-ending needs, humans constantly sought to fulfill them; however, according to Maslow, 'the appearance of one need usually rests on the prior satisfaction of another more pre-potent need' (p. 370). In other words, needs or drives, as they are sometimes referred to, were situated in a hierarchy, with lower needs having to be met before higher needs could be addressed. The central import of Maslow's work was his hierarchical analysis of that which drives or motivates individuals to fulfill their needs.

Of Maslow's hierarchy of basic needs, the ones placed lowest in the hierarchy are considered, in his words, the most pre-potent and thus must be fulfilled first. They include physiological needs such as food, water, shelter, and warmth. For the 'human being who is missing everything in life in an extreme fashion, it is most likely that the major motivation would be physiological' (1943: 373). If the basic physiological needs are met or gratified, then higher ones emerge almost immediately, which according to Maslow's hierarchy are the safety needs, most importantly security and freedom from fear. In other words, people prefer 'a safe, orderly, predictable, and organized world' (1943: 378) and will be unable to function at a higher level unless that state of existence is achieved and maintained. Next in the hierarchy, needs of love, affection, and belongingness emerge after the safety needs are stabilized.

The love needs, in Maslow's scheme, are followed by the emergence of the esteem needs, which center on the 'desire for a stable, firmly based, (usually) high evaluation of themselves, for self-respect, or self-esteem, and for the esteem of others' (p. 381). From a product-marketing and fashion-behavior standpoint, this Maslow level becomes very important. At this hierarchical level, people begin to express achievement, seeking reputation and prestige, with the concomitant need for recognition and attention from others. We know that conspicuous consumption, including the fineries of dress, is an important means of expressing achievement and drawing recognition of accomplishment from others. Thus we conclude that fashion behavior comes into play only when more pre-potent survival and love needs are met.

The next and final level which emerges beyond the esteem needs is the capstone of Maslow's hierarchy. This uppermost level addresses the highest form of achievement for human potential. Maslow referred to those who successfully reached the previous esteem needs level as essentially 'satisfied people'; however, beyond the esteem needs for recognition and accomplishment, some individuals are internally driven, either through discontent or restlessness to seek 'to become everything that one is capable of becoming' (Maslow, 1943: 382). This highest level of human potential was referred to by Maslow as 'self actualization,' and can take many different forms, including endeavors in academics, art, other forms of creativity, such as writing or music, and even athletic accomplishment. In summary, self-actualization is an ongoing attempt beyond status recognition to reach the conceptual goal of personal completion. Here again, dress can be an extension of representation of personal completion.

The identification of the needs hierarchy gave industry and marketers a deeper understanding of how to segment a heterogeneous population of consumers, and create differing products for individuals located within the various strata of Maslovian need. One of the more successful marketing models based to a large extent on Maslow's theory was the VALS™ framework. Maslow's hierarchy was used to distinguish the original VALS groups and David Reisman's *The Lonely Crowd* (1965), an important tract on sociology at the time, influenced the naming of the original VALS consumer groups. Developed and managed originally by Stanford Research Institute (now SRI International), and currently by spinout SRI Consulting Business Intelligence (SRIC-BI), their first system segmented consumer types by their values and lifestyles, hence the acronym VALS.

Today, SRIC-BI uses a revised VALS framework categorizing consumers based on psychological characteristics that correlate with purchase behavior and several key demographics. Psychological characteristics were found through extensive research (conducted by a team from SRI, Stanford University and University of California, Berkeley) to be better predictors of consumer behavior than values (which gain or lose popularity with people over time). The connection of personality traits, a fundamental discipline in psychology with the consumer's proclivities, was the significant accomplishment of the revised VALS system. Here we see the possibility that fashion changes could be introduced with specific personality types in mind as the product is developed.

Until the introduction of VALS, marketers tended to view consumers as a homogeneous group, or at the very best they segmented the population by demographic attributes such as age, gender, income, and geographic location. With the application of VALS the new discipline of psychographics was brought to bear in the marketplace. In essence, psychographics could characterize people by their respective sense of self. The VALS psychographic information was then used by the marketing, advertising, and product development functions of companies producing consumer goods and services to tailor their products to specific types of consumers (Atlas, 1984). In addition, Japan-VALS™ and United Kingdom VALS™ have been developed for those cultures. GeoVALS™, which estimates the percentage of each VALS groups by US Zip Code and block group, was also developed.

The US VALS system divides the adult population (eighteen years and older) into eight basic consumer groups. These groups can be broken into more refined clusters based on a secondary classification or lumped together to create groups with larger market share. The eight basic groups are arranged in a hierarchy shown in Figure 2.1. Six of the VALS groups are centrally stacked in two layers of three with one group, Innovators, serving as a top capstone, and Survivors positioned at the bottom. The vertical dimension represents 'resources' including age, education, income, degree of health, self-confidence, and consumerism or their willingness to buy. Generally speaking, groups at the top of the framework consume more than groups on the bottom half. The hori-

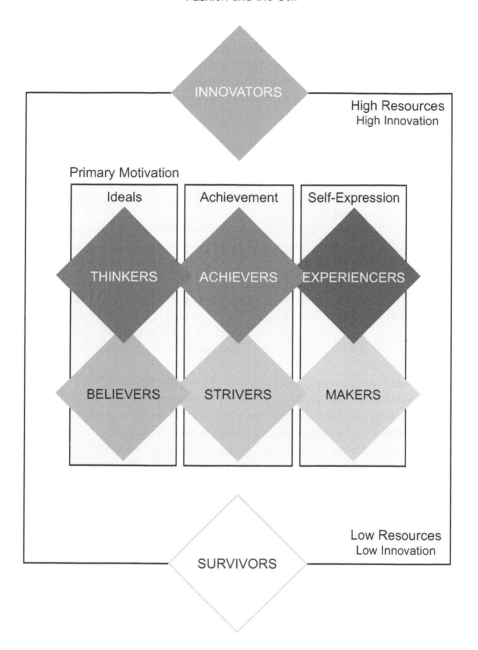

Figure 1.1 Diagram of the VALS™ Framework. Source: SRI Consulting Business Intelligence (SRIC-BI); www.sric-bi/VALS

zontal dimension of the VALS hierarchy varies as a function of what SRIC-BI terms a consumer's primary psychological motivation driving their consumption. VALS identifies three 'primary motivations':

1. The *ideals* motivation, where knowledge and principles guide consumption.
2. The *achievement* motive, where acquisition of products and services is driven by a desire to fit in and demonstrate success to a respected peer group.
3. The *self-expression* motivation, where the primary driving force behind consuming is social and/or physical activity, interacting with the need for variety and risk taking.

Brief descriptions of the VALS types and their consumption influences are given below:

1. *Survivors* lead a quiet, modest life, are uncomfortable with change, and focus on needs rather than desires. They tend to be older and are often retired. They have limited impact in the marketplace, trusting in familiar brands and products, particularly those that can be acquired at a discount.
2. *Believers* are motivated by ideals. They are conventional sorts, who value traditions, family, religion, patriotism and community. They have considerably more money than survivors but like them tend to consume familiar and well- established products and services.
3. *Thinkers* are also motivated by ideals. Valuing order and awareness, they are pleased with their position in life, value knowledge and learning, require lots of information about a new product before trying it and tend to purchase durable, practical products, with a high value-to-cost ratio. They are not motivated by status of fashion but by comfort and practicality.
4. *Strivers* are motivated by achievement. With money as their key measure of success, *Strivers* are active and impulsive consumers who purchase products to emulate those more successful then themselves. They are fashion conscious but shop for discounted prices.
5. *Achievers*, as their name suggests, are motivated by achievement. Unlike the *Strivers* they possess the personal capabilities to rise to higher levels of resource-related success. Conservative and family focused the *Achievers* value stability, responsibility and are somewhat risk averse. *Achievers* are well dressed – clean, neat, in-style but do not seek to draw undue attention to themselves with fashion- forward style. They want the best for themselves and family and use respected

brands as well as prestige products to demonstrate success to their peers.

6. *Makers* are motivated by self-expression in a physical way. Makers value down-home self-reliance and possess practical skill to build, fix or craft their homes, vehicles and any number of physical projects. Many *Makers* work in the trades and they are more likely to hunt and fish than other VALS groups. They have a traditional family orientation. They buy functional clothes and are not fashion forward, with preference given to value over showiness.

7. *Experiencers* are motivated by self-expression. *Experiencers* are fashion forward and risk takers, seeking the new and the interesting. Active both socially and physically, they are high-functioning consumers in the fashion, entertainment and social milieus. Consumption is dictated most by interest in innovative, leading-edge, cool style. Experiencers want to stand out in the crowd.

8. *Innovators* are located in the uppermost position in the VALS framework, with maximum access to resources and innovativeness. They are, in Maslovian terms, actualized and capable of responding to circumstances with all three VALS motivations at varying levels of energy. Not risk averse, but open to new ideas and innovations, they are involved and sophisticated consumers. Expression of taste and culture in activities and consumption are hallmarks of Innovator behavior.

In overview, we see that VALS allows us to see different consumption behaviors in terms of psychological make-up, which is defined to a large extent as a function of motivations. The motivations vary across different types of people and are also influenced by access to resources. Clearly VALS is used for more than an understanding of fashion and influences on apparel-purchasing behavior; however, it is important to note that the VALS framework has been directly applied in the textile and apparel business. Solomon and Englis (2000) have used the VALS methodology to study 'how (apparel) consumers' preferences are influenced by their desires to attain aspirational lifestyles' (p. 65). As a fashion-change theory, VALS creates a framework for analyzing and predicting the appeal and adoption of fashion trends among distinct groups of consumers, with Achievers wanting their clothes to show that they are successful members of a responsible community (à la Ann Taylor). Strivers are style conscious and drawn to status-marking products; Experiencers are drawn to fashion items expressing individuality and creativity; and in contrast Makers look to practicality and value.

Psychological Approaches to Fashion Change in the New Millennium

The psychological theories related to fashion adoption and change presented in this chapter will often underlie theories drawn from other disciplines due to the integral relationship between dress and the self. Thus this chapter is foundational, a cornerstone upon which the book is built. The movement away from conformity and toward expression of individuality, seemingly so much of part of the new century, is really driven by individuals who are motivated to distinguish themselves. On the other hand, the proliferation of fashion choices in the present time period and the rapid rate of fashion change have steadily increased the relevance of psychological theories that stress our attraction to novelty and our desire for ever newer versions of sexual expression. The now well-developed relationship between popular culture and fashion creates a more solid link between lifestyle, psychological motivations, consumer products, and our dreams – making these theories increasingly relevant in this era of instant imaging and Internet communication.

The six fashion-change theories summarized below, while relevant to the contemporary time period, are largely vested in foundational work by Freud, Flügel, and Maslow. Classic theoretical writing on the perception of novelty, the conflict between the motivations of modesty and display, the pleasure-driven libido, and the human needs hierarchy are central to an understanding of application of psychology to fashion change in the twenty-first century. Following the summary of theories are new millennium case studies, illustrating the application of these theories to contemporary dress expressions.

Summarization of Psychological Theories

Theory One: Fashion Change Motivated by Novelty

Fashion change, according to this motivation-based psychological theory, is caused by the human perception process, and the attraction of 'newness' as a stimulant. René König (1973) argued that fashionable behavior was a fundamental form of human psychological functioning, grounded in human perception's hard-wired receptivity to the new and innovative that is habitually adopted at points of stability and stasis.

Theory Two: Fashion Change Motivated by Modesty and Display

This theory, labeled the 'lust-shame theory' by Steele (1985), is based on Flügel's argument that a component of the fuel feeding fashion change is the psychological conflict between the human motivation to cover the body, and the motivation for display. According to Flügel's logic the human conflict embedded in the contradictory motivations toward both modesty and display creates ambivalence within the self regarding dress styles. Fashion changes emerge out of this conflict as the self continually reinvents itself, in an endless attempt to resolve the two conflicting motivations.

Theory Three: Shifting Erogenous Zones, Emergent Sexualities

The original theory developed by Flügel established that there are primary erogenous zones, most notably the genitals, and secondary zones such as breasts or the derrière. Fashion change occurs according to this interpretation in order to maintain male curiosity and sexual interest in women's bodies. Valerie Steele (1985) has recently refined the theory by suggesting dress incites sexual curiosity through the simple process of concealment, which creates curiosity. Responding simultaneously to the innate human need for novelty and sexually-driven curiosity, the fashion business moves the erotic focus around the garment over the course of time, stimulating new fashion trends. Finally, and most importantly, Steele concluded that sexually-driven curiosity need not be aroused only by the exposure of erogenous elements of the body. Instead, basic fashion changes in dress features such as color, drape, or trim can also elicit curiosity; nevertheless it is still caused by the underlying, unconscious, libido-driven, erotic response.

Theory Four: Libido, Fashion Change Driven by the Desire to Look

This theory, based on Freud's theory of personality, interpreted fashion change as driven by the pleasure-seeking libido. According to Freud, libido-driven 'looking' is a core element of the sex drive (Steele, 1985), with the female-dressed body playing the tantalizing role of representing sexuality to the viewer and the wearer alike. While both men and women experience libido-driven pleasure as a result of the use of dress to represent female sexuality, the sources of the pleasure are very different. Both are fundamentally based in the sexual objectification of women's bodies, and the use of dress and appearance to accentuate and mark sensuality. The pleasure women experience is indirect, based on imagining themselves as objects of male gaze. The pleasure men experience is more direct, with women's clothing eliciting an erotic male response.

Theory Five: Buy Your Dreams, Fashion as Who We Want to Be

This twentieth-century model of fashion change is based on the application of Freud's unconscious motivation theory to consumer behavior. Advertising campaigns initially developed in the 1920s by Edward Bernays, nephew of Sigmund Freud, along with his colleague Bruce Barton (Curtis, 2002; Zeitz,

2006), appealed to the unconscious, underlying psychological motivations of people, beginning the still effective aspiration-based advertising approach linking fashion products to lifestyle dreams. Fashion change according to this theory is initiated by a popular culture dream machine, continually feeding consumers new desires and new images of themselves as fast as mass-production can make the product.

Theory Six: Fashion as an Expression of the Desire to Conform

Based on a Freudian-inspired theory that products have the power to satisfy inner human desires, this consumer behavior model of fashion change is based on the assumption that buying products similar to others reduces anxiety and improves self-image by keeping the pleasure-seeking libido under social control, resulting in higher levels of individual security. Predicting fashion change thus becomes centered on detecting and following patterns of conformity, driven by the psychological need to fit in and feel secure.

Theory Seven: Fashion Change Directed Toward Distinct Consumer Groups

The connection of personality traits, a fundamental discipline in psychology, with consumer buying behavior, is the core thread underlying this approach to forecasting and understanding fashion change. Based to a large extent on Maslovian motivational theory, the VALS market segmentation model presented in this chapter identified consumer types by their values and lifestyles, focusing on three fundamental psychological motivations of achievement, self-expression and commitment to ideals. Forecasting the adoption of a consumer to a fashion trend is thus based on analysis of their psychological motivation, and the appeal of the product to their particular market segment.

Psychological Theories in the New Millennium: Four Case Studies

The New Cleavage: A Turn-of-the-century Erogenous Zone

At a lunch with the director of product development for a popular blue jean manufacturer, the topic of 'the new cleavage' (exposure of the crack of the derriere) came up as an emerging trend. Curious, we pursued the conversation, learning about the purposeful design of a jean that carefully exposes just the right amount of cleavage – and a little bit of thong. The not accidental duel emergence of thong underwear and the low- slung blue jean trends signaled the emergence of a new erogenous zone. The power of the erogenous zone theory is demonstrated by the transformation of the male working-class stereotype of a 'plumber's butt' into a popularly accepted and widely adopted version of female sexuality.

According to the shifting erogenous-zone theory, the pleasure-driven libido is driven by sexual curiosity, a psychological motivation stimulated by shifting the erotic focus of apparel to different parts of the female body, and by different styles of concealment and display. The explanation for this fashion trend from this theoretical point of view would be that the duel development of thong underwear paired with intentionally revealing blue jeans styles created a tantalizing new version of sexuality to increase fashion interest and sales in both blue jeans and underwear. Alex Kuczynski captures the look at its peak in a fashion editorial: 'The thong, with straps worn high over the hips, exposed by fashionable low-rise jeans and Juicy Couture sweat pants, became a public icon' (2006, S1).

Kuczynski also charts the look's demise in his style article. Entitling the article 'Now You See It, Now You Don't', the focus of the fashion column was on what lingerie company founder Adam Lippes termed 'thong fatigue,' then going on to explain:

> The thong got skinnier and skinnier, and women got tired of it. And they got sick and tired of seeing string hanging out of the top of every celebrity's jeans. It's just gross. I think it went too far over the edge and enough is enough. (2006, S1)

The eventual shift away from the low jean style toward a new erogenous zone and/or style of concealment and display is central to this fashion-change theory, with curiosity driven libido ever anticipating a new version of sexuality.

Blackspot Shoes: Sneakers for the Socially Conscious Vegan

Consumer behavior commentator Rob Walker recently highlighted the emergence of a brand of shoes for the anti-brand consumer, Blackspot Shoes (2006a). His fashion analysis articulated the self-conscious presentation of this brand to consumers as the non-materialist, non-capitalist alternative:

> [These shoes are] a considered choice: the shoes are made from 'vegetarian materials,' including hemp and recycled tires. They are manufactured in a 'safe, comfortable union factory' in Portugal and sold by the creators of Adbusters, a magazine best known for its withering critique of the advertising business and of mindless materialism. Instead of a logo—or as its logo—the Blackspot is decorated with a rough circle meant to suggest the obliteration of branding. (Walker, 2006a: 24)

Blackspot shoes first emerged as a brand in 2004, with the release of a low-top sneaker, the anti-Nike boot shoe called the 'Unswoosher' – perhaps the perfect embodiment of company philosophy was available on the market in March 2005, and was doing well in terms of sales.

This shoe brand's consciously constructed political correctness was deliberately positioned to appeal to the morally conscious consumer within the VALS model. However, the labeling of Blackspot as the 'hottest urban brand' by Forbes may move the appeal into the Experiencers VALS category – those consumers motivated to purchase by self-expression and a commitment to following the latest fashion trends.

'Girls Just Want to Belong'

Club Libby Lu is a mall-based experience retailer, specializing in creating packaged parties for 5- to 13-year-old girls. The chain of seventy-seven is rapidly expanding, with eleven mall-based stores in 2003 and eighty-seven as of 2006. While a limited amount of fashion product is on sale at the store locations, the principle draw of the retailer is the in-store party featuring fantasy makeovers for all girl participants. Girls have five choices that Walker points out 'do not test limits of gender empowerment' (Walker, 2005b). Fashion accessories are fundamental components of each look. For example, Sparkle Princess wears a tiara, Drama Queen includes glittery sunglasses, and She Rocks! is outfitted with a headset microphone (sparkly of course).

This trend in fantasy dress-up parties for young girls, with its stress on fitting in, confirms the continuing relevance of the psychological motivation of conformity. Despite the wide range of fashion alternatives open to young girls, Club Libby Lu's founder Mary Drolet stressed the importance of conformity to her target market. 'This is an age where friends and being part of a club, or just kind of belonging, is very important' (Walker, 2005b: 22). The lack of challenge to the traditional definition of a girl as a 'pretty princess' fits with the continuing socialization of women toward conformity. It is likely that this trend is embraced by VALS Achievers who value status and traditional roles, and are willing to spend considerable money on their children.

Dreams of Domestic Bliss and French Street Markets: Anthropologie

Anthropologie, a chain with 82 stores across the country, has taken the sensibility cloyingly referred to as French flea market chic, cleaned it up and made it available to mainstream American shoppers. According to the company literature, the company, founded in 1992, sees its customer as a woman who is 30 to 45; she is 'affluent but not materialistic,' well educated, well traveled and 'relatively fit'. (Kuczynski, 2006: E4)

The appeal of the individual object, the vintage collector item, is captured in the trappings of the retail environment as well as the trims and finishes on the clothing. The result is that the Anthropolgie customer feels like she is experiencing authentic and one of a kind culture – as she shops and as she wears the brand.

The dream is deeply embedded in the social fabric of the century, with an intentional attempt to create the illusion of continuity to the past, and an illusion of stable domestic life:

> This is where Anthropologie steps in: It helps the shopper create the illusion of household continuity by allowing her to re-imagine a place where Grandma might leave out her pre-fluoride tooth-powder, to simulate a life in which Mom and Dad still live together in a house with European tea cups and flocked bedspreads. In a world of Anthropologie furnishings and clothing, the consumers can reclaim lost childhoods, lost marriages, lost virginities. The store's philosophy takes the colloquial and sad world of regrets and realities and wraps it up in a swath of vintage calico, tied with a satin bow. (Kuczynski, 2006: E4)

So while the dreams are different than those marketed by Bernays in the 1920s, retail organizations still appeal to consumers' underlying psychological needs through the design of products and retail environments that speak to contemporary angst and insecurities.

3

Fashion Change as Search for Meaning

Trend-spotting is a little like the ancient Roman art of divination. You stir the ashes. You consult the entrails of birds. A pattern emerges, and perhaps even one that contains unexpected meanings about where the culture is headed.

Trebay, 2006a: E1

From an anthropological perspective, dress and appearance, and fashion trends in particular, are visible embodiments of cultural systems and meanings. How we construct ourselves expresses a world view and a value system that are key to understanding meaning within a distinct milieu and time period. The role of the cultural anthropologist interested in dress is to put together disparate puzzle pieces into a whole exposing a pattern of appearance based on an accepted cultural world view. Fashion trends, in contrast with more stable dress patterns, are harbingers of shifting cultural attitudes and systems. Thus we can learn where a culture is headed, by reading the future on the bodies on the runway and in the streets.

One of the key tasks for a trend analyst is to isolate recurrent dress patterns that appear and reappear on the fashion landscape, carrying slightly different meaning on each appearance. By unraveling the history of these recurrent styles and their meanings, one can begin to anticipate and predict how they will be used in the future. One of the most potent sources of recurrent fashion imagery emanating out of the United States is the Western frontier, drawing inspiration from both Native American and cowboy mythology and culture. Utilizing this rich treasure trove of meaning, the first half of this chapter will review the history of anthropological theories as related to the meaning of dress and fashion change by using its recurrent adoption of Native American dress and symbols by white culture as an extended example.

While some recurrent trends emanate out of inspiring historical moments, others recur due the ability of a fashion look to capture a salient message. Recurrent symbolism based on class difference and gender difference under-scores seemingly ever-emerging punk trends, first based in London, but spreading worldwide. The second part of the chapter will focus on two recent embodiments of the punk trend that are diametrically opposed to each other in terms of cultural context and meaning. The first termed 'A Tremor of Rebellion' by Guy Trebay (2006a), examines threads of rebellion in women's fashion in the fall 2007 American collections. The second focuses on the appropriation of punk by the conservative Christian youth movement, as a means of expressing commitment to the ideals of Christ as a counter-culture hero. Both contemporary case studies demonstrate the power of past meanings when interpreting the form and content of current or emerging trends, and stress the importance of tracing the development of recurrent trends as a means of forecasting future fashions.

Native American Runway Princess: Meaning in the New Millennium

In the summer of 2002, an Air France magazine cover featured a French fashion model in a full American Indian headdress, and fringed and beaded fashions. In the summer of 2005, along the River Rhone in Lyon, France, French 'American Indians' in headdresses were singing traditional songs to the passing art market shoppers. Understanding the meaning of this relatively recent appropriation of Native American dress and its appearance in France involves exploring early borrowing of Native American dress within the United States. The first section of this chapter, focused on Native American dress and meanings, will introduce you to the work of anthropologists who have contributed to understanding fashion change related to individual search for meaning through dress and appearance. Through the use of this extended case study the key theoretical frameworks used by anthropologists to both understand and predict fashion change will be presented and analyzed.

Going Back to the Beginning: Understanding Functional Anthropology

Dress and appearance became a part of the study of anthropology as scholars began to focus on the role of clothing and adornment in marking important categories of people within different cultural groups. Emil Durkheim (1915) discerned that different cultures provide individuals with different methods of perceiving and sorting out the world into categories. As you grow up in your own culture, the categories you learn to sort people into seem natural and non-negotiable. For example, in much of the world a binary gender system is in place, wherein children are taught to sort people into categories of male or female at an early age. In these cultures, different styles and trends are associated with male dress and female dress, and the assumption that these categories are 'natural' is accepted. In all cultures one of the *functional* roles of dress is to mark membership in a particular gender category, to enable individuals living within a group to, on the most fundamental basis, interact with each other based on gender expectations and roles.

In small numbers of cultures, including some Native American tribes, a third gender was recognized, which is marked by distinct dress and appearance traditions. 'Berdache' is a generic name used to label a Native American third gender of biological men living as women, who wore a distinct style of dress drawing from both male and female dress styles, and had specific roles in society including counseling and therapy. The term 'Two Spirit' is sometimes now preferred, making reference to the dual female/male spirit living within people classified within this third-gender category. The following is a self-description of the berdache (or Two-Spirit) dress styles worn by Michael One Feather as he grew up in the mid twentieth century on a reservation:

> I always dressed differently. I never liked the clothes they [other people] wore. I always created my own clothes. I designed my clothes to be very flamboyant. I looked at magazines a lot to design my own clothes . . . I knew that I did not look like the rest of the boys, and I was glad I did not look like them. I dyed my hair and curled it. It was different than from either girls or boys—unique, that's what I wanted. (Williams, 1986: 75)

Two-Spirit gatherings featuring distinct third-gender dress styles have gained momentum in the late twentieth and early twenty-first century. The ninth annual Montana Two-Spirit Gathering occurred in October 2006 and included a powwow with participants dressed in traditional styles of women's dress (Leland, 2006b, archives). From the functional point of view, the distinct dress of this third-gender category reinforces the validity of this three-gender system and also marks the identity of its members to facilitate normal everyday interaction.

In addition to gender, cultures have many other ways of dividing people into categories. Common examples include age, class, religious affiliation, religiosity (level of religious commitment), political stance, and value system. In all these examples, dress functions as a way of marking that a person is a member of a particular category. For example older women in both the United States and Europe have created Red Hat Societies in which red hats and purple clothing are used to formally mark entrance into middle and older age with fun and spirited apparel (Lynch, Stalp, and Radina, 2007). These category systems help people living within cultural groups to interact easily, with dress functioning as a sign system allowing for rapid sorting of people into known and accepted groupings important to the given culture. Rituals, ceremonial occasions marking significant events such as weddings, graduations, and important holidays, are often events which are dressed for, where categories deemed important by a society are visually displayed for all to see and appreciate.

While the functional approach offers an explanation as to why dress differences emerged in human societies, and how dress functions to validate and make visible the invisible world of beliefs and perceptual categories, it does not explore why dress of individuals sometimes deviates from acceptable categories within a culture. Or why people in one cultural group might choose to borrow elements of dress from a group of people outside their own culture. How do you explain, for example, the adoption of Two-Spirit dress by a white suburban transgender teenager in twenty-first-century America? What is missing from the functional anthropological approach is the recognition of the formative ability of cultural artifacts, such as dress, to initiate and facilitate cultural change in behaviors and attitudes. It is in this area of transformative dress that fashion change happens, as will be traced by the review of cultural anthropology that follows.

Cultural Explanations for Fashion Change

In this section, which is focused on cultural anthropology, we will present four theories directed towards understanding why fashion changes as people within cultures seek meaning in their lives. In all four cases, examples of outsiders adopting the dress of Native Americans will be used to explore and explain how dress changes are often initiated by a search for meaning. The ideas of Mary Douglas (1966) are presented first, as she began the process of exploring what happens when people or their experiences no longer fit within the accepted behaviors and categories in their own culture. Two theoretical models of how ritual helps initiate change are then discussed: Clifford Geertz's (1973) concept of ritual as both a model of and model for reality and Victor Turner's (1988) interpretation of ritual serving as both formative and reflective performance. Finally, this section closes with a discussion of Grant McCracken's (1988) Meaning Transfer Model in which the fashion system acts as a vehicle for the transfer of meaning to individuals through the adoption of fashion trends.

Mary Douglas: Anxiety as a Source of Fashion Change
Anthropological explanations of fashion change and fashion adoption must first start with an examination of the work of Mary Douglas (1966). Douglas recognized the great power of the margins, the zones where an accepted categorization system starts to unravel and be questioned consequently resulting in cultural anxiety. Not all people and experiences fit neatly into an accepted group within a given cultural system. Those deemed and recognized as valuable are given sets of clothing to mark their identity for all to see. Those who do not *quite* fit often modify themselves in order to fit – but the true anomalies challenge existing systems, often through their dress and appearance, and have the potential to cause change. According to Douglas rituals are created not only to validate or display dominant and accepted categories of identity, but also at points of cultural anxiety, where people and their experiences are no longer fitting neatly into the accepted categorization system.

The first well-known group appropriation of Native American dress by white Americans did not occur as a fashion trend, as will be examined later, but rather at a point of cultural anxiety, when rebel English colonists were first attempting to separate themselves from an identity based on their home country and assume a newly emergent American identity. Using Douglas' ideas, the category 'American citizen' did not exist at this time in American history, therefore those individuals who no longer felt allegiance to England had yet to define a new identity. In this marginal zone the first public documented use of Native American dress to mark white American identity took place.

The now well-known story of the Boston Tea Party, in which white colonists dressed in the apparel of Native American Indians and raided the cargo on British-owned sea vessels docked in Boston Harbor, is an example of dress being used within ritual to challenge the existing categorization system. To date, if you were of English heritage and lived in New England your primary allegiance was to old England. As colonists worked to break away from England in order to establish a new American identity, the donning of Native American dress liberated them from the constraints of the old categorization system. According to Deloria, dressing in Indian dress allowed the rebel colonists to 'leave their colonial status behind and to define and become Americans' (1998: 69). This early adoption of the symbols of an out-of-doors, ruggedly masculine, Native-American look became an ongoing part of American identity which later resurfaced as a part of fashion trends of the nineteenth, twentieth, and twenty-first centuries.

Another way that individuals who cannot find a home within a culture's classification system can resolve the anxiety related to living in the margins, is to seek outside cultural validation. In other words, if the culture that you live in doesn't provide a place for you in its system of recognition, find a cultural system that does! The adoption of symbolic aspects of Two-Spirit (or berdache) traditional dress by contemporary transgendered members of the Bay Area American Two Spirits is an attempt to create an accepted and visually displayed, third-gender category within the United States, modeled after the Native American example. Conceivably trends like this can move into the more fashion mainstream as those outside as well as inside the sub-culture are exposed to the dress styles linked to berdache identity. For example, Doc Marten boots, originally worn by women as a symbol of lesbian identity, moved relatively quickly into a broader fashion trend adoption pattern in the 1980s and 1990s (Browne, 2004).

Clifford Geertz: Ritual as a Source of Fashion Change
Clifford Geertz's ideas about how ritual helps to formulate cultural change are useful in exploring how fashion change can be interpreted as a search for meaning. Culture is defined by Geertz as 'an historically transmitted pattern of

meanings embodied in symbols, a system of inherited conceptions expressed in symbolic form [such as dress] by means of which men [and women] communicate, perpetuate, and develop their knowledge toward life' (1973: 89). According to Geertz we create rituals to carry the meaning of the past into our present lives, and develop new meanings as we experience changes in our culture and in our everyday lives. Using Geertz's definition of culture, dress when worn within ritual is a form of symbolic behavior and as such a cultural pattern that expresses, transmits, and helps create cultural attitudes and stereotypes. Depending on the level of acceptance of the attitudes and stereotypes presented within a ritual, the dress styles worn within the ceremonial context can become broadly based fashion trends existing outside the boundaries of the formal ritual.

Using the work of Geertz, the question becomes how dress styles worn as a part of a ritualized ceremonial event trigger a more widely adopted fashion trend. Geertz argues that the power of ritual is to fuse cultural *models of* everyday reality with *models for* transcendent or idealized reality. As individuals participate in ritual Geertz argues that the symbolic dress that fuses the two models together, in other words dress that in some sense combines everyday and idealized reality, helps participants imagine or experience transcendent or transformed versions of everyday life. Thus meaning is infused into daily experience through the power of ritual. What startles and transforms the participants is the juxtaposition of the idealized and the normative occurring as symbols from both everyday life and ritual crossover, and then reflect on each other. In the words of Geertz, 'In a ritual, the world as lived and the world as imagined, fused under the agency of a single set of symbolic forms [in this case, dress], turns out to be the same world' (1973: 112). The coming together of the real and the ideal in a single set of symbols is what creates transformation and heightened consciousness.

From the perspective of dress studies, what happens within a given ritual is the meeting of the real and idealized/or imagined conceptions of identity as expressed through dress and related behavior. Participants draw from a range of available dress options to create symbolic ensembles that function as visible embodiments of actual or hoped for cultural identities. The comparison of normal everyday life and expectations with the idealized identities made visible through dress results in self-reflection and possible transformation of normative cultural categories and roles. Contributing to the power of ritual to transform cultural norms are the debates on appropriate dress which also occur in the audience as they observe and react to performed ritual.

This use of ritual, as a means of raising consciousness and empowering transformed identities, can once again be illustrated using an historical example of white Americans dressing up as Indians within a ritualized context. This example comes from the early history of the Boy Scout movement in the

United States in the first decade of the twentieth century. Urbanism and indus-trialization during this time period were rapidly changing the socialization of young boys, moving toward what some considered an effeminate version of masculinity void of the frontier spirit of early American manhood. The early American Boy Scout movement developed in part as a response, seeing as its mission the reintroduction of rugged out-of-doors manliness to the education of young men in America. One of the early leaders was Ernest Thomas Seton, who focused on exposing young boys to the dress, traditions, and skills of Indians, as a means of recapturing essential American character in young men growing up in post-Frontier modern America (Deloria, 1998).

Hand-making costumes and dressing up as Indians was a key component of Seton's boys' camping program. The idea was that as young men made the costumes they would be transformed as they attempted to reconcile the mean-ings and experiences carried by the Indian costumes with their daily modern lives. Using Geertz's concept of *model of* and *model for*, meaning was created for the young men through the making and the wearing of the costumes. Reflection on the *model of* masculinity they had learned growing up in urban areas in post-Frontier America occurred as they compared it to the idealized *model for* masculinity captured by the out-of-doors American Indian experi-ence. Fashion trends such as fringed and beaded outerwear and accessories emerged as these young men return to everyday life, with a desire to continue to express their newly found version of frontier masculinity in daily dress. Trends related to this meaning, masculinity based on models for manhood inspired by Native American culture, continued to generate meaning and fashion change throughout the rest of the twentieth and beginning of the twenty-first century. For example, in the 1950s a Davy Crockett craze triggered by a popular television program swept the United States, resulting in the production of a whole range of trended products including fringed leather vests and coats (Anderson, 1996).

Victor Turner: Fashion Change as an Expression of Cultural Conflict
Victor Turner (1988) focused his lifetime study of ritual on exploring how cere-monial aspects of our lives are used to express and at least temporarily resolve deeply seated, but often not blatantly stated, cultural conflict. Richard Schechner stressed that Turner saw ritual as a catalyst for changing position or role for the participants. In Schechner's words, 'For Turner ... the basic human plot is the same: someone begins to move into a new place in the social order; this move is accomplished through ritual' (1977: 120–3). Ritual, in Turner's work, therefore becomes an arena wherein dress is used to experiment with emergent and controversial identities that signal new social order, or new social consciousness. As these images of new identities are displayed within ritual, the audience is forced to recognize and debate merit or appropriateness, with

participants often using the ritual to display ambivalence and unresolved conflict.

Again, the history of white Americans dressing up as Indians provides us with an example of fashion-change theory in action. In the 1950s white Americans hobbyists in the United States began to study traditional Indian dances and make copies of Native American dress, performing at powwows, sponsored by regional hobby associations. According to Deloria (1998), hobby interest in Native American dress and dance emerged during this time period in American history as an expression of the ambivalent feelings of dominant white culture toward Native Americans and blacks. While both Native Americans and blacks fought side by side with white soldiers in World War II, they came home to a segregated world. White Americans both denounced and accepted blatant racism during this period, with many moderate white Americans seeking ways to maintain the status quo, yet appear progressive in terms of racial equality. The Native American hobby movement, as well as other movements, focused on appreciation of black culture, allowed the middle-class white American to both express respect for the authentic 'Other,' yet keep a racial distance – thus bringing into harmony the racist elements of segregation and the growing awareness that peoples of color deserved respect and equal rights.

Turner's idea that ritual expresses underlying conflict is thus captured in this historical example, wherein white powwow dancers are able to both pay tribute to the authenticity of Native Americans and their traditions, and reinforce the validity of a society that marginalizes Indians from white mainstream America. The contrast between Native American and white mainstream identity becomes the basis for the respect given to Indians within white powwow performances. The threat of Indians becoming a real part of the social and economic fabric of America is thus mitigated by a dramatic presentation of the American Indian as idealized 'Other,' a being existing outside of normal everyday work, life, and schools in the United States. By presenting themselves in a ritualized ceremonial context dressed as Indians, white hobbyists express the in-between shifting status of Indians in this post-war period, when they are struggling to gain equal status in the workplace. Respect is given to 'old-fashioned, authentic' Indian culture by the hobbyist, but space in the real world of work is closed, as these Indians are presented as living in an idealized 'Other' world, with no real place in this one. Again, the influence on fashion occurred as these themes are integrated into everyday western- inspired dress styles as well as major popular culture trends such as the Davy Crockett (Anderson, 1996) trend of the 1950s.

McCracken's Meaning Transfer Model: Post-Modern Shopping for Meaning
The freedom to appropriate the dress and dance traditions of American Indians

by hobbyists in the 1950s discussed above was a part of a larger trend toward seeing cultural traditions as learned behavior. Deloria contrasted this attitude popularized by cultural anthropologist Alfred Kroeber (1919) with earlier reliance on race as a way of determining identity:

Under the older racialist regime, truly becoming Indian meant passing—devoting one's entire life to acting out a fraud . . . now, however, it seemed that the line between white and Indian did not have to be a rigid biological border. Being Indian was most of all a matter of behavior . . . If authentic Indian culture was, as Kroeber claimed, learned behavior, then individual non-Indians could also learn it, grasp hold of the authentic, and thus consolidate a unique personal identity. (1998: 141)

While certainly the hobbyists behavior can be interpreted as an expression of underlying cultural ambivalence regarding the status of American Indians in the post- World War II period, Deloria (1998) pointed out that the behavior was also an expression of the hobbyists' search for meaning and personal identity in the culture of conformity of the 1950s in the United States:

Postwar Americans turned their anxious eyes toward individuals and their quests for meaningful lives. These quests for meaning took a variety of forms, but they often involved personal searches for authentic experience. For whites of all classes, the quests for personal substance and identity often involved forays into racial otherness. (1998: 131–2)

The severing of cultural traditions and meanings of dress from their sources of origin, and the liberal interpretation of cultural traditions by individuals seeking to define their own personal identities, accelerated in the latter half of the twentieth century, leading into the early years of the twenty-first century. This trend was coupled with skepticism toward inherited meaning systems, leading, argued Deloria (1998), to the inclination for sub-cultures and individuals to take an eclectic approach to creating identity, drawing from the wide repertoire of meaning systems and symbols available in mass-produced consumer products such as fashion.

Grant McCracken's Meaning Transfer Model imbued consumer products with the ability to carry cultural meaning from influential cultural figures or groups to consumers through the purchase or acquisition process. McCracken posited that the culturally constituted world changes over time, with different groups of people, or cultural figures, becoming influential at different time periods. McCracken's model (see Figure 3.1) reads from top to bottom, with meaning transferring from influential cultural groups to consumer goods, and finally to consumers through four different acquisition rituals.

At the top of the model is what McCracken referred to as the culturally

FIGURE
MOVEMENT OF MEANING

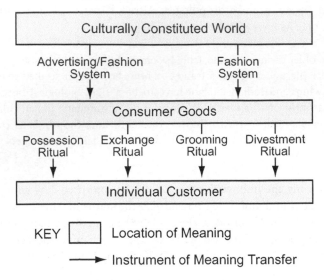

Figure 3.1 McCracken Model of Meaning Transfer

constituted world. Similar to other anthropologists we have talked about in this chapter, McCracken focused his analysis on categories of people. He argued that the cultural world we live in is populated by different influential cultural groups at different times, with the culturally constituted world made up of shifting identities. Again drawing an example from the long history of white Americans dressing as Native Americans, in the late 1960s and 1970s a cultural group emerged out of the hippie movement that used Native American dress and other traditions to mark their counter-culture identity.

This counter-culture group adopted not only the dress styles, but in many cases the living arrangements of Native Americans, at least as idealized within the white American imagination. Deloria recalled visiting a commune in the Northwest United States populated by members of this group, and emphasized the importance that was placed on consuming products carrying 'Indian' meaning:

> I liked to visit the Indian camp, where people in headbands, fringed leather jackets, and moccasins padded quietly about, calling each other names I cannot quite recall but that had the kind of faux-Indian ring—Rainbow, maybe or Green Wood—that I would later associate with suburban tract developments. The tipis were pleasant enough, although they tended to leak when it rained. Perhaps the Indians had been mistaken in choosing the Plains tents, so inappropriate to the wet climate, over the comfortable cedar-plank Indian homes one learned about in

we compare the *model of* life we daily experience with the ideal *model for* life we were exposed to within the ritual.

Theory 3: Fashion Trends as Expressions of Cultural Conflict

Victor Turner (1988) also focused his attention on ritual performances, but instead concentrated on the role of rituals in the expression of underlying cultural conflict. According to this theoretical model, fashion changes emerge from cultural conflicts in the form of dress and appearance symbols. The power of these symbols to capture popular sentiment and acceptance determined whether the conflicted identities become fashion trends, or are experienced as relatively isolated expressions of discontent.

Theory 4: Buying Meaning: Transfer of Identity Symbols through Trends

Grant McCracken's (1988) meaning transfer model emphasizes that the groups that make up the modern cultural world are in flux, and that as these groups change, our fashion styles change. In this model, as a new cultural group enters the mass-media stage and is recognized as important, designers target their look, creating a line of fashion products linked to the new emerging cultural identity. Advertising and marketing executives then sell the look to the public, who purchase, along with the product, the meaning associated with the cultural group. Thus consumers adorn themselves in meaning as they purchase and wear new fashion trends.

Twenty-first Century Punk: Four Case Studies

Punk styles first emerged in London in the late 1970s as a way of visibly and symbolically protesting accepted categorizations of class and gender in Great Britain. Responding to the extremely high jobless rates, the focus on poverty, and publicized moral decay captured in the news media, marginalized working-class youth dramatized their plight in the creation of a visible style expressive of their frustration and position as the English underclass. In his analysis of English punk style of this period, Dick Hebdige pointed out that 'it was fitting that the punks should present themselves as "degenerates"; as signs of the highly publicized decay which perfectly represented the atrophied condition of Great Britain' (1979: 87). Female punk styles, popularized by the British designer Vivienne Westwood, were visible challenges to both class and gender, with symbolic elements from the street world of pornography and sex workers juxtaposed with punk hair styles and schoolgirl uniforms.

Within weeks of each other, two *New York Times* fashion stories in the spring of 2006 focused on the appropriation of punk in emerging fashion styles among two distinct cultural groups. In the first story on women's fall 2007 collections, Guy Trebay argued that fashion is expressing a movement toward an 'interest in cultural flux' and a willingness to subvert the conservative establishment in Washington (2006a). The second article, appearing three weeks later, focused on what was termed 'Extreme Christian Clothing,' an adoption of punk styles by a Christian countercultural movement identifying with Christ as a rebel figure (Leland, 2006a). The simultaneous embodiment of punk to express allegiance to the values of the Christian Right, and opposition to the conservative spirit exemplified by the Bush Administration, illustrates the powerful and flexible symbolic weight of punk to express attitudes and values of counter-cultural youth movements.

In the following four case studies of punk, you will be once again reacquainted with the four cultural fashion-change theories introduced in this chapter. This section of the chapter will begin with using the work of Mary Douglas (1966) to both understand and predict the potential impact of the new punk styles found in fall 2007 women's collections on the wider Euro-American marketplace. The second case study will use the work of Clifford Geertz (1973) to explore the enactment of ideal versions of self within the American evangelical youth movement, with a focus on the potential of this movement to spur a widely embraced Christian punk trend. This case study is followed by an examination of the role of cultural conflict in the fall 2007 female punk styles, and the tie of this conflicted identity to the punk styles of the past. Finally Grant McCracken's (1988) meaning transfer model will trace the movement of meaning from the Christian Punk group through the fashion system into the lives of American teenage consumers.

Cracks and Margins: 'Raunchy Chic in the Face of a Conformist Era'

> If there is anything in the success of Transamerica, Brokeback Mountain, a spate of transsexual plot lines on cable television, drag kings in cabaret and movies like the Miramax production, Kinky Boots, it seems to show that Americans are regaining their interest in cultural flux. This is not to say a revolution is going on . . . But even small subversions come as welcome at a cultural moment as static, obedient, and politically benumbed as our own. (Trebay, 2006a: E7)

Trebay's fashion editorial and headline 'The fall fashions throw raunchy chic in the face of a conformist era' (2006a: E1) underscored the emergence of punk influences in women's fall 2007 collections as emblematic of seeds of subversion within a largely complacent and conservative American population. Citing examples such as the unexpected embrace of the homoerotic film *Brokeback*

Mountain, Trebay goes on to argue that a significant body of women's wear fall trends were similarly challenging conservative categorization systems through a recalling of punk symbolism and meaning.

Since its initial appearance in London in the 1970s punk styles have been revived as visible embodiments of subversion by cultural groups marginalized by mainstream culture. Using the ideas of Mary Douglas regarding the power of the margins, what these revival trends do is mark the existence of cultural groups posed outside of conventional categorizations systems. In the same sense that *Brokeback Mountain* forces us to reconceptualize the American cowboy, the fall 2007 women's collections analyzed by Trebay force a rethinking of femininity in the twenty-first century.

After characterizing a majority of the women's fall 2007 collection as 'fundamentally alike . . . in the their packaging of [female] sexuality' and a celebration of 'feminine passivity,' (2006a: E1) Trebay switches gear and highlights the challenges to femininity gracing the runway. Beginning with the collection of Luella Barteley, whose designs included 'messed up party dresses and ironically worn strands of pearls,' Trebay focuses on the small number of rebellious collections, perhaps signaling a trend toward an opening of gender to discourse and meaning. Challenges to traditional femininity included diverse reinterpretations of punk by Marc Jacobs, who featured oversized knit caps and chains, skirts worn over trousers, and the black lipstick models of Alice Roi.

Linda Fargo, the new director of Bergdorf Goodman, is quoted in Trebay's article, throwing some light on the question of whether these challenges to femininity will take root and create fashion momentum, and like Trebay recalled the early punk movement led by Vivienne Westwood:

> There are a lot of choices out there this season . . . There's a lot of 1940s, there's a lot of Cristobal Balenciaga influence with the swing coats and balloon shapes.' But there is also something compelling, Ms. Fargo added, about the appearance of shows of women wearing black lips and black nails, motorcycle jackets with Frankenstein zippers, buffalo plaids of the sort that Vivienne Westwood was toying with in what seems like a century ago. (Trebay, 2006a: E7)

Also like Trebay, she attributed these fashion challenges to conservative femininity to a shift in political climate, a movement toward rebellion:

> 'Perhaps when you look at what's happening politically in this country, you can understand why people are looking for something that's less about conformity,' Ms. Fargo said. (Trebay, 2006a: E7)

Again, making reference to the relevance of Mary Douglas' ideas to this case study, where this potential fashion trend emerges is in the cracks and margins, with designers purposefully creating feminine identities that don't fit the norm and that challenge existing categorization systems. The attention paid to the trend by Trebay, as well as Linda Fargo, raise expectations regarding the potential impact of this look on future collections and the marketplace.

Runway as Ritual: Expression and Resolution of Gender Conflict through Fashion

The idea of a runway as a conceptual and ritualized space wherein ideas and identities are manipulated is a part of contemporary fashion culture, with such presentations referred to as 'substance runway shows' by Ginger Duggan (2005[2001]). Because of the centrality of dress in the marking of male and female gender many substance shows (Duggan, 2001) involve explorations of gender through fashion. Whereas in a traditional spectacle show normative ideals of male and female beauty tend to be displayed, substance shows often deliberately disrupt normal expectations by challenging the audience to consider alternative gender identities.

Victor Turner's concept of ritual as an arena wherein conflict is displayed and resolved, leading to transformation, is a helpful construct to apply to these types of fashion experiences. In the case of the fall 2007 punk style fashion shows analyzed by Trebay (2006a), what is presented on the runway is a new millennium remake of the original punk trend of the 1970s. Designers including Luella Bartley, Alice Roi, and Mark Jacobs all reinterpreted in different ways the earlier punk styles to express contemporary versions of feminine identity.

The British designer Luella Bartley, citing the influence of garage-band cult musician Holly Golightly, used a vocabulary of party dresses in disarray and mixes of cheap and classic accessories to create a challenge to conventional passive femininity. Alice Roi, working on a similar theme, but relying heavily on make-up for effect, also cited alternative music as an inspiration for re-imaging the feminine. Marc Jacobs reintroduced Bohemian and grunge to create feminine elegance dependent upon mixes of masculine and feminine forms of dress. DJs working the fashion shows reiterated the link between many fall 2007 women's collections through play selections drawn from early punk, commenting that 'There's a lot of New Wave again, but it's new New Wave' (Trebay, 2006a: E7).

Conflict resolution of the gender ambiguity of the twenty-first century is achieved in the eclectic mix of messages portrayed on the runway by Bartley, Roi and Jacobs. Elements of traditional femininity are juxtaposed with masculine elements and discordant messiness to achieve an elegant rebuttal of the passive female fashion object. In this case the runway is treated as ritual space wherein the conflict embedded in the cultural definition of femininity is visually expressed, but then resolved through the designer's ability to create elegance and beauty using an untraditional mix of fabrics, masculine and feminine shapes, and accessories.

Rebels With a Cross: A New Counterculture

'If evangelicalism means a commitment to the radical doctrine of Jesus, you have to be subversive.' In the increasingly clamorous Christian marketplace rebellion is where you find it: in full-contact skateboard Bible study groups; in Christian punk, Goth and hip-hop CDs; in evangelical tattoo parlors; in sportswear brands like Extreme Christian Clothing and Fear God; in alt churches or ministries called Revolution, Scum of the Earth, and Punk Girl; in a podcast called Xtreme Christianity, which turns out to be a fairly conventional weekly sermon delivered by a Baptist minister in a suburb of Kansas City, Mo. (Leland, 2006a: E1)

Clifford Geertz's contribution to cultural explanations for fashion change centered on the ritualized juxtaposition of *models of* life as it has been, or is being experienced, with *models for* a more idealized conception of how a life should be lived. Within the newly emergent Christian subcultural punk movement, Christ's life as a rebel is visually enacted on the body in a range of apparel carrying messages of punk rebellion. These Christian rebel fashions are worn in a range of non-traditional ritualized environments wherein participants spiritually commune and express a connection to Christ as a figure of salvation and transformation. Through the wearing of these punk styles drawn from the secular world of street-level rebellion into a sacred context infused with symbolism of Christ as a counterculture hero, these teenagers fuse models of the real world they live in with a model for a better life as exemplified by the life of Christ. The coolness of their look links them to the real world of street fashion. The identification of the look with Christ's life fuses their lives with a model for a better life, a life of sacred purpose.

The creation of nontraditional services and youth programming oriented toward the musical tastes and recreational patterns of teenagers has resulted in the emergence of this counterculture movement, with an evangelical orientation toward youth, and open to the use of marketing techniques to attract adolescent taste and commitment:

Anyone looking for the spirit of American counter culture—as a romance, identity or marketing principle—need look no further than the nearest evangelical bookstore, youth ministry or clothing line. A decade and a half after Nirvana's success exposed the strength of secular alternative-culture, their evangelical counterparts are having their own coming out in rebel gestures that sometimes recall the early church, sometimes . . . well early Nirvana. (Leland, 2006a: E1)

The likelihood of the trend of Christian-inspired punk-look fashion having a significant impact on American culture appears relatively high. Levels of religious involvement of American adolescents is high (Regnerus, Smith and

Fritsch, 2003) with 76 percent of adolescents reporting that they believe in a personal god, and 74 percent reporting that they pray regularly (Gallup and Bezilla, 1992).

The movement of this trend from marking religiosity to a fashion commodity is also made more likely by the large-scale adoption of evangelical nontraditional approaches by mainstream Protestant congregations throughout the country. As pastors and congregations have moved away from traditional liturgy and ceremony toward more informal and contemporary approaches to services and educational programming, larger numbers of Americans have been exposed to alternative Christian culture within their home congregations. The more mainstream the counter-culture look becomes, the more likely it will be broadly adopted within the peer cultures of teenagers. Thus the experiences of a teenager participating in a religious ceremony within which dress is used to make reference to both his real life as a skate boarder, and the idealized life of Christ as a rebel figure, become translated into a popularized trend produced and marketed by such companies as Extreme Christian Clothing.

Extreme Christian Clothing: The Movement Becomes Trend

Grant McCracken's Meaning Transfer Model (1988) moves the looks created by sub-cultural groups such as the Christian Punk counter-culture movement through the fashion system to young consumers buying the look as trend. Using this model, rising levels of religiosity among American youth coupled with the movement of Protestant churches toward Evangelical nontraditional orientations help to create an environment wherein young people began to see their faith through a different lens, envisioning Christ as a rebel figure, and seeking a visual vocabulary to express their version of faith.

The fashion system's response to the emergence of this cultural group in the culturally constituted world has been the creation of companies specializing in production of T-shirts emblazoned with logos and images carrying the message of 'in your face' punk-inspired faith. Writing about the opening of an Extreme Christian Clothing shop in the college town of Lawrence, Kansas in 2005, a local journalist contextualized the event by providing information of the preponderance of websites serving the same consumer group popping up on the internet:

> An internet search for the phrase 'Christian clothing' alone results in 8.9 million links to stores, manufacturers and others selling a wide range of merchandise similar to many of the items sold at Extreme Christian Clothing. (lawrence.com, April 2, 2005)

The number of consumers seeking out and purchasing these products has been rising dramatically, with companies catching the trend early sometimes seeing 70 percent gains from one year to the next. Chris Rainey, the director of marketing for an Arkansas-based religious apparel company called Keruso Inc., explains his company's growth, linking the meaning of commitment and fashion statement in the mind of the consumer teenager:

> 'There has been such a rise in spiritual interest across the country, especially the youth looking for ways to express their faith and values,' he said. 'They are wearing T shirts both as a fashion statement and a faith statement.' (Washington Times, April 16, 2005)

Making a similar connection, trend analyst Catherin Stellin, vice-president of a fashion-forecasting company in Los Angeles, stated in the *Washington Post* in 2005 that the edgy punk-style T-shirts were a growing trend as 'Teens and those in their early 20s see consumerism as a way to express convictions,' this comment clearly substantiating McCracken's model with its argument for purchase of meaning through consumer objects (*Washington Times,* April 16, 2005). Thus this case study illustrates the transfer of meaning from the culturally constituted world, through the fashion system, to a teenager buying a Christian punk T-shirt in Lawrence, Kansas.

4

Fashion as Collective Behavior

'Well, I try my best to be just like I am, But everybody wants you to be just like them.'

Bob Dylan, 'Maggie's Farm' (1965)

The purpose of sociology is to develop a scientific understanding of the factors affecting group behavior, as well as understanding the interpersonal relationships occurring within those groups. Collective behavior is one of the several broad subdivisions within the overall discipline of sociology. Analyzing social movement or the emergence of new forms of social order which encompass fashion change is a primary focus of the study of collective behavior. It is especially important to note that from the study of collective behavior, the original theories of fashion emanated; consequently, it is an exceptionally important perspective from which to consider fashion change (Blumer, 1939).

Sociologists have identified several different types of groups that behave collectively; however, it is the study of just one of those particular group forms, referred to as the mass, which has been most edifying for the development of a sociological understanding of fashion theory. The mass is an anonymous aggregate of people with no rules or formal organization. Members of the mass are typically independent of each other with minimal interpersonal contact. Individuals within the mass go about seeking there own needs through a process of selection driven by indistinct inclinations and sentiments. Mass selections could include decisions such as which film to see, which digital camera to purchase, or which new apparel fashion to adopt. When the decisions made by individual members of the mass coincide, as they frequently do in the form of fashion, mass behavior can develop considerable importance (Blumer, 1939).

The convergence of individual decisions from within the mass is a form of social movement, of which there are several types identified by sociologists. Some social movements create new forms of order. On the other hand, Herbert Blumer (1939), a noted sociologist, identified fashion as a form of expressive social movement, which does not seek to change or create social order, but rather serves as more of tension relief through some type of outward or expressive behavior. In our case, this expressive behavior is exhibited in the form of dress.

Collective behavior and its subset expressive social movement serve as a broad umbrella, under which most sociologically based fashion theories fit. This chapter will present the several major theoretical positions developed from within the context of collective behavior, starting first with a discussion of fashion functioning as both an expression of individuality and group identity, followed by summaries of three theoretical approaches to fashion change from a sociological point of view: (1) fashion change driven by emulation; (2) fashion change driven by conspicuous consumption; and (3) fashion change as a response to identity ambivalence and cultural conflict.

Fashion as an Expression of Individuality and Group Identity

This chapter opened with an excerpt from 'Maggie's Farm', a highly personal, signal song written by Bob Dylan, announcing to his colleagues in the folk genre that he was moving on to other musical pursuits, despite their pressure on him to continue to conform to the expectations of their particular musical community. In addition to changes in his musical style, his transition out of traditional folk music and into 'plugged-in' electric, more rock-influenced music was characterized by a change in outward appearance from a working-class Woody Guthrie folk style to that of a British-invasion-influenced Carnaby Street rocker. This is only one of a number of chameleonic appearance changes witnessed throughout Dylan's career. We open this chapter using Bob Dylan and his ever-changing outward appearance as a case in point for fashion functioning as a form of collective behavior, both in terms of marking group membership and conversely establishing individuality.

Creating credibility through appearance styles was essential to the young Dylan, due in part to his geographical and cultural separation from the epicenter of the music scene during his critical younger years. Pity Robert Zimmerman in the late 1950s, a young man who sensed his manifest destiny; however, by accident of birth he finds himself in his late adolescence living in relative obscurity in the Mesabi Iron Range in Hibbing, Minnesota, a 'small-ville' American town if there ever was one. Young Zimmerman eventually breaks away from Hibbing and goes on to become a significant cultural symbol, poet, and songwriter known as Bob Dylan, developing his initial folk-singer chops in the warrens of the Dinkyville, Minneapolis, ascending to folk idol in Greenwich Village, and eventually achieving national icon status as a rock star. Throughout the course of his career Dylan transitions through a series of simultaneous musical and physical metamorphoses, with his appearance changing in parallel with the evolution of his music.

While in Hibbing, Dylan self-described his appearance as that of a typical high-school greaser with hair slicked back, engineer boots and leather jacket. Later, a plethora of photographic evidence from his Greenwich Village days indicated Dylan's transition from a greaser to a hard-scrabble Woody Guthrie look-alike folk singer, typified by dusty suede boots, worn twilled trousers, faded chambray work shirt and a shapeless corduroy cap. Later, as his traditional folk protest songs gave way to lyrical images of the surreal, he plugged in a Fender electric guitar and fashioned a Beatle-booted, Carnaby Street look best symbolized by a brown and black, large-patterned, houndstooth suit worn onstage during a tour in England. Essentially, what Dylan accomplished through his various alterations of appearance was to establish, on his command, varying social positions to correspond with his musical evolutions through the adoption of fashion from the group to whom he wished to assign himself.

Fashion viewed from within the context of the group behavior is best characterized by a tension-created ambivalence between an individual's wish to preserve a semblance of individuality and the contradictory need to signal membership with a larger group (König, 1973). A sociologist would suggest that Bob Dylan, with each of his physical manifestations, accomplished both contradictory purposes. He simultaneously achieved some degree of individualism with his newly adopted appearance, but he also assured himself membership in a broader group of similar or like-minded individuals by conforming to a new set of dress expectations. So, for example, with the hard-scrabble folk look he adopted to fit the New York folk scene, Dylan differentiated his appearance from the Doris Day-like Tin Pan Alley corporate music world, but simultaneously paid homage to the authenticity minded folk crowd, who viewed Woody Guthrie's working-class hero visage as the primary form of acceptable folk singer appearance.

For our purposes, Dylan's excerpt from 'Maggie's Farm' does a nice job of expressing the ever-present conflict people experience as they attempt to define themselves as both individuals and members of groups. Once you have been accepted into a group, group expectations begin to assert some degree of control over your decisions, particularly if you are seen as a central emblem or icon of group identity. From the time of his arrival in Greenwich Village, the geographical and intellectual focus of the 1960s folk music revival, this young man from the Midwest in fairly short order made himself into an iconic performer and spokesperson for the folk music genre, in part by carefully adapting the appearance and stylized affect that the idiosyncratic folk community demanded. Though Bob Dylan had done an incredible job placing himself squarely in the center of the expectations of the collective folk community, eventually his individual internal motivations drove him to venture into other musical endeavors, ultimately resulting in both changes in appearance and musical style. Because his carefully cultivated behaviors and appearance were so central to group self-identity, his defection caused a tremendous disruption within the fabric of the folk community and quickly resulted in a high degree of applied pressure on Dylan to reverse himself and return to the fold.

Therefore, central to all sociological explanations of fashion change, is the notion that dress functions both to mark us as members of a social group and define us as individuals; nevertheless, this dynamic concept does not in and of itself explain fashion change (Simmel, 1904). To that end, three core theoretical approaches are presented in this chapter to explain the causes of fashion change from within the sociological context: (1) fashion change based on emulating of dress styles of others, including trickle-down, trickle-across, and bottom-up theories; (2) fashion change based on conspicuous consumption; and (3) fashion change based on identity ambivalence, and cultural conflict.

Fashion as Expression of Status and Power: Emulation of the Powerful

The notion that people establish social status through dress was initially suggested by Herbert Spencer in 1879. The self-taught Spencer (1924) was, in fact, the first to claim that it was possible to scientifically explain the group behavior of people, thus establishing sociology as a nascent discipline. Spencer also suggested that those with higher social status wield a higher form of political power within a collective group. Furthermore, it is possible to differentiate social status and its concomitant political power through dress and appearance, in other words fashion. Spencer's view of the origin of fashion is as old as the first hunter who ornamented himself with the evidence of a kill to demonstrate skill and accomplishment, which in turn establishes status. Other hunters, according to Spencer, also wishing to prove their efficacy, would follow the first and ornament themselves too, thus adopting the fashion which denotes excellent hunters, thereby achieving the same relative status of the original hunter. In essence, Spencer was the first to suggest that personal ornamentation, be it tattoos, jewelry, bones, hides, furs, and/or apparel were capable of establishing social status and group authority (Carter, 2003). Spencer further suggested that fashion springs from the act of imitation driven by power and status competition between social classes. In other words, those of the lower ranks seek to gain footing by emulating the upper classes through imitation of their dress. Thus Spencer gives us one of the earliest expressions of 'trickle-down theory' where status is sought by emulating those in a higher social position. In other words, the fashions of those in higher social positions trickle downward and influence those in the lower social orders.

Herbert Spencer's fashion theory is applicable for analyzing Bob Dylan's adaptation of Woody Guthrie's hard-scrabble appearance. The folk music community, consisting of both singers and scholars, was collectively fixated upon the notion of authenticity, both in the music and the affectation of the folk performer. Affectation included both delivery of the song and appearance of the singer. In the mid twentieth century, few folk singers were held in higher esteem than Woody Guthrie. Both Guthrie's appearance and music were considered the epitome of folk music authenticity among folk music aficionados. From his theoretical perspective, Spencer would have suggested that Dylan, with his adaptation of Woody's appearance, honored him with imitation, and generated his own aura of authority by adapting the appropriate fashion of a proper folk singer. When Dylan made this calculated change in appearance he was talented but very much an unknown entity in the sphere of folk music. To counter his unknown status, Dylan began the process of winning favor and notice 'by copying the actions and equipment of the powerful' (Carter 2003: 31). In sum, Dylan asserts himself with his new appearance as being a legitimate member of the folk-singing community.

The first official articulation of the now classic class-based, 'trickle-down theory' is credited to Georg Simmel, a German philosopher, who wrote a seminal paper in 1904 appropriately entitled 'Fashion' (Simmel, 1904). Simmel's work treated fashion as a social force with an all-pervasive impact on the lives of people, and served as one of his many contributions toward establishing sociology as an independent and respected discipline (Johnson, Tortore and Eicher, 2003). Underpinning Simmel's notion of fashion theory was his conclusion that imitation was a major driving force of human social adaptation. At many levels of behavior, including dress selection as well as a myriad of other aesthetic judgments, people tended to imitate each other. In fact, this mimetic behavior helps achieve two contradictory goals. By imitating those in a chosen social class, union is signaled with a desirable group and simultaneously delineation or exclusion from other less attractive social groups is accomplished. This demarcation separating people from lower, less desirable social strata helps fulfill the psychological need referred to as individuation. Simmel argued that fashion was actually a by-product of the conflicting social demands of union and segregation. In fact, Simmel postulated that there was really no other objective or aesthetic reason for fashion to exist other than to meet the aforementioned social demand.

Simmel viewed fashion as an integral component for the construction of class social structure. In other words, dress and appearance were key elements for distinguishing social classes from each other and for signaling membership within. In general, members of a particular social class followed the same fashion, thus appearing similar to each other but different from other social classes. What drove fashion change, according to Simmel, was a relatively simple dynamic: those in the lower classes sought to gain status by imitating or copying the upper classes. A member of the lower class signaled the wish to enter the upper class by dressing, appearing and emulating them, which in turn created a separation from the social class from which they desired to leave. Of course, those in the upper strata resented this symbolic invasion from the lower classes and sought to re-establish a new barrier of demarcation by moving on and establishing new forms of fashionable behaviors and appearance. So according to Simmel, the 'game goes merrily on' as one class pursues the upper while the chased flee further away, using fashion change as the key class differentiator (Simmel, 1904). The fashions adopted by the superior class are said to trickle down eventually to the lower aspirational class who will adopt the newest fashions to again reclaim their aspirations for higher social status. This process of cyclical chase and flight creates a dynamic, ever-changing fashion engine (McCracken, 1985).

Criticisms of the trickle-down theory based on its assumption that fashion always flows from those of higher, to those of lower status began to occur as fashion professionals attempted to rework the class-based theory to fit the more fluid social structure of the later twentieth century. In response, new fashion theories emerged. For example, instead of either trickling down-wards or across, Field (1970) suggested that fashion influence actually trickled upwards from lower to higher status levels in a process referred to as the status float phenomenon. His hypothesis, which has been widely accepted among fashion industry professionals as one of several reasonable explanations for fashion movement, was supported, though somewhat super-ficially, in his publication (Field, 1970) by a series of historical examples. In his lead illustration, he pointed to African-American subculture as having influenced speech, music, dance and dress. Another fashion trend that trickled upwards, according to Field, was the youth influence on the dress of older males. Examples he gave included hair styling, facial hair, and casual clothes fashion. He used the general popularity of guitar playing as another case in point of fashion diffusing upwards from youth culture. Another low originating influence that moved upwards, according to Field, was working-class dress being adopted by the upper classes. He also cited ready-to-wear clothing and the adaptation of long trousers as having moved upwards status-wise from the working class. Field concluded his work by suggesting that 'the number of borrowings traceable from the lower status groups is probably only limited by the amount of research devoted to seeking them' (Fields, 1970: 52).

Adding further weight to Field's work was Carol Tulloch's (1992) research on the impact of black street style on British and global fashion. Her analysis of British subcultural street styles among immigrants of African descent suggested both 'bottom-up' and 'trickle-across' forms of fashion diffusion. According to Tulloch, Britain's black street style originated from a sense of otherness felt by African immigrants. The distinctive sense of subcultural style witnessed on British streets developed initially among African slaves in the West Indies as a form of emotional self-defense contrived to limit slaveholder invasiveness to the extent that any limitations were possible. This style expressed itself in forms of music, language, physical manifestations, and dress. After the demise of slavery, black style served the continuing purpose of creating communal identity for a people newly launched into the existential challenge of establishing a new social and economic position in a free, but continuingly prejudiced world.

The influence of black style impacted Britain following a large-scale immigration of West Indian blacks during the 1940s. Almost immediately the immigrants began influencing the surrounding white culture. Within a decade the influence of black style on white British teens could be seen in the styles of subcultures 'such as the Jazz Fiends, Beatniks, and West End Boys' (1992: 86). Tulloch speculated that white youth adapted black street style to express individuality and to escape symbolically from existing adult social boundaries. Continuing to follow the evolution of black street style into the late 1960s, Tulloch noted that the fashion became more radicalized, exemplified by Afro hairstyles, later dreadlocks, and the even more threatening urban guerilla look of the Black Panthers. All of which symbolized a rejection of the pervasive, largely impenetrable, hegemonic, white social and economic structure. Tulloch observed also that this radicalized and subversive style crossed national boundaries becoming an emblematic link among disaffected black youth around the world. By fashion moving upwards from black subculture to a broader social milieu, we see bottom-up fashion diffusion, and the intra-cultural adaptation of dress among black youth around the world exemplified a form of trickle-across fashion movement.

Over time, because of a steady flow of criticisms, 'trickle-down' theory fell into disfavor among the scholarly community. Nevertheless, even despite voluminous criticisms and modifications to the original theory, trickle-down was given new life and relevance by Grant McCracken in the late twentieth century. The 'Revised Trickle Down Theory' presented by McCracken (1985, 1988) served as a rehabilitation of the original Simmel (1904) model, although with several cautionary stipulations in terms of comparisons to the original. First, fashion movement would not occur as traditionally believed between social strata, but instead would be seen to occur along the lines of other power-based dimensions, such as gender or ethnicity. Second, the groups through which fashion trickled down would not necessarily be distinguishable by social status as speculated in the original theory. In addition and very importantly, the lower-positioned group would imitate the fashion of the superior group by copying status symbols and or styles, but not in their entirety. Instead, elements of those styles or symbols would be only partially appropriated, so that the borrowing lower class captured status but still maintained essential elements of its own basic identity.

McCracken voiced other concerns regarding the original trickle-down theory. He noted that the name of the theory was misleading, indicating that the actual movement of fashion diffusion was upwards instead of downwards as the term trickle down implied in our past understanding of the theory. Upward chasing of the higher class by lower-class imitation caused the higher class to move on to newer and more distinctive fashions. Also, classic trickle-down theory, as Simmel (1904) described, did not account for the multi-layered, socio-economic system that actually exists. Instead, Simmel focused primarily on the uppermost socio-economic class and its relationship to the adjacent lower class. Examining the diffusion of fashion change through multiple layers of socio-economic class remained unexplored by Simmel, eliminating, according to McCracken, some rich possibilities for further exploration of the dynamics of fashion diffusion. Finally, trickle-down theory was hampered by its inability to help accurately predict where the upper class would move fashion-wise to differentiate themselves and escape the stigma of having been copied by a subordinate class.

Despite McCracken's recognition of trickle-down theory's flaws, he nevertheless envisioned high value in a rehabilitation or reframing of the original model to a more reliable and workable form. As a strength worth keeping, he noted that trickle-down theory placed fashion analysis squarely within a social context, and as a result, the theory offered fashion specialists a predictable early warning of impending fashion change via observation of the varying social-economic strata. In other words, knowing what the fashions of the upper classes were would indicate the future fashion of subordinate classes. The propensity for the subordinate classes to imitate the upper-positioned classes as a status-building device provided trickle-down theory with a logical and predictable pattern of behavior that propelled fashion change.

The rehabilitated version of trickle-down theory, according to McCracken, accounted for both the imitative behavior of the lower-positioned, subordinate group as well as the differentiating behavior of the fleeing upper or superordinate group. For the rehabilitated theory to be sensitive to both imitative and differentiating fashion movement, McCracken decided that a change in theoretical context was required. The cultural context, he decided, must be considered beyond simply using social status as the key marker for fashion movement. More specifically, he pointed out that cultural context involved considering the symbolic meaning of the fashion elements that trickled downwards. Consideration of cultural context was exceptionally important because cultural meaning embedded in dress symbolism could be used to differentiate numerous culturally derived categories such as social status, gender, occupation, workplace authority, and responsibility, politics, or even economic power. Across those various cultural categories, fashion differences in the form of dress can be used to discriminate higher and lower status, because as McCracken pointed out, fashion both marked and defined the differences in cultural categories.

The distribution of workplace power and status between men and women was the key example that McCracken used to demonstrate his rehabilitated trickle-down theory. He pointed to the traditional and heavily meaning laden dress worn in the workplace which creates a culturally categorical and stereotypical distinction between men and women. For example, the classic fashions of men in workplace leadership positions typically consisted of austere, precision-designed, painstakingly tailored suits of expensive worsted fabrics which symbolized gravity, focus, responsibility, and mastery. In contradiction, traditional women's workplace fashions were more embellished, colorful, softer and less structured, and therefore communicated whimsicality, as well as diminished rationality and intellectual substance, all leading to the notion that women were not up to the requirements of leadership-track responsibility. In sum, as long as women wore their traditional and stereotypical fashions in the workplace they would continue to hamper their potential for career growth because of the lack of capability that their dress symbolized.

Confirming the veracity of his revisions to trickle-down theory, McCracken noted that as women, the subordinate group, aspired to gain power and status in the workplace, they were witnessed shedding their old symbols and appropriating new ones from men, the superordinate group. As women began to assume greater levels of responsibility in the workplace, their new dress fashions began to reflect some of the attributes of men's tailored fashion in features such as structures, colors, and fabrics, while still maintaining the fundamental elements of women's attire. As a result, women reconstructed their identities to enhance male perceptions of their competence and the equitable distribution of workplace power. As McCracken concluded, women were motivated to assimilate male vestiges of power through fashion change and simultaneously to drop symbolic liabilities, thus on balance they acquired symbolic advantages and gained status in the workplace.

Chase and flight, a central tenet of the original trickle-down theory, remains applicable within the new rehabilitated version. In other words, taking cultural context again into consideration, McCracken suggested that it would be possible to show that a higher-status, superordinate group would move onwards to adapt new fashion symbols in response to theirs having been appropriated by a lower-status group. As proof, he pointed to the 'heroic elegance' look in men's tailored fashions as a reaction to women's borrowing elements of menswear for workplace attire. The heroic look, which included enhanced and refined qualities such as elegant and sumptuous suit fabrics, was adopted by men as an assertive response to women's appropriation of their power symbols, thereby reclaiming their previously held higher status and authority position.

In sum, acquisition of power and status through fashion is still the foundation upon which trickle-down fashion is built. Instead of fashion trickling down from higher to lower levels of social status, the rehabilitated trickle-down process tracks status movement between culturally derived categories. Rather than fashion moving wholesale between categories, elements of fashion that symbolize status trickle downward; however, in response the higher status group in many cases flees away to adapt new symbolic vestiges of power and status to reassert their authority.

From this theoretical standpoint one might argue that Bob Dylan's incessant reinvention of himself was driven by the wholesale copying of his musical and appearance style by lesser-known and talented performers. One of his most notorious copiers was Donovan Leitch. As others became ersatz Bob Dylan copies like Leitch, Dylan himself moved on to a new identities, new looks, and in many cases a reinvented musical style. As others gained status and credibility by adopting the 'Dylan look,' he found an alternative identity ever different than those chasing him.

Trickle-Across Collective Selection Theory

As we have discussed, the original 'trickle-down' explanation served as the primary form of fashion change theory for several decades until it came under criticism by a series of writers, most notably Blumer (1939, 1968, 1969), who challenged the prevailing belief that emulation of the upper social classes was the *only* means of driving fashion change. To begin with, Blumer examined the dynamics underpinning fashion movement and conjectured that fashion had a potentially dramatic influence on collective human behavior. To that end, Blumer argued that fashion was a significant social phenomenon with an impact spreading far beyond the apparel we wear, being 'found in manners, the arts, literature . . . philosophy . . . [and] certain areas of science' (1939: 275). By helping prepare the collective populace to cope with change in an orderly manner, fashion, according to Blumer, served a major social purpose of bringing order to a rapidly altering, potentially chaotic world.

Similar to Simmel, Blumer noted the mimetic nature of fashion, with people choosing to behave fashionably via the imitation of a sophisticated elite leadership, which in turn offered the imitating individual a form of endorsement or respectability. He noted that 'it is this endorsement which under-girds fashion' (1969: 277). In other words, through the adoption of a particular fashion people seek group membership, which in turn gives them an important and calming sense of self-endorsement achieved through belonging. Blumer agreed with Simmel that change is a key element to fashion's existence; however, he demurred from Simmel's explanation of inter-class competition as the prime engine for fashion change, claiming that Simmel's theory was out of synch with modernity, given the absence of a rigid social class system existing in the United States.

Blumer instead developed the basis of his theory through the study of marketplace behavior of textile and apparel industry professionals, specifically retail buyers and apparel designers. He noted, for example, that retail buyers participated in an intense and independent process of seasonal selection from a massive array of product choices, and somehow, surprisingly often made selections similar to those among their peer buyers. He observed this same selection process among apparel designers by noting the resemblance of their independently created designs. In sum, though working independently, the designer's creations and buyer's purchase choices indicated common influences, which suggested that more than random chance was at work influencing both design and purchase decisions! In fact, Blumer postulated that design and purchase decisions were indicative of a common social experience driven by 'prevailing and prospective tastes of a consuming public' (1969: 279). These collective tastes were a reflection of social and cultural events, such as literature, the arts, politics, and current events, as well as movement within the fashion industry, such as availability of new fibers or fabrics, all of which combine in Blumer's analysis to be expressions of what he referred to as modernity or the 'spirit of the times' (1969: 283). He went on to state that fashion was constantly moving forward to maintain proximity or congruence with modernity.

Blumer was blunt in his criticism of Simmel's model of fashion change, which as we know depended heavily on the fashion selection of social elites trickling down to the lower classes for eventual imitation. The 'tail wagging the dog' would have been an expression Blumer might have used as a description of Simmel's model. In essence, Blumer countered Simmel's theoretical position by implying that the upper social classes did not drive fashion selection, but instead had to be skillful at adapting to fashion change in an effort to maintain the façade of being fashionably elite. Adapting to fashion change was a matter of anticipating and reflecting the collective tastes of the general population instead of driving those tastes. In sum, Blumer described fashion as a 'collective groping . . . for the future' rather than a 'channeled movement laid down by prestigeful figures' (1969: 281). He wrestled away the conception of fashion change movement from Simmel's 'class differentiation' procession toward a new model he referred to as 'collective selection.' Fashion then, according to Blumer, was a selection or an 'unwitting groping' for new forms of outward appearance in an attempt to find an expression congruent with modernity, namely the broad spectrum of complex social experiences and interactions encountered by the collective populace (1969: 282). Further, Blumer was particularly adamant in his belief that the collective process of selection overrode individual psychological motivations as an explanation for fashion's movement.

The term 'fashion trend' was used by Blumer to describe the predictable forward movement of fashion as people strove to be up to date. He described currently fashionable goods as being directly related to or springing from fashionable items that were historical predecessors from a very recent past. Fashion trends, or subtle changes in style from the recent past, could then be analyzed in an attempt to predict future fashions. Attempting also to understand trends or transitions in collective tastes of the public was an additional approach to fashion prediction suggested by Blumer. Despite his admonitions, Blumer was disappointed to note that fashion trend analysis and prediction was a sadly neglected area of study. In the same vein, Blumer accused sociologists, in general, of being both ignorant of and indifferent to the impact of fashion on collective behavior.

Blumer's other major contribution was to define the 'six essential conditions' for fashion to exist as a collective behavior. Not all social conditions were conducive to fashion movement; however, if the following conditions were present fashion would likely exist (1969):

1. People within the social sphere should be receptive to change and be 'ready to revise or discard old practices, beliefs, and attachments, and . . . to adopt new social forms' (1969, p. 286).
2. Models of new social form must be available for repetitive presentation and subsequent consideration.
3. People should have the freedom to select among competing new models of social form.
4. Selection from among new models of social form is not a rational or scientific process. In other words, clearly defined decision rules for selection based on the merit of a new model do not exist.
5. As Blumer (1969) articulated it, 'prestige figures' should be available to select among competing models, which in turn would cause others to follow in kind, making similar selections.
6. The social sphere should be responsive to alterations in the state of modernity caused by factors such as outside events, entrance of new social participants and the occurrence of new social interactions.

In earlier sections of this chapter, you will remember that the initial theories (Simmel, 1904; Spencer, 1924) developed to account for fashion change centered primarily on the belief that social elites were motivated to select fashions that were novel and would distinguish or differentiate themselves from each other as well as the lower-class masses; however, the lower classes seeking to gain status through imitation copied the appearance of their social superiors. Thus fashions were said to trickle downwards from the upper to lower social strata. We learn from Blumer one of the most serious criticisms of the trickle-down fashion change theory: while Blumer believed that fashion elites do help point the way to new fashion directions, they do not create fashion as the trickle-down theorists suggest. Instead, fashion elites were early responders to a collectively developed mass taste. Thus, instead of fashions trickling downwards, fashion is said to develop among the broad social mass through a convergence of collective taste. Therefore, Blumer's explanation for Dylan's Woody Guthrie style of dress, which he wore during his Greenwich Village years, would probably be that elements of American culture as a whole were moving toward an alternative folk-inspired identity as a result of a shift in collective values and tastes. Dylan, as a leader within his peer group, served as an early responder to this collectively selected look.

Another notable challenge to the trickle-down theory was offered by Charles King (1963) who, like Blumer, interpreted fashion change as happening more along the lines of a process of collective selection *within* social groups, rather than simply the emulation of those of higher status or power. While conceding that the trickle-down model may have been a more relevant explanation a century or more ago, King countered that with changes in apparel industry manufacturing and marketing practices, pervasiveness of mass communications, and alterations in class structure, the theory lacked applicability as a useful model by the mid twentieth century. He was particularly critical of the time-dimension aspect of trickle-down theory, in which it was traditionally theorized that the upper classes adopt new fashions first, as 'symbols of distinction and exclusiveness' (1963: 110), to be followed later by the lower classes. King methodically discussed the elements that impeded the workings of trickle-down theory, which he alternatively referred to as a 'vertical flow process' (1963: 110). For example, he pointed out that the erosion of clearly delineated social classes in the United States blurred the directional movement of fashion information. In addition, King pointed to another overriding modern phenomenon: that the ready-to-wear apparel industry now played a significant role in driving fashion change. Anticipating the collective tastes of modern apparel consumers, the industry itself presented a series of seasonal fashion offerings, which tended to supplant the leadership role of the upper class. Furthermore, the industry produced fashionable products at varying price points so that more people outside the traditional upper class now had the wherewithal to purchase the latest fashion goods. In other words, the affordability and acquisition of quality fashionable goods was more available to a much broader swath of people than solely the upper classes, which was supposedly the case when trickle-down theory was initially postulated. Further invalidating the trickle-down process was the undermining of the centrality of upper-class fashion leadership by mass communication systems such as television and print media which increased the rapidity with which fashion dictates from around the world were broadcast to all levels of social strata simultaneously, instead of from the top fashion leadership in a downwards direction.

After dismissing the relevance of trickle-down theory, King conducted his own consumer research to identify where fashion leadership resided. Exploring the purchasing influences and behavior of women's millenary across varying economic strata in the United States, King discovered that early buyers of fashion products existed among all economic class levels, which confirmed his notion that the upper classes did not purchase new fashionable items first and trickle down their fashion choices to the less financially endowed. Through survey research, King also identified influential consumers, or those individuals who persuaded others to adopt or follow their fashion whims. He found that influential consumers existed at all social levels and that they tended to influence those within their own social sphere. In sum, King theorized that each social stratum had its own consumer leaders and that fashion influences traveled across the strata from those leaders to other members of the same group. Thus, King coined the expression 'trickle across' (1963: 163) to best capture the dynamics of fashion movement as he observed it. King's model could be used to account for the adoption of folk-style dress in New York during the Greenwich Village years as a trickle-across phenomenon, driven by influential consumers like Bob Dylan who led the movement from within his own sphere of influence.

Fashion as Expression of Status and Power: Conspicuous Consumption

Thorstein Veblen is best known for developing the highly influential conspicuous-consumption theory to account for the pecuniary behavior of socially and economically powerful people. Pecuniary behavior relates to human activity centered on or relating to money. Contained within his overall work on the collective behavior of the rich and powerful is a wonderful analysis of fashion-change dynamics that still resonates today with fashion scholars. Despite Veblen's significant impact on our sociological understanding of fashion, it is important to note that Veblen wrote from the perspective of an economist, his intellectual discipline, thus his explanations of group behavior are, by and large, economic or in his terms 'pecuniary' in nature (Carter, 2003). In fact, his theory of fashion was very much focused on how wealth was capriciously expended to influence perceptions of outside observers. Central among Veblen's interests was the extravagant flaunting of wealth by the moneyed or leisure class. This extravagant public display of wealth, according to Veblen, was primarily for enhancing social worth or standing, and he referred to this behavior as conspicuous consumption. Most importantly, from our perspective in this book, the use of extravagant clothing was one of the key forms of this outwardly conspicuous behavior.

Veblen initially published elements of his theory in an essay entitled 'The Economic Theory of Women's Dress' (1894)[1] and later in more fully developed form in his book *The Theory of the Leisure Class* (1899). In his work, Veblen explored the group behavior of the 'Leisure Class,' which he defined as 'an

---

1. Compared to men, women's dress played an even more important role in establishing social status by communicating to the observer that women were incapable of executing any form of 'productive employment' (1899: 171). According to Veblen, the woman partner in a marital relationship effectively represented the pecuniary strength of the male spouse when she was perceived as a person of leisure. In essence, the woman's primary role

amalgam of the rich, the hyper-rich, the owning class, the ruling class, the business class, the aristocracy, the nouveau riche, and high society' (as quoted in Carter, 2003: 44). Again the central premise of Veblen's theory was that the leisure class applied most of its energies toward enhancing their social worth via conspicuous consumption. In his oft-cited book chapter entitled 'Dress as an Expression of the Pecuniary Culture,' Veblen elaborated on how central the conspicuous consumption of clothing was for expansion of social standing because 'apparel is always in evidence and affords an [immediately visible] indication of our pecuniary standing to all observers at the first glance' (1899: 167). Because of its readily observable and obvious nature, dress in Veblen's analysis, more than any other personal expression, can be used to demonstrate conspicuous consumption which as he construed was directly indicative of social worth.

Despite the fact that Veblen's theory has usually been lumped in with other 'trickle-down' theories, Veblen observed in contrast that the competition engendered by conspicuous consumption was typically within social class, rather than between social classes. He observed imitation as the force which pushed novel designs from point of origination to diffusion among other members of a social class. If competition was felt among the upper classes via imitation by lower groups, such as nouveau riche, Veblen observed that the upper classes created space by finding even more extravagant ways of exercising conspicuous consumption. It is this activity that caused Veblen's theory to be associated with other trickle-down formulations (Carter, 2003).

According to Veblen, dress can announce social standing in different ways. Veblen used the term elegance as a general-purpose measure of the ability of dress to represent conspicuous consumption. For example, elegance can be a function of elaborateness of dress which is in turn indicative of its expense. Even more importantly, in Veblen's dress scenario elegance implied that the wearer was not engaged in the pursuit or accretion of wealth. The highest form of social standing demonstrated that requisite wealth has already been attained. In other words, elegant dress should 'convey the impression that the wearer does not habitually put forth any useful effort' (1899: 170). Frayed sleeves, soiled trousers, or inked-up sleeve cuffs detract from dress elegance and diminish the perception that the wearer is a member of the leisure class.

Veblen's particular contribution to fashion change theory was his argument that the highest status dress styles were those that were new, carrying the aura of novelty as well as expense. It was this 'principle of novelty' and its never-ending quest, combined with the previously mentioned propensity for imita-

---

was that of male ornament, signaling social status through dress that communicated a life of leisure. Veblen considered the purpose dress artifacts such as the skirt and corset to immobilize the wearer and prevent the execution of non-leisure activities. In sum, Veblen's theory was built upon his observations of an extant patriarchal world, where women were consigned to the role of non-productive symbols of male wealth and social status.

tion within a social class, that drove fashion change in Veblen's world as he observed it. Influenced somewhat by Darwin, Veblen speculated that clothing styles were continuously evolving and that this evolution was the driving force which underpinned the constant search for novelty. The ultimate goal, according to Veblen, was to achieve an aesthetic ideal at which time the evolutionary end point would be reached and fashion change would cease to exist.

Bob Dylan's folk period dress style was, in an important sense, posed as a reaction to American consumer culture's embrace of conspicuous consumption as a symbol of status. Dylan's dress, drawing from the working-class attire of such folk heroes as Woody Guthrie, had embedded within it symbols of the life of a man who earned his living through physical labor, which in turn made a cogent political and social statement about class and power within the United States. As a fashion trend leader and a powerful cultural icon of the period Bob Dylan's dress was copied by others, allowing them also to rebel symbolically through dress against the mass conspicuous consumption that dominated the post-World War II American landscape.

Fashion Change as a Response to Identity Ambivalence

The work of Fred Davis (1985, 1992), which was another important examination of the intersection between collective behavior and fashion, rounds out the theoretical discussions in this chapter. Because Davis' work was based on the supposition that people construct a social identity for themselves, his theory falls squarely into the study of collective behavior. Davis set his theoretical stage by defining the notion of a social identity. Social identities, according to Davis, constructed in part through fashion, simultaneously differentiated and integrated people within the broader spectrum of social possibilities. A complex arrangement of personal attitudes and distinguishing characteristics, social identities were not passively assigned by society but instead built through a series of individual decisions. It is important to note however that identities are not constructed in a vacuum but are affected by external social influences. Furthermore, social identities are dynamic and constantly evolving over time because external forces continuously impinge upon the individual altering the sense of self. These impacts on social identity happen to many of us simultaneously; consequently, group identities evolve collectively with time. Influential social forces such as needs, wants, fears, anxieties and dissatisfactions collectively impact many individuals in a similar manner and often elicit a collective response.

According to Davis, fashion was remarkably integrated into the process of identity construction, and also played a role in the collective response of people to the sorts of external social forces mentioned above. Through the process of identity construction, dress served an instrumental role by communicating, in part, individual attitudes and attributes, but in a coded way. In other words, combinations of garments in an ensemble, how they were worn, and other visual elements such as shape, fabric, texture, and color combined to create an elaborate but subtly coded indication of identity construction. The codes embedded in an individual's dress communicated meaning in a symbolic form from which a perceived identity construction could be interpreted by others. Nevertheless, Davis cautioned that the symbolic meaning of dress codes could be difficult to understand and categorize because no firm socially accepted rules existed for interpretation. In fact, because dress coding was so difficult to parse out and understand, Davis used the term 'undercode' to describe more accurately the subtle nature of dress's embedded meanings. Adding further complication, interpretation of dress codes could also be influenced by context and the unique characteristics of the observer. Even so, Davis allowed that collectively, individuals were capable of making reasonable and generally correct interpretations of dress undercoding. For example, most of us would not construe a man wearing a tuxedo as a man preparing to dig a drainage ditch.

According to Davis, for fashion to exist, a noticeable change in dress had to occur which reflected a new collectively derived notion of form typically in ensemble, fabric, texture, and/or color. In Davis' view of fashion, though, the importance of what changed was not so much the form of dress, but rather the encoded meaning embedded in the dress. It is also important to note that fashion, as defined by Davis, was not the gradual seasonal adjustments of dress components like hem lines or lapel widths, but instead consisted of larger-scale changes that elicited surprise, drew attention and/or sparked imagination. Serving as a major contribution to fashion theory scholarship was Davis' focus on the fashion engine or what propelled fashion forward. At the center of the fashion engine was the constructed social identity, which was mutable and ever shifting as people were impacted by external forces. Changes in stage of life, interpersonal relationships, economic circumstances, politics, and current events are all examples of tectonic shifts that Davis thought could cause disruptions in our view of our selves and where we fit collectively with our socially derived identities. Davis also wrote of commonly experienced strains, paradoxes, and ambivalences that destabilized social identity and required a collective response. And, of course, Davis suggested that fashion was one of the most effective forms of symbolic social response to identity destabilization through the presentation of newly embedded dress codes. In sum, fashion, according to Davis, was driven almost entirely by the winds of external change which destabilized social identity and in turn elicited a collective symbolic response encoded in new expressions of dress!

External pressures that destabilize our sense of who we are and where we fit in the grand scheme of things create what Davis defined as identity ambivalence, or an oscillatory view of self, undergoing continual internal negotiation.

This ongoing internal tumult is often expressed externally in fashion as the view of self evolved. Typical forms of identity ambivalence that can fuel the engine of fashion involved, for example, tensions resulting from shifting perceptions of gender, status, and/or sexuality.

Historically so much of the intersection of fashion and collective behavior involved claims of status. Consequently, it would be interesting to consider Davis' take on this phenomenon to serve as an example of a typical ambivalence that destabilized social identity and subsequently resulted in fashion change. Not surprisingly, Davis devoted a good deal of attention to ambivalence regarding social status. The ambivalence he spoke of involved the tension created between contradictory behaviors of either claiming or deflecting claims of status, all of which he believed served as an important fashion engine. For example, among some of the wealthiest individuals in American culture, modesty and understatement were considered much more preferable than ostentatious exhibition of financial means. This deflection of status was rooted in an acetic sensibility stretching back to the Protestant Reformation, where aversion to an outward display of wealth was considered a higher form of moral character. This valuing of simplicity has lead to the development of fashion classics such as Coco Chanel's little black dress, which insinuated 'social superiority . . . in the raiments of penury' (Davis 1992: 64).

Fred Davis might also use the concept of collective identity ambivalence to explain the adoption of working-class apparel by Bob Dylan and other folk musicians of the 1960s. Focused on status, Davis would argue that folk revival dress emerged out of conflict related to the 1950s rigid class structures, being symbolized by external emblems of class mobility such as dress, cars and new houses in the suburbs. These emblems of status may not have been reflective of the social identity for many young people at that time, creating ambivalence in identity construction. Woody Guthrie, and his deliberately constructed working-class appearance, quite possibly became an emblem of authenticity for these young folk musicians, most of them born and raised in 1950s affluence.

Searching for Status and Social Identity in the New Millennium

Many of the collective behavior theories presented within this chapter were developed in earlier time periods but still resonate in today's new millennium. The desire to mark group identity, individual identity, and status remain central tenets of collective behavior and continue to serve as engines behind fashion change and adoptive behavior. The increasing globalization of fashion made possible through web-based computer technology has also increased the potential for international application of these theories. The increasing commercialization of identity, linking who we are to what we buy, perhaps gave rise to the surge in conspicuous consumption that we will read in a case study later in this chapter. Finally, identity ambivalence, the continual shopping for who we are that characterizes this era of post-modern identity, makes the work of Fred Davis particularly relevant for the analysis of fashion change.

Summarization of Collective Behavior Theories

Theory One: Emulating the Powerful, Modified and Revised Trickle-down Theories

The use of dress and appearance as a means of forging connections to those of power and influence drives this theory and its many interpretations. First developed in the late 1800s during a time of class conflict and class mobility, the theory has continued to be reinterpreted in line with ever-emerging social realities. In current form the theory is best articulated by Grant McCracken (1985) who argued that fashion change was still driven by the copying of the dress of those in power by those with less power, with new fashions emerging as the more powerful group continues to reinvent their look and remain distinct. Slight variations of this theme, including the bottom-up theories of Field (1970) and Tulloch (1992) still argue essentially that what is motivating fashion change is emulation based on attraction to the power carried by the dress styles of influential people.

Theory 2: Following Your Peers: Collective Selection and Trickle-across Theory

Fashion change from this theoretical point of view occurs as a result of collective selection of looks and fashions that ease or facilitate the adjustment of people to ever-changing versions of modern social life (Blumer, 2003 [1939]). Simultaneous adoption of fashion at all price points is central to this theory, with fashion leaders functioning to instigate trend adoption within distinct peer sets (King, 1963).

Theory 3: The Drive to Show Off: Conspicuous Consumption

Conspicuous consumption theories of fashion change, largely built on the seminal work of Veblen (1899), focus on the collective need for marking status through visible forms of affluence such as fashion. Novelty, access to the newest and the cutting edge, is related to both cost and status in this model, thus fashion changes incessantly as status-driven consumers seek the newest version of a given fashion product category.

Theory 4: Finding Who I am: Unstable Identity as a Fashion Change Agent

Fred Davis' (1985) contribution was to move the focus to the unstable identities that characterize the post-modern condition. His theory argued that fashion changes emerge as a collective response to identity ambivalence, with new fashions expressing ever-changing versions of identity in social categories wherein individuals feel compromised or conflicted regarding their level of power and status.

New Millennium Case Studies

The New Gilded Age: Luxury Goods Make a Come Back

In 2002 the *New York Times Magazine* declared that the Gilded Age was making a comeback, best characterized by income disparity between the rich and poorer now rivaling and sometimes surpassing that of the late 1800s. The egalitarian middle-class society so dominant in the 1950s and 1960s, argued economist Paul Krugman, was rapidly disappearing as the income differences between the super rich and the rest of the country widened (2002: 64). Krugman's article was visually illustrated by examples of house designs by architect Thierry Despont who specializes in extravagant displays of wealth in mansions with up to 60,000 square feet, approximately the square footage of the White House.

Not focused on by Krugman was the concomitant return of luxury fashion products which also exemplify the growing extravagant show of wealth; however, others have noticed. For example, in a fashion article in the style section of the *New York Times*, the author asked, 'Who pays $1,200 for a handbag, and why?' (La Ferla, 2005: E1). The ultra-expensive handbag appeared to be part of a broader trend in women's wear, with fashion analysts claiming that 'in the women's fashion luxury market there has been a migration from one category to the next . . . A few years ago it was shoes. Last year it was jeans. This is the year of the handbag' (La Ferla, 2005: E1). The question becomes not whether women are going to spend high sums for luxury goods, but rather what will be the next product category that will attract the lavish spending of the well-to-do?

The *New York Times* fashion analyst pointed out that part of the reason for the focus on the handbag, or other accessories as a mark of status, was the more general trend toward casual looks, that do not in and of themselves announce the status of the wearer:

One reason for the rise of these bags is that the rest of fashion has moved toward a more dressed-down look, so that even jeans may be appropriate for a dinner party. A four-figure bag imparts the corrective message: I am not a graduate student. 'You can go out with blue jeans and cowboy boots, and that high-priced bag makes it all OK,' said Cece Cord, a social figure in New York. 'A bag is sort of like a portable house. It represents you.' (La Ferla, 2005: 9)

The return of Veblen's conspicuous consumption theory as a means of predicting fashion trends is aptly illustrated by this consumption trend in luxury goods. In this case the role of the fashion forecaster becomes one of anticipating what bag will be hip next season, or predicting which new product will become the replacement emblem of status for the next year.

Collective Selection of Surf Style: A Twenty-First Century Look

The casual beach look made first recognizable by Tom Wolfe's 1965 book *The Pump House Gang* was an expression of the surf lifestyle, as much as the sport. Fashion writer Guy Trebay described the 1960s surfers as 'legitimate counter-culture types, a wave-riding minority of oddballs, semi-sociopaths, dropouts, athletically gifted isolates with the occasional drug or messiah problem, or just all-around good-time freaks' (2006: E1). In retrospect, the mass adoption of the surf look is astonishing. Surfer appearance is big business now, with sales statistics indicating a 90 percent increase in self-described surfers during the time frame between 1987 and 2005, with a current national total of 2.7 million surfer devotees.

Surf lifestyle is now longer sub-cultural but is instead big business. For example, Quiksilver, a surf-wear company founded by two former surfers, is now reporting profits of $541 million per quarter. They sell their product using lifestyle messaging, but the audience has broadened beyond legitimate surfers. The current marketing strategy welcomes the non-surfer into their style arena, along with committed beach bums. The founders of Quiksilver describe their company as being 'producers of clothing, accessories, and related products for young-minded people and developers of brands that represent a casual lifestyle driven from a board-riding heritage' (Trebay, 2006c: E5). In sum, this large-scale change in self-declaration of surfer identity that has translated into a huge fashion trend can be viewed as an excellent example of collective behavior response to the more general embrace of dressed-down casual looks for men.

Red Hat Society Fashions as a Response to Aging Ambivalence

The cultural meaning of female aging in the United States is strongly affected by mass media dominated with ideals of youthful beauty, and fashion products primarily designed for young bodies and young lifestyles. As a result, older women do not see themselves or their lifestyles depicted in the fashion system, leading to feelings of being marginalized and invisible. In addition, aging for women in contrast with men has been made more difficult in the US due in part to a culturally maintained reliance on attractiveness as a measure of female accomplishment (Kaiser, 1997) throughout the lifecycle. Red Hat Societies drawing membership from women over fifty have emerged as a group response to the identity ambivalence surrounding the female aging process. In concert, fashion products designed specifically for Red Hat Society members have grown in popularity, and offer a good contemporary case study of fashion emerging out of identity ambivalence, the theory established earlier by Fred Davis (1992).

The Red Hat Society got its official start in 1997 when Sue Ellen Cooper, a midlife, white, California native bought a red fedora on a whim in an Arizona thrift shop while on vacation. She discovered that wearing the hat made her feel free to have fun again, as she had when she was younger. Cooper wanted to share this experience with her friends, so she started a tradition of buying her female friends red hats for their fiftieth birthdays, and sharing with them the Jenny Joseph poem 'Warning,' which links aging to having fun. In particular Cooper was drawn to the poem's opening lines which speak to the wearing of bright, conspicuous dress as a fun spirited way of approaching older age:

When I am an old woman, I shall wear purple,
With a red hat which doesn't go, and doesn't suit me. (Joseph, 1992)

Eventually, Cooper's group of friends named themselves the Red Hat Society and began meeting in public spaces wearing their red hats. Their activities quickly earned them public and media attention, and interest from women throughout the country. The Red Hat Society has grown to include chapters officially registered on Cooper's website with a total official membership of 850,000 women. There are also many other unofficial chapters throughout the country (Walker, 2005a). As Red Hat Society membership has grown, Rob Walker (2005a) points out that the group's subversive ability to make the surrounding culture look at female aging differently has grown proportionately.

As Red Hat Societies have grown in popularity the breadth and availability of red-hat merchandise has also increased. In interviews older women expressed delight with the growing availability of red-hat fashion items through catalogues, the Internet, and traditional retail environments. Red Hat Society conventions feature prominent displays of red-hat merchandise for sale as a part of the proceedings, and 'shopping, shopping, shopping' is often a feature of the Red Hat Society chapter meetings. For these older women, accustomed to seeing special merchandise created for younger markets, to be granted so much attention by retailers, direct-mail organizations, and local businesses is perceived quite positively (Lynch, Stalp and Radina, 2007). The freedom from conventional fashion is expressed in comments like, 'when you get older you don't have to stick to the norm, and you don't have to follow fashion' (Lynch, Stalp and Radina, 2006), thus opening up the possibility for this market segment of older women demanding a more active and enjoyable set of products to embody their Red Hat identities.

Hispanic Culture Rises to Chic: The New Millennium Version of Trickle Down

Quince Girl, a magazine guide published annually for young Hispanic women planning their traditional 15th birthday celebration, the quincenaera, released its first issue on March 1, 2006. Signaling the emerging trend of large-scale showy quincenaeras among the Hispanic American population, the magazine showcases national trends in fashion and event planning for this important coming-of-age ritual.

The original quincenaera dates back to the pre-colonial era in Spain and is experiencing revitalization in the United States. Teenage Hispanic girls, who not long ago had dropped the ritual in favor of the more mainstream symbols of adulthood, like a new car, are returning to their cultural roots and insisting on the more traditional 15th birthday celebration. The ritual that is in many ways modeled after a wedding ceremony, without the groom, includes a processional entrance down the center of the church and a symbolic dance with the father of the 'queen for the day.' Appearance is central, and young women invest in colorful formal wear and a tiara, sourced often at web-based or local bridal stores. The recent revival of the quincenaera emerged first among wealthy Hispanics but has been adopted by other Hispanics on lower rungs of the economic ladder. Thus we see trickle-down effects are occurring as young women from middle-class backgrounds are exposed to the rituals of the wealthy and follow suit to capture the power and status of those wealthier than themselves. The exposure of quincenaera rituals to all rungs of the socio-economic ladder occurs through national advertising channels on the web and in magazines like *Quince Girl*. All of this exposure signals a change in the fashion dynamics within the United States. Now we witness growing immigrant populations exhibiting trickle-down effects within their own communities. In other words, rather than copying mainstream trends from outside their community, ethnic populations are creating their own status-based fashion trends internally.

Rob Walker (2006b) wrote that the revitalization of this traditional version of coming of age is in large part due to a shift in how Hispanic culture and rituals are perceived within immigrant communities, as well as a more general trend toward extravagant marking of teenage rites of passage within the

United States. The identity shift toward recognizing ethnicity in shopping and dressing patterns noted by Walker (2006b) was captured by Marilyn Halter (2000) who identified a new millennium trend of shopping for identity, with immigrants eager to mark themselves as not simply American, but as members of elite ethnic groups within the United States.

5

Style: The Endless Desire for a New Look

The new fashionable figure is growing straighter and straighter, less bust, less hips, more waist, a wonderfully long, slender suppleness about the limbs . . . The long skirt . . . reveals plainly every line and curve of the leg from hip to ankle. The petticoat is obsolete, prehistoric. How slim, how graceful, how elegant women look! The leg has suddenly become fashionable.

Quoted in Steele, *Fashion and Eroticism*

The above quote, published in *Vogue* in 1908, captures the dramatic beginning of the modern silhouette which would come to dominate female ideals of beauty beginning in the two opening decades of the twentieth century. The quote also captures the important linkage between body form and fashion, and how within modern fashion the two inter-relate and by so doing express ever-changing ideals of beauty. The emergence of not only new fashions, but ever-changing versions of ideal body shapes leads us into exploring the body as a formal design problem solved stylistically in different time periods, in different ways. Style change is thus a modification of how the body is approached and presented as a design problem, with cloth and construction techniques used to create line, shape, and idealized form.

The emergence of style evolution in Western costume history corresponded to the emergence of fashionable dress in Europe between 1200 and 1400. Prior to that time dress for both men and women relied heavily on ornamentation and surface design for visual interest. The creative manipulation of shape to fit, enhance, or alter body form was absent in early European dress. Instead, the emphasis was on expressing wealth, station, and power through wearing intricately patterned woven silks, in some time periods heavily encrusted with surface ornamentation and trims. Between 1200 and 1400 fashion 'began to operate symbolically and allusively through fashionable shape and ornament, using its own suggestive applied forms in dynamic counterpoint to the shapes of real bodies' (Hollander, 1995: 31). With this change toward exploration of the relationship between body form, shape, and line, dress in the West entered into a more sophisticated dialogue with other visual arts such as sculpture and painting. At the same time, as a living, breathing form of sculpture, dress styles began to evolve in relationship to each other, with styles of the past leading into styles of the future.

This chapter will challenge you to consider style changes as self-perpetuating, sometimes preceding or anticipating social changes. The first half of the chapter will focus on case-study examples from the first two decades of the twentieth century to illustrate how art historians interpret style-based fashion change. Further, using the ideas of both Valerie Steele and Anne Hollander, introduction of new style trends will be linked to the development of new cultural norms and values through presentation of new ways of looking at the dressed body. The second half of the chapter will begin with a summarization of style-based explanations for style change, followed by a series of applied contemporary case studies.

Understanding Style: An Art Historical Approach to Fashion Change

Style is defined by art historians as those elements of form, line, meaning and shape that serve to unify or group a set of art works together as being made by a single artist, or by a group of artists who have a shared aesthetic vision (Finch, 1974; Gombrich, 1979; Munro, 1970). Art historical style analysis includes comparing similar works of art from the same time period, as well as contrasting work of a given style with preceding, competing, and subsequent styles. The assumption is made by art historians that a tradition of craft and a history of ideas influences artistic endeavor, with artists building innovation on a foundation of shared technical history and conceptual understanding. Changes in artistic style are thus seen as evolutionary, with contemporary innovation emerging out of and building upon past styles, and even radical movements seen as reactions to the past rather than isolated extreme movements. Change is thus interpreted as internal to the creation process, not caused by external events or the individual creative spirit of a single artist.

Historians and art historians, most notably Valerie Steele and Anne Hollander, have argued persuasively for approaching fashion change as an internally style-driven process. Both Steele and Hollander largely dismiss notions that external events, changing cultural attitudes, or concepts of femininity and masculinity directly cause fashion change, but rather argue that like other plastic arts, fashion styles change in response to previous styles. What is emphasized from an art historical perspective is tracing the evolution of aesthetic rules underlying creative fashion making, in order to understand the common treatments of line, shape, form, and meaning, bonding different dressmakers together into a unified style.

Linking the creative fashion process to the literary arts where genres and forms create literary movements, Hollander states:

One might say that individual appearances in clothes are not 'statements', as they are often called, but more like public readings of literary works in different genres of which the rules are generally understood. A genre naturally develops as groups and individuals modify it, but always in terms of previous examples within it and rules that define it. Thus Western clothing is not a sequence of direct social and aesthetic messages cast in a language of fabric, but rather a form of self-perpetuating visual fiction, like figurative art itself. (1975: xv)

According to Hollander's thinking the evolving 'fiction' of dress is expressed in the varying relationships of clothing forms on the body, and the meanings each time period associates with those recurring forms (Hollander, 1995). Thus meaning is embedded in a stylistic flow of ideas, which inter-relate the body to a series of formal solutions in cloth.

While both Steele (1985) and Hollander (1975 and 1995) assign style the role of instigating fashion change, they interpret how it works differently. Steele attributed the continual striving for a new look we currently experience in the West to the role of dress in stimulating sexual interest. According to her analysis, 'novelty arouses sexual curiosity and causes the individual to be "seen" more clearly again' (1985: 247). This clear vision of a new look rekindles aesthetic and sexual interest, stimulating a broader adoption of the style. Steele also expressed a sensitivity and understanding of the role of craft and artistic community in stimulating and developing stylistic direction within the plastic art of dressmaking. As designers experiment with the body as a three-dimensional design problem, drawing from stylistic patterns of the past and integrating emerging technical and formal influences, solutions to style are born.

Hollander also argued that sexuality 'is always the engine of fashion,' with eroticism usually expressed in 'formal opposition to whatever has lately been conventionally defining male and female' (1975: 40). Like Steele, Hollander saw fashion as a way of refreshing the perception of the male and female sexual body, and by so doing stimulating movements of style toward ever new or reinterpretations of the relationship between dress and the body. Rather than seeing fashion as a form of rebellion against normative and 'unbearable' styles, Hollander (1975: 49) argued that style change is rather a reaction to conventionality and boredom – with a new look that creates interest again.

The role of representational images of dressed appearance, in advertising, painting, lithographs, and other pictorial medium, in communicating style and forming style is given great weight by Hollander. Unlike Steele, she assigned huge formative power to visual depictions of fashion, and the role of images in stimulating style change and adoption behavior. Rather than embedding the change process within the plastic art of dressmaking, Hollander moved agency into the world of paintings, lithographs, photographs, and film:

Like any visual art, the art of dress has its own autonomous history, a self-perpetuating flow of images derived from other images. But any living image of a clothed body derives essentially from a picture or, rather, from an on-going, known tradition of pictures of clothed bodies, rather than directly out of satisfying a desire for good-looking covering, invented anew each generation or each decade. Dressing is always picture making, with reference to actual pictures that indicate how clothes are to be perceived. (1975: 311)

While both Steele and Hollander interpreted style change as erotically motivated, Hollander moved the stimulus for change from novel design solutions to innovative forms representing the dressed body with 'change ... spurred and led by images in pictures, more and more of which offer themselves to feed the eye and create dissatisfaction' (1975: 359). Hollander goes as far as to argue that illustrations and other pictorial media have the power not only to lead style change, but to precede changes in society 'as unconscious desire for change appears in the illustrative bodily realm before anyone articulates and reasons the need (1995: 28).

Hollander posited that anti-fashion styles (Polhemus, 1978), looks posed in dramatic rebellion to cultural norms, are endemic to the change-based fashion process, often emerging to visually shock the eye, in order to prepare the eye for upcoming style shifts (1975). She goes on to point out that anti-fashion looks when first appearing as counter-cultural or rebel dress are not widely accepted, and in fact are often viewed as either perverse or ugly when first introduced. Some anti-fashion looks die, but others are harbingers for the look to come, and re-emerge in a more widely acceptable form after their first introduction by marginal sub-groups. Hollander pointed out the 'those who devise anti-fashion clothing are themselves not exempt from the influence of the general taste, even as they flout it.' And further, 'they are likely to propose a way for clothes to look that is not really revolutionary but evolutionary, and likely to emerge anyway in fashion before too long' (1975: 364).

Seeking the New Look: Style Change in the Early Twentieth Century

The emergence of the thin modern silhouette in the early twentieth century, along with the tubular fashions that went with it, is a style change arguably accomplished by the combined creative vision of a host of both known and anonymous designers and artists of the period. The debates surrounding who first abolished the corset are perhaps most well known, with at least three celebrated and vocal contenders in Coco Chanel, Paul Poiret, and Madeleine Vionnet (Evans and Thornton, 1989). The intention of this extended case study will not be to sort out the credit for the new modern look. Instead we will illustrate through case study examples how in multiple ways the evolution of style in this period worked to redefine the relationship of the female body to dress and adornment, in the end creating a modern interpretation of female beauty and eroticism.

The modern look that eventually took center stage most significantly draws style elements from menswear in order to distance the modern ideal of female eroticism from the nineteenth-century ideal which relied heavily on its contrast with the male ideal for its appeal. The twentieth-century ideal of beauty also draws from modernism with its spare lean style, lack of decorative ornament, and modern line. The style evolution leading to the free use of menwear style to create sexually charged and interesting looks for women begins with our first case study that traces the symbolic breaking down of the rigid division of menswear and womenswear by the introduction of bifurcated underpants for women. This case study is followed by an examination of Hollander's thesis of representational art leading style change, through an analysis of the impact of the graphic art depictions of Paul Poiret's fashions in the popularization of the new modern silhouette. A focused case study of the contribution of Coco Chanel to the twentieth-century female ideal follows. This set of related case studies ends with an application of Steele's idea that style change is at least partially embedded in the craft and art of dressmaking, using Sonia Delaunay's print and apparel designs as a case study example.

The Naughty Case of Underpants: Anti-fashion Becomes Acceptable Trend

Style was defined earlier in this chapter as those elements of form, line, meaning and shape that serve to unify representational art or costume into movements or periods of creation. The emphasis on *meaning* within the definition stresses the importance of considering the history of meaning that is linked to treatments of the body with cloth, in order to both understand and forecast style changes. The emergence of women's underwear as a popular style occurred relatively late in costume history, with the first popular and widespread adoption, both in Europe and the United States, in the later half of the nineteenth century. Within this opening case study of the style chapter the focus will be on the impact of the historical meaning of bifurcated (trouser cut) styles on the timing of the style trends in women's wear, and what that trend came to symbolize and mean.

The first popularization of bifurcated styles for men was led by Charlemagne, crowned as the first Christian king of unified Europe in AD 800. In earlier Roman and Byzantine empires, civilized men wore woven wrapped or tunic-style garments, with bifurcated styles relegated to the working and soldier classes. Charlemagne introduced trousers into the accepted lexicon of styles for civilized male leadership in the West, drawing from his own Germanic tradition of roughly woven or animal-skin trousers which allowed physical mobility and horsemanship. Combining this Germanic dress style with Roman and Byzantine leadership dress, Charlemagne reconfigured the masculine silhouette with trousers introduced as a style symbolizing active and aggressive masculinity as defined in early Europe, and wrapped Roman imperial styles evoking leadership based on legislative and decision-making power (Russell, 1983).

The introduction of bifurcated styles for men begins the process of sharply separating the style history of menswear and womenswear. Donning bifurcated garments, 'wearing the pants,' became synonymous to being in masculine control, with dresses associated with the less seriously regarded roles of women in European history. Wearing 'dresses' and wearing 'pants' became taboo for the opposite sex, with perversion and lack of sexual credibility associated with cross-dressing. These gender-based dress patterns extended also in the adoption of bifurcated underwear styles, with 'the separation of women's legs, even by a single layer of fabric' being considered 'obscene and unholy' up until the second half of the nineteenth century (Hollander, 1975: 132).

The relatively slow adoption of bifurcated underwear styles for women can thus be attributed to the heavily masculine symbolism embedded in the wearing of trousers by men. The wearing of any form of bifurcated styles, including undergarments, became the 'measure of a man,' and thus forbidden and taboo to a proper woman. The question then becomes how, when, and why did bifurcated underwear styles for women emerge as a fashion trend?

The first emergence of bifurcated underwear styles for women were worn as naughty tantalizers by isolated numbers of fast women in sixteenth-century Europe (see Hollander 1975 for an imprint of a courtesan of the period wearing underpants). Both Steele and Hollander stress the sexual charge granted the wearing of underpants by women due to their style history in menswear – the forbidden nature of the male style thus serving to further accentuate female curves and female body differences for the male gaze. During this period, the association of unholy ideas with fabric passing through the legs of mature women continued to stop widespread adoption of the style, thus confining this early experiment to women on the fringes of respectability. As stated earlier in this chapter, anti-fashion styles are often precursors to later more popular trends, functioning to lead the way through association of the style with meaning. The association of the bifurcated underwear styles with sexuality in the sixteenth century raised its head again in the early Victorian period with 'good women' wearing plain and modest styles, with fancier styles still associated with faster women. In both cases the underwear is sexually charged by its very form, which assertively laid fabric through the forbidden legs of even the most proper women. The fact that 'proper' women wore less fancy styles does not negate the sexual charge, which is primarily created through form and fit on the body.

The trend throughout the Victorian period is to link more clearly female underpants and sexuality by increasing the decoration and luxury of the underwear worn by even the most proper married woman. Steele reported that while undergarments from this time period were 'essentially modest and unassuming' [by our standards], there was a 'gradual and subtle increase of decoration over time' (1985: 194). By the 1880s, she reported that 'more decorative and seductive underwear was perfectly appropriate for the respectable married woman' (1985: 194).

Understanding why the style was relegated to anti-fashion in the sixteenth century, but emerged as popular fashion in the Victorian period, involves exploring the relationship between the historical meaning of the style and cultural receptivity to the connotations carried by the form. In contrast to the sixteenth century, men's and women's lives were socially divided between the public world of work for men, and the domestic sphere for women in the Victorian period. The intensification of the social differences between men and women in the Victorian period made adoption of the forbidden underpants particularly seductive.

Appearing first in the nightclub world of dancers and prostitutes, fancy underpants eventually developed into an acceptable way for a 'good' Victorian wife to keep her fellow at home through a socially sanctioned expression of sexuality. By the early decades of the twentirth century, the time period of this extended case study, Mrs Eric Pritchard, writing in the *The Lady's Realm*, an upper-class English magazine, 'stressed repeatedly that 'lovely lingerie' did not belong 'only to the 'fast,' and that 'dainty undergarments . . . are not necessarily a sign of depravity. The most virtuous of us are now allowed to possess pretty undergarments, without being looked upon as suspicious characters' (Steele 1985: 195). Mrs Pritchard goes on to link the wearing of beautiful undergarments with sexual satisfaction within marriage.

During this period of popular and widespread adoption of male bifurcated-style undergarments for women, expressions of other versions of female sensuality played with crossing over to masculine role or appearance to create impression and sexual edge. The British Blondes, peroxide blonde showgirls from England, appeared on New York stages as soldiers and pirates. In the words of William Dean Howell, these stage cross-dressed women had 'all the easy attitudes of young men,' and were described by him as sensual 'creatures of a kind of alien sex' (Banner 1983: 125). The gradual acceptance of female sexuality in the later Victorian period leads into the more modern outlook of the twentieth century, along with it styles of dress that continue to borrow design elements and silhouette direction from menswear styles.

The Power of a Picture: Paul Poiret's Launching of the Modern Silhouette

Great battles have been waged over who deserves the credit for introducing the svelte female body and style of the modern era. This case study will use Anne Hollander's ideas on the formative power of visual representation to focus on the role of popular lithographs of Paul Poiret's fashions served in the transformation of the old-fashioned, turn-of-the-century, wasp-waisted silhouette into the boyish lines of the twentieth century.

As stated more briefly earlier, Hollander attributes great power to images –paintings, photographs, lithographs – in formulating and moving forward style changes in body ideals and related dress. According to Hollander (1975), depictions of the dressed body within Western figurative art are not merely representational but rather play, in Hollander's words, a 'vital' role in the continual recreation of the relationship between the body and cloth. The common interpretation of clothing styles depicted in paintings and other artwork as reflections of cultural and economic changes was refuted by Hollander. Instead she argued the visual arts present new images of the ideal dressed body to the public, who in turn use the images to fashion a new more contemporary look.

Poiret is well known as a 'brilliant publicist,' whose 'attack on the corset succeeded where others had failed' (Evans and Thornton 1989: 128). Certainly Poiret himself, in his autobiography, claimed the contribution to the new style:

> It was still the age of the corset. I waged war upon it . . . It was . . . in the name of Liberty that I proclaimed the fall of the corset and the adoption of the brassiere which, since then, has won the day. Yes, I freed the bust. (1931: 76–7)

What is important to note, however, in the credit granted Poiret by Evans and Thornton, is the significance given to marketing, and Poiret's skill as a publicist. While most costume historians argue that many designers were experimenting with corset-less modern looks in this era, what was unique about Poiret was his use of graphic representations of his styles to sell the look to a still hesitant international audience. Careful always to link his designs to the art world, Poiret commissioned well-known artists Paul Iribe and George Lepape to create fashion plates of his work for exclusive clientele (Troy, 2003; Behling, 1977).

The significance of the new ideal and its pronounced contrast to the past is captured by Victoria Steele in her summarization of the commentary of French fashion magazines of the era:

> For centuries the ideal had been the 'fat' woman, who 'symbolized the family'.[1]

1. Contradictions to the position taken by these popular fashion magazines can be found in the academic literature. For example Lois Banner argues that the Romantic ideal of the early eighteenth century was a slight and young ideal.

Now the new ideal had resulted in 'a different conception of love'. At present the thin woman seduces us with her disquieting and alert glamour. She comes and goes . . . Nothing rejuvenates like thinness. (1985: 230)

However, despite the build-up of support for the new-style thin ideal, Steele pointed out the convincing argument of French fashion historian Marylene Delbourg-Delphis that 'the early twentieth century woman was only "beginning" to want be thin, and that this [ideal, this new look – new style] was still 'more a desire than a reality' (1985: 229). Steele instead points out the very real gap between the representations of modern female style, and the reality of most figures of the time period:

The 'idealized' graphic art of 1908 to 1914, characteristic of Poiret's deluxe pamphlets and certain avant-garde French magazines, did not accurately portray the figures that most women had at that time. And some people complained that the new 'sheathlike' fashions were 'very trying to the average figure.' (1985: 229-30)

Thus Poiret, through his visual marketing strategy, created a need for a new look, a desire to appear modern, that transcended the power of his individual designs to create the new look. Certainly it can be argued that Poiret played a role, along with others, in the freeing of female fashion style from cinched corset silhouette, allowing designers freedom to work with a 'new vocabulary of shapes and styles' (Steele: 227). But perhaps his greater contribution was creating popularly consumed imagery of the modern silhouette, which broadcast the desire for being modern to a wide audience.

Poiret's moment on the fashion stage was relatively short as Chanel's image of the modern woman, more effective agent than a decorative accessory, took center stage after the First World War. Poiret's treatment of women as decorative objects lost its appeal as the twentieth century new woman took center stage. However, the notion that visual representation of Poiret's designs played a formative role in creating a desire on the part of women to look and act modern is persuasive, and aptly illustrates Hollander's concept of the generative role of visual representation in creating fashion change.

Chanel as Style: The Expression of Modern Eroticism and Beauty

Coco Chanel's contribution to fashion of the twentieth century is often looked at in retrospect, and interpreted as a reflection of the social changes in women's lives over the course of the century. Her early borrowing of menswear-style details and shapes are seen as marking the entrance of women onto the public stage of work and out of the confines of domesticity. This case study will challenge that interpretation of her work, by using Valerie Steele's ideas to focus on

Chanel's contribution to an evolutionary style change that in the end created a modern ideal of feminine beauty and eroticism.

The entrance on the fashion stage of the modern look, in large part heralded by the popularization of Chanel's fashion look between the two World Wars, is often interpreted in sociological terms as the birth of the new modern independent woman. While certainly the roles that women played in World War I were liberalizing, perhaps more significantly female beauty and eroticism were redefined in modern terms by the style created by Chanel. Thus when summarizing Chanel's contribution to fashion, Steele focused her attention on the casual young athleticsm captured by Chanel's look:

> The real secret of Chanel's success was not that her clothes were simple or even comfortable, but that they made the rich look young and casual. Women throughout the western world had a new image of themselves that made the formal an ostentatious elegance of the prewar period look old-fashioned. The ideal body was not so much boyish as it was the style of a sophisticated school girl. (1988: 247)

In explaining the meaning of this new look, Steele draws from F. Scott Fitzgerald's description of Jordan Baker in the *Great Gatsby*, a wonderfully concise portrait of new modern feminine erotic appeal and beauty. As cited by Steele, Fitzgerald described his female ingénue wearing her 'evening dress, all her dresses, like sports clothes—there was a jauntiness about her movements as if she had first learned to walk on golf courses on clean crisp mornings' (1988: 247).

From this point of argument Chanel's place on center stage during this era comes not from single-handedly abolishing the corset (in which others played a role), and inventing sportswear (although she contributed in this arena), but rather redefining beauty and eroticism on modern terms using the visual vocabulary of fashion. This point of view, that shifting ideals of beauty and eroticism instigates style changes, was articulated by Valerie Steele:

> All of my research has led me to believe that the concept of beauty is sexual in origin, and the changing ideal of beauty apparently reflects shifting attitudes toward sexual expression. At the deepest level, the meaning of clothing in general and fashion in particular is also erotic. (1985: 5)

The lasting impact of her image of beauty is testimony to how well she encapsulated the move toward an active, dynamic, liberated concept of female beauty and sexuality – an ideal that still feels modern today.

The story of the creation of the modern beauty ideal begins with Chanel's personal experiments with fashion and a new look in the prewar years. The status of Chanel, who started out her design career as a mistress from a poor provincial background, impacted her attitudes toward conventional fashion of the early twentieth century, with its emphasis on looks that announced privilege and status. When combined with the growing style of modernism in the arts, which emphasized simplicity and movement away from sentimentalism and nostalgia, Chanel first dressed herself and then other women in styles that expressed modern anti-decorative functionalist design and the erotic appeal of a sporty, democratic spirit.

The stylistic borrowing from menswear, so central to the new look created by Chanel, infused a new eroticism into women's day and evening fashions that was already influencing undergarments in the Victorian period (as discussed in a previous case study). In a photograph in the Charles-Roux biography, Chanel is captured in 1910 'at the races, a parading ground for high fashion at the time, wearing a tie and a man's coat—too big in the shoulders, too long in the sleeves' (Evans and Thornton 1989: 122). While the look certainly challenged the normative roles of women of the time, it was, perhaps more importantly, 'glamorous' in its 'borrowing from the male wardrobe . . . within the terms of classical male dandyism', which signified 'personal independence within a rigid order' (Evans and Thornton 1989: 124). In this sense, Chanel's own personal style can be interpreted as a stylistic development from the earlier time period, moving from borrowing menswear elements in undergarments to outer garments, in search of renewed erotic charge and stylistic interest. The internal engine of style change is noted by Steele:

> Symbiotic with changing ideals of erotic beauty, the evolution of fashion has an internal dynamic of its own that is only very gradually and tangentially affected by social change within the wider culture. (1988: 5)

Thus the work of Chanel is seen not as primarily a reflection of the changing lives of women, which in the 1920s were still not remarkable liberated, but a continuation of stylistic experimentation focused on infusion of cross-over style elements from men's tailored styles into women's fashion looks to add erotic charge and interest.

The evolution from Chanel's own personal style to the wider adoption of her look by others largely occurred between the World Wars in Paris. The look she created and sold was expensive, but expressed a casual, democratic, active ideal of beauty favored by wealthy women during this time period. The idea that the look was associated with feminist inclinations was pasted on later; what is central to the style as it emerged was that it expressed a new feminine ideal, and a new image of eroticism for the modern American and European social stage.

The social changes in women's roles 'catch up with' the ideal of beauty put forward by Chanel in the later years of the twentieth century, as women began more significantly to create inroads into the roles and behaviors of men in Western society. As introduced earlier, according to Steele and other style-based writers, fashion change is not primarily driven by external social and cultural events, but rather is a self-perpetuating process or continual reinvention of ideals of beauty and eroticism. From this vantage point, style can lead behavior, with designers and individual fashion leaders inventing looks expressing ever-changing ideals of beauty and sexuality sometimes in advance of behavior and social change. As stated by Steele:

> It is often asserted that as beliefs and behavior change, so also does appearance. There is evidence, though, that appearance may change 'in advance' of widespread changes in belief systems and behavior. (Steele 1985: 47)

Thus Chanel's style becomes a harbinger rather than a reflection, with its ability to capture in plastic three-dimensional form, lasting visions of modern sexuality, and beauty that eventually transform and impact daily lives of modern women.

Sonia Delaunay: Textile Designs of the Jazz Age

The final style case study drawing from the first decades of the twentieth century will focus on the apparel and textile designs of Sonia Delaunay as a means of illustrating Steele's argument that 'Fashions evolve by means of a symbiotic relationship between the world of craft . . . and the more gradual evolution of cultural ideals of beauty' (1985: 47). Within this example we will illustrate the importance of innovations within the craft of printmaking to the contributions of Sonia Delaunay to the development of the modern ideal of female beauty and eroticism.

Sonia Delaunay was a Russian-born abstract painter working in Paris as the modern female look emerged on the fashion stage. Delaunay's migration over to fashion design was facilitated by the coming together of several related artistic traditions in the early twentieth century. First of all, Delaunay as a painter became interested in cubism, and experimented with expression of cubist ideas in cloth, in the creating of a quilt for her son – thus moving her towards an interest in designing-two dimensional textile patterns. Secondly, a group of designers including Paul Poiret, Coco Chanel, and others had moved the fashion ideal toward a modern angular silhouette, which provided a suitable canvas for large-scale textile designs, which were flat and painterly. But, perhaps most significantly, the adoption of newly developed screen-printing craft techniques in the early twentieth century allowed relatively inexpensive short runs of large-scale print designs in multiple colors (Damase, 1991).

While certainly it can be argued that Delaunay's textile designs, with their emphasis on movement, angularity and motion further developed the modern look for women in the early twentieth century introduced by others, it is also important to see her textile designs within the printing craft tradition in France during this era. Steele emphasized the importance of craft to explaining and forecasting style changes:

> The conscientious art historian would not analyze an artist's work simply in terms of that individual's psychology (or the psychology of his audience). Nor would he relate it primarily to larger cultural concerns—social economic or political. He would also have to take account of the artistic tradition within which the artist worked. Similarly, the fashion designer and the dressmaker worked within a 'world of craft' with its own traditions. Whatever connections they might have with the wider culture and with social change, styles of dress are clearly more directly related to earlier styles and to the internal processes of fashion change. (1985: 22–3)

Thus Delaunay, as well as other graphic artists of the period such as Iribe and Dufy, was working within a community of artists whose creative direction was in part influenced by the emerging technical and craft traditions of the period. Because of innovations in printing process, these artists were able to experiment creatively with textile design, utilizing printing houses mostly headquartered in Lyon, France. In another time period, within a different community of artists, and a different tradition of craft, it is unlikely that the style contribution made by Sonia Delaunay would have been accomplished.

Moving Style into the New Millennium

Style changes are modifications in the manner that the body is approached and presented as a design problem, with cloth and construction techniques used to create line, shape and idealized form. As reviewed earlier in this chapter, the emergence of style evolution in Western costume history corresponds to the emergence of fashion dress in Europe between 1200 and 1400. During this time dress emphasis shifted from decorating dress items to reflect status to manipulating the form, shape and line of garments. Those arguing that fashion change is style-based view fashion change as internally driven, with new styles building upon or reacting to the styles of the past. There are, however, distinct interpretations of what drives style change, particularly as captured in the scholarship of Valerie Steele and Anne Hollander. This chapter will conclude with a summarization of four interpretations of style change included in this chapter, followed by contemporary case study applications of the four theoretical positions.

Summarization of Style Theories

Theory One: Style Change Initiated by Changing Images of the Dressed Body

A unique contribution by Anne Hollander to style theory was her argument that images of the dressed body can initiate style change. According to her theory, pictorial depictions of the dressed body have the potential to affect how viewers see themselves and others, in some cases leading to novel constructions of fashionable identity. Thus new styles are first depicted in pictures of emergent ideals of beauty, which are then used as a reference for creating modern looks.

Theory Two: Style Change Initiated by Shifting Ideals of Beauty and Eroticism

Valerie Steele argued persuasively that changes in ideals of beauty and eroticism initiate style change. Fashion change according to this theory is always posed in relationship to the past ideal, with the novelty of new looks inspiring renewed erotic interest. The argument from this point of view is that feminine fashions emerge to spark sexual interest, with older styles falling into disfavor as the sexuality they express grows predictable and uninteresting.

Theory Three: Style Change Initiated by Changing Dressmaking Traditions

Valerie Steele approached the study of dressmaking as an art, with an emphasis on examining the stylistic relationships between dressmakers working within a shared tradition. Similar to shifts in painting styles, she argued that stylistic changes in apparel design are at times a communal response from a group of related designers who through interconnected artistic experimentation come up with new ways of configuring fabric on the body. Using this approach it is important to understand the relationship between designers, and one must struggle to detect the aesthetic relationships between separate bodies of work.

Theory Four: Style Change Initiated by Changing Technology

Innovative technological advances adopted by influential designers have the potential to create new looks and style change, according to Steele. Fashion change from this theoretical position is triggered by a technological advancement that results in a novel expression of the relationship between fabric and the body by a single influential designer, or a set of related dressmakers.

Style Change in the New Millennium: Four Case Studies

Anticipating or forecasting style-based trends requires an historical perspective in terms of the relationship of the body to dress. Shifts in ideals of beauty are important to watch for, and the related changes in how the body is addressed as a design problem. Novel dressmaking traditions are also important to follow, particularly as they emerge as a movement within a group of related designers. Finally technological innovation has the power to recreate the relationship between dress and the body, giving rise to the possibility of new trends and new visions of the dressed body.

The four case studies that follow offer contemporary applications of the four style-based fashion-change theories included in this chapter. Hollander's argument that visual representations of the dressed body are powerful initiators of style change is moved into the twenty-first century in the first case study that focuses on the role of mass-media images of plastic-surgery enhanced female celebrities in instigating a trend toward a bustier, less athletic feminine ideal. The second case study uses Valerie Steele's ideas to trace the emergence and development of a new feminine eroticism with ties to soft porn and American 'raunch.' The third case study, also using the ideas of Valerie Steele, examines changes in dressmaking traditions within knitwear design, leading to broadly based style changes. Finally the impact of new technology on the body of work of a related set of knitwear designers is examined, again illustrating an explanation for fashion change articulated by Steele.

The New Plastic Silhouette: Ideals of Beauty of the New Millennium

Shifting ideals of beauty such as the dramatic movement from the more voluptuous ideals of feminine beauty of the Victorian era to the modern thin ideal bring with them dramatic fashion changes, as dress interacts with the body in the expression of a new style. According to Anne Hollander, these changes were often inspired by images of the dressed body, pictures that inspired a new look, a new interpretation of beauty. The pictorial images of beauty that the consuming public is now commonly exposed to are most often photographic images, often utilizing such touch-up techniques as air brushing to achieve ideal body shapes and looks. Plastic surgery enhancement of the breasts and other parts of the body to increase sexual attractiveness have become increasingly common among celebrity figures, thus changing the images we are exposed to on a daily basis, and therefore our attitudes toward our own bodies. The 'pictures' we copy thus require a change in our body as well as our dress.

Evidence is mounting that the century long commitment to the thin more athletic ideal of beauty that emerged in the early 1900s is being challenged by a bustier more voluptuous ideal. Breast implants, while not yet normative in all parts of the country, are becoming more widely accepted. Health concerns related to the silicone implants which caused a decline in surgeries in the early 1990s appear to be quelled, with wide adoption of the trend in saline implants, particularly in Southern California, Texas and Florida:

> Surgery for breast enlargement (including breast lifts) has grown by 257 percent since 1997, reaching 432,403 patients last year [2004], according to the American Society for Aesthetic Plastic Surgery. Saline implants, filled with water, have largely replaced silicone in the United States. In total surgeons have performed about 1.3 million augmentations in the last decade, not enough to have a broad impact on the American clothing market in a population of 149 million women. But the implant trend has affected the styles sold in designer boutiques in certain cities and regions where surgeries are most popular. (Wilson, 2005a: S1)

Fashion on the racks of stores in regions strongly affected by this trend is beginning to reflect the new ideal, with larger sizes being offered:

> In regions where breast augmentation is most popular the wave of implants is skewing the selection of designer clothes sold at some stores, favoring sizes and styles more ample on top and creating a new market for alterations. With many plastic surgeons saying that Los Angeles is the country's implant capital, the Beverly Hills branch of Neiman Marcus sells more dresses in Size 12 than any other, while Sizes 8 and 10 are the most popular for designer evening wear at other Neiman branches, said a buyer for the chain, who linked the phenomenon to customers who had surgically increased their busts. (Wilson, 2005a: S1)

More significantly, however, are considered changes in dimensions of dress forms, and potential style changes related to the aesthetic of dressing a body which is busty, but slim – a somewhat unlikely combination of the voluptuous ideal and modern athleticism. The current mismatch between runway styles and this new millennium ideal is captured by Brian Bolke, a high-end Dallas boutique owner:

> For women who love fashion, breast enlargements and designer dresses do not go together. These women have great bodies, but they are not the bodies that designer clothes are made for. There is a ton of adjustments going on, because this area [Texas] is not known for small chests. Either women are having dresses completely butchered, or we're selling them separates with a top and skirt in different sizes. (Wilson, 2005a: S1)

While at present this trend has regional rather than national or international impact, it is important to recognize the prevalence of the trend among women representing female ideals within our culture. Using Anne Hollander's argument that fashion change is triggered by changes in how ideals of beauty are represented, while we may not be responding to paintings of women, we may very well respond to continual exposure to photographs of celebrities sporting new implants, and long thin legs. This new look, like the thin ideal of the twentieth century, will require a design response, a new relationship between the now changed body and fabric. And while not all women may choose to get breasts implants, a new way or refiguring the body to emphasize the breasts is already on the runway, and already given attention by consumers.

Transformation of the body through plastic surgery has extended into the most private domains, the genital area. This recent trend in designer laser vaginoplasty, a labia conturing technique, is attributed by plastic surgeons to more broadly based exposure of the American women to soft pornography, and to body exposing fashion styles such as the ubiquitous thong:

> primarily, doctors say, aggressive marketing and fashion influences like flimsier swimsuits, the Brazilian bikini wax and more exposure to nudity in magazines, movies, and on the Internet are driving attention to a physical zone still so private that women do not dare, or care, to look at themselves closely. 'Now women shave,' said Dr. Gary J. Alter, a plastic surgeon and urologist with offices in Beverly Hills, California and Manhattan who has come up with his own 'labia contouring' technique. 'Now they see Porn. Now they're more aware of appearance.' (Navarro, 2004: S1)

'Raunch': The Emergence of a New Eroticism

> If you ever watch television when you have insomnia, then you are already familiar with 'Girls Gone Wild': late at night, infomercials show bleeped out snippets of the brand's wildly popular, utterly plotless videos, composed entirely from footage of young women flashing their breasts, their buttocks, or occasionally their genitals at the camera, and usually shrieking 'Whoo!' while they do it . . . it's all girl-on-girl, we never shoot guys . . . And no pros. It has to be real. (Levy, 2006: 13–15)

Steele argued that style changes initiated by changing versions of feminine eroticism are posed in relationship to expressions of sexuality of the past. The flapper of the 1920s that we analyzed earlier in the chapter was posed in relationship to the nineteenth-century domestic public dichotomy, wherein good women clothed in proper Victorian dress were the keeper of the home, and public 'bad' women dressed in racy attire were the madams of the street. The flapper style was embraced in part in its time period due to the challenge to that division, a movement of the domestic into the public and with it a more open regard for women's sexuality and eroticism.

Similarly the emergence at the turn of the twenty-first century of what has been classified as raunch eroticism (Levy, 2005) must be seen posed in response to twentieth-century conceptions of female sexuality and empowerment. Embodied in everything from centerfold images of female Olympic athletes, to college women flashing their breasts for *Girls Gone Wild* crews during spring break, to Hooter's well-endowed waitresses, to televisions shows focused on sexually promiscuous housewives, the cultural presence of a new erotic ideal is undeniable. Tantalizing its audience with the blend of 'real' women with pornography, we are in its grip, and particularly young women are adopting its fashions and styles.

At the first level of adoption of this new look by young women are products emblazoned with logos marking the wearer as a part of ranch culture such as *Girls Gone Wild* T-shirts and hats, hooters T-shirts, and newly designed Playboy bunny logos. Following close behind are companies such as Abercrombie and Fitch who begin marketing their apparel with blatant sexuality, and in 2003 producing a catalogue that could only be viewed by those of legal age. Finally are newly emergent entrepreneurs like Dov Charney, CEO of American Apparel based in Los Angeles, who bases his entire advertising strategy on bridging the gap between pornography and the mainstream, using advertising to sell a lifestyle to a market segment he refers to as Young Metropolitan Adults. Characterizing this group of consumers as on the cutting edge of urban hip culture, Charney stressed that they 'have embraced an aggressively sexualized world, a continuum that includes the hip, subversive and degenerate aesthetic of so-called "pervey" cultural phenomenon—those parts of culture linked to the perverse' (Wolf, 2006).

Products made by American Apparel include a range of body hugging basic apparel, with the first signature T-shirt design sold in 2003 at a storefront gallery exhibiting photographs in a hip neighborhood in New York. As of January 2006, Charney has 100 American Apparel stores in hip cities in the United States and abroad with total sales in 2005 of $250 million. His factory based in Los Angeles employs 3,500 workers and is the single largest onshore garment factory now open in the United States. While certainly the clothing hugs the body, style writer Jaime Wolf argued that it is the advertising that establishes the link to ranch culture, and to sexualized cyber identities found on websites like Myspace or Facebook:

> The ads are also highly suggestive, and not just because they are showcasing underwear or clingy knits. They depict young men and women in bed or in the shower; if they are casually lounging on a sofa or sitting on the floor, then their legs happen to be spread; frequently they are wearing a single item of clothing but are otherwise undressed; a couple of the young women appear to be in a heightened state of pleasure. These pictures have a flashbulb-lighted, lo-fi sultriness about them; they look less like ads than photos you'd see posted on someone's Myspace page. (Wolf, 2006)

With the adoption of this new look, the clear line between 'good' and 'bad' women is once again challenged. In the opening to his book on the styles and culture of the 1920s Joshua Zeitz (2006) recalls the public deriding of the flappers of the period as immoral women of the streets, in effect feeding the style frenzy as women flocked to become this controversial ideal. In the same sense the controversy surrounding the sexually explicit video tape of Paris Hilton and her boyfriend, and the infamous *Girls Gone Wild* films are feeding the movement toward raunch style, and the blending of mainstream femininity and pornography.

Deconstruction Fashion: Knitwear Redefined

Radical designers and radical ideas appear at intervals in fashion, as in other design disciplines, throwing existing ideas into question, challenging assumptions and the aesthetics of established taste. Shocking as they are at first, we gradually absorb these new ideas until they become less strange to our sensibilities, and slowly there develops a fundamental shift in perceptions and we reach another plateau of acceptance. (Black, 2002: 90)

Valerie Steele's assertion that one of the triggers to fashion change is stylistic movement of a related set of designers is echoed in Sandy Black's fashion analysis on contemporary knitwear design. Citing the trio of Issey Miyake, Rei Kawakubo and Joyhi Yamamoto, Black (2002) argued that a synergy of design philosophy and practice by these three fashion innovators spawned a widely accepted modern avant-garde look that has transformed knitwear design, and influenced the broader design landscape. Among the aesthetic innovations introduced by this set of designers and adopted by their protégés and the wide design community are: (1) asymmetry in terms of left-to-right-side body balance, and hemlines; (2) utilization of non-traditional textiles and yarns; (3) combining of contrasting weight fabrications; (4) the cutting up of traditional tailored shapes into broken and unfinished sections; (5) the purposeful use of unfinished edge to create aesthetic effect; and (6) distortion of the proportions of the body through fit and shape (Black, 2002).

This style revolution called by some 'deconstruction fashion' involves both creative and intellectual experimentation on the part of a set of related artists/designers, but also, according to Black, is facilitated by the nature of knitwear design itself:

Knitted fabric can, uniquely, be made in the round (without seams) or it can be manipulated and twisted into sculptural new shapes for clothing. Seams can be displaced and repositioned . . . Pieces can be reconfigured with internal darts and lines of relief stitches can be contoured around the body. At its simplest level of single jersey fabric, knitting is particularly malleable. Individual garment pieces can be shaped at will and, according to choice of yarn and finish, can either result in something perfect and balanced or something distorted and untamed. (2002: 92)

Early and revolutionary work coming out of this designer workshop included Rei Kawakubo's 1981 sweater full of holes. This sweater, while appearing deconstructed and threadbare, in actuality was physically sound with each hole carefully constructed using traditional casting-on and casting-off knitting processes. This type of look was later widely adopted in punk, grunge, and post-punk looks, heralded by such designers as Alexander McQueen. Other deconstruction trends initiated by this innovative set of designers include the now common unfinished sweater cuff, left to curl up around itself, rather than being finished with a more classic knitwear cuff finish of a cable stitch.

These deconstruction influences moved not only into a redefining of knitwear design and finishes, but into woven design and finishes as well. As articulated by Black 'witness the mass-produced fashions that incorporate raw and frayed edges . . . Ripped denim jeans were shocking when first seen, but although they may have coded meanings, they no longer cause the same consternation' (2002: 90). Thus the radical experiments of a workshop of creative designers create a stylistic shift that becomes widely adopted and accepted as a mass fashion.

Technology Moves Trends: Knitwear Reconfigured

In many cases creative designers take the lead in discovering innovative ways to use existing technology, resulting in new trends such as the deconstruction fashion look outlined above. Steele also argued that technological developments can initiate fashion-trend development, spurring designers to approach design differently. In the words of Black, 'Design developments can clearly be linked to technological developments: technology can lead design, or design and fashion can lead technology' (2002: 178). In the knitwear industry, according to Black (2002), two of the most significant new developments are seamless, integral garment knitting on flat knitting machines and A-POC tubular clothing made from warp-knitted circular construction.

As currently practiced in the industry, both knitting technologies are highly dependent upon computer-aided design (CAD) capabilities. Integral garments, as described by Black (2002), are produced using either Stoll of Germany or Shima Seiki of Japan patented knitting systems and are based on seamless tube construction. Two tubes are for the sleeves, and one tube is for the body of the garment, with variations of stitch structure and size to create the shape and form of the garment. Seamless dresses and other forms of outerwear have revolutionized the runways, with designers taking advantage of this new technology to achieve body hugging new twenty-first-century looks. A-POC tubular knitwear design also uses CAD to create a designer/consumer interactive garment. This revolutionary warp-knitted circular-knitwear process first developed by Issey Miyake, involves the creation of a knitted tube that separates into a range of different styles. Black captures the agency given to the individual consumer purchasing an A-POC design:

> All the A-POC designs can be varied according to choice—round neck, V-neck or loose collar, short or long sleeves, short or long length, and so on. A computer-generated video shows the process of releasing the wardrobe from the cloth. The innovative retail concept of the A-POC shops is that they are to be seen as a laboratory in which the customer can view many examples of the variations on each theme and can cut their own garments from the piece or roll, with the help of the well-informed sales staff. (2002: 123)

This technology inspired trend in knitwear, while currently in an experimental phase, and not widely available, has the impact of not only radically redefining knitwear, but also transforming the shopping experience.

6

Fashion as Performance

Fashion is defined as the art of the perfect moment, of the sudden and surprising and yet obscurely expected harmonious apparition—the Now at the threshold of an immediate future. But its realization is, at the same time, its destruction. By appearing, and giving definitive form to the moment, fashion is almost already part of yesterday.

Vinken, 2005

The aesthetic and academic exploration of fashion as performance began to gain attention beginning in the 1990s as scholars and artists working in performance studies, film studies, gender studies, and the performance arts took notice of the theoretical and expressive possibilities of dressed appearance. The multi-disciplinary breadth of this exploration, including performing artists as well as academicians from diverse fields, presents a challenge to organizing this chapter. For the purposes of clarity we utilize Richard Schechner's division of performance into two main realms, those: (1) 'looking at human behavior—individuals and social—as a genre of performance'; and those (2) 'looking at performances—of theatre, dance and other "art forms"— as a kind of personal or social interaction' (1985: 296). To state it differently, Schechner discerned a useful distinction between performances of everyday life, which we witness without buying tickets, and those performances which are staged for an audience. Fashion, we will discover, is part of both types of performances, and within those performances seeds are planted giving rise to fashion change and related cultural transformation.

The relatively late emergence of fashion studies within performance scholarship can be attributed to the following converging attitudes. Firstly, the ephemeral nature of fashion made it vulnerable to dismissal by scholars interested in studying the 'lasting' and 'significant' aspects of culture; secondly, the link of fashion to consumer culture often meant it was relegated to analysis as a consumer behavior; and finally, for second-wave feminists, fashion was interpreted as symbolic of the subjugation of women to male gaze and desire (Church Gibson, 1998), making its study somehow a validation of sexist attitudes and behaviors. Ironically, the very attitudes which delayed the serious regard of fashion as a form of performance are now the essence of the emergent interest in fashion as performance. Fashion *is* fleeting and ephemeral, but as such it is the ideal embodiment of the modern condition – and what must be embraced as *real* in the late twentieth and early twenty-first century (Lehman, 2000). Fashion *is* the most visible and fluid form of 'commodity fetish'. Living in the age of the consumer, fashion allows us to embody our desire, buy our identity – in the most intimate sense, and is the consumer product most linked to the performance of everyday life. Finally, *yes, yes, yes,* fashion is about gender construction, and about dressing for others to see, and within this process, scholars, designers, and artists have found the potential for transforming gender through performance.

In some ways what has occurred is a rediscovery of what was already noticed once before, by some of the most thoughtful artists, designers, and scholars of the early twentieth century. Post World War I artists and writers who were struggling to unleash themselves from art based in the static classical traditions, saw the momentary ephemeral nature of fashion as the perfect embodiment of the new modern aesthetic. Ulrich Lehman, in discussing the conceptual connections artists and writers saw between their ideas of modern art and fashion, stresses the performative, the transistory nature of sartorial expression:

> for the artist in modernity, beauty lies expressing in the contemporary and no recourse to the ancient ideal of sublime beauty is permitted. Fashion is the supreme expression of that contemporary spirit. It changes constantly and remains necessarily incomplete; it is transitory, mobile, and fragmentary. This quality ties it in with the pace and rhythm of modern life. (2000: xii)

The notion that modernity is about the ephemeral played a large conceptual role in the emergence of performance art during this post-war time period, as artists working in diverse mediums together defined a new twentieth-century direction for creative expression. Early explorations of the link between fashion and art resulted in performances including the work of designers such as Sonia Delaunay and Paul Poiret, as well as artists and writers of the period.

This chapter will focus on late twentieth and early twenty-first-century examples of the role of performance as an instigator to fashion change. Using Schechner's ideas, the case studies are divided between those that are integrated into everyday life, that happen without a ticket on the stages that surround us; and those that are formal staged productions, requiring tickets. Opening case studies will be performances of everyday life, including performances enacted as a part of surrounding popular culture, performances which help create the spirit of the time or Zeitgeist; and finally how subcultures enact performances that impact the wider culture through challenging assumptions and normative behavior.

Performances of Everyday Life

Wearing our Identities: Popular Culture as Performance

Gwyneth Paltrow, wearing folk-style headdress of fall flowers, declares on the cover of October 2005 *Vogue* 'I HAVE SOMETHING THAT'S SO REAL.' MADONNA (written in red and all caps), is 'REINVENTED FOR THE VERY LAST TIME' as a 'Marvelous Mom and English Lady of the Manor' on the cover of August 2005 *Vogue*. The full-spread coverage of these two twenty-first-century female popular cultural icons sells fashion. Wearing Valentino Couture and Estee Lauder Pure Color Crystal Lipstick, Gwyneth is 'real' as she lies in the flower bed with flowers scattered in her hair on a French estate outside of Paris. Madonna as 'Marvelous Mom' and 'Lady of the Manor' wears Galliano polka dots and plays with her son who is dressed as a medieval knight, defending her on the Manor. How do the lives of celebrity icons like Madonna and Gwyneth function as a form of performance popular art within our culture, and how do they contribute to fashion change?

Fashion coverage in early nineteenth-century women's magazines took a didactic tone, and focused on telling women what was in fashion, and how and where to wear it. Middle- and upper-middle-class women, eager to imitate the dress of the upper class, read fashion magazines for guidance in following the current rules of fashion and social etiquette. Elizabeth Wilson contrasted this function of early fashion coverage with what exists today, accurately capturing the purpose of the 'Lady of the Manor' and 'I am so Real' *Vogue* fashion spreads, which was to create in the viewer the desire to capture the life of their popular culture icon, through buying and wearing their look:

> Fashion is a magical system, and what we see as we leaf through glossy magazines is 'the look'. Like advertising, women's magazines have moved from the didactic to the hallucinatory. Originally their purpose was informational, but what we see today in both popular journalism and advertising is the mirage of a way of being, and what we engage in is no longer only the relatively simple process of direct imitation, but the less conscious one of identification. (2003: 157)

The continual definition of gender identity, captured aptly in the Madonna cover headline, 'REINVENTED FOR THE VERY LAST TIME,' is noted by Wilson as she discusses the impact of fashion photography (2003: 158), noting the sensual relationship between the viewer and fashion imagery, with modern photography stimulating a continual dialogue on what it means to be a woman, and increasingly a man, in Western culture. The nineteenth-century focus on accurate depicture of a fashion product, so that it could be copied and disseminated, is replaced by what Wilson terms 'images of desire'(2003: 157), that captured a lifestyle and attitude of popular culture icons, making the viewer feel that consuming the fashion will also capture the dream.

The full performance of both Madonna and Gwyneth is of course much more permeating than these two fashion spreads in a popular fashion magazine. Both have long histories of popular culture performance, both on formal stages, and in informal contexts such as talk shows, interviews, and unsolicited media coverage (see Schwichtenberg, 1993; Gilligan, 2000). Fashion thus becomes embedded within a wider range of leisure entertainment, with fashion change happening on multiple levels and in multiple places, as designers, mass-market product developers, teenagers in the rural Midwest, and European elite all pick up on the look of popular culture icons all at the same time, and through different mass communication channels. Fashion is thus an ongoing constant performance, as popular culture cult figures move in and out of publicity's glare and popularity. In some cases changes happen as cult figures alter their identity, such as Madonna, for example. In other cases, cult figures are replaced with those capturing more closely the Zeitgeist, the spirit of the age.

'Adorned in Zeitgeist': The Contribution of Barbara Vinken

> Fashion has become what art had wanted to be: the Zeitgeist expressing itself in visible form. Its stage is no longer the opera or race course. Fashion is now made, worn, and displayed, not by the bourgeoisie or the aristocracy, but on the street. (Vinken, 2005: 41)

The tracing of changing styles through Western costume history is often accompanied by explanations for the new looks focusing on changing world views and changing times. The simple argument is that as the so-called 'spirit of the times' or zeigeist changes, styles in fashion, architecture, music and other arts also change to express the new mood of the age. As an early example, Max von Boehn, in his three-volume history of costume series, argued that dress and other visual arts conform to the 'spirit of the age' (1933: 62, see also Uzanne, 1898). Style changes are thus seen to reflect rather than precede cultural and social changes, and to be reactive rather than formative agents in the change process. More recently, Barbara Vinken has revitalized the term 'Zeitgeist', focusing on the performance aspect of fashion, with the dressed body performing and therefore playing a role in formulating the spirit of the times. Rather than being a reflection or expression of the times, within the scholarship of Vinken, fashion becomes the very embodiment of the ever-changing moment:

> Fashion is defined as the art of the perfect moment, of the sudden surprising and yet obscurely expected harmonious apparition—the Now at the threshold of an

immediate future. But its realization is, at the same time, its destruction. By appearing, and giving definitive form to the moment, fashion is almost already part of yesterday. (2005: 42)

The agency of fashion, the role of fashion as instigator of cultural change, is dated by Vinken to the 1970s, when she argues post fashion began to dominate the streets. With the post-fashion era Vinken argues that 'the fashion designer loses his [her] absolute power' and 'fashion becomes a co-production between the creator and those who wear the clothes' (2005: 35). With this movement to the streets, rather than within the imagination of particular designers, post fashion becomes more formative as it is used as an emblem of changing identities and attitudes of the wider cultural population.

Like many others, Vinken embedded fashion and its development as a designer-based industry within an analysis of cultural construction of femininity, and gave the Victorian designer Charles Frederick Worth the credit for 'creating an aura around fashion and promotion as a new art for modern times' (2005: 19). In these early years of the couture industry, argued Vinken, fashion concerned itself with marking female sexuality and artifice in clear contrast to the perceived authenticity and physical and intellectual potency of men. Women's secondary sexuality characteristics were overly emphasized by corseting and bustles, and posed in dramatic contrast to men's sober business looks of the period. The Vinken-labeled 'fetish of femininity' emerged, with fashion becoming an arena marked by the interplay between the natural and artificial, with women's bodies molded to satisfy male gaze and desire. The established pattern of males lusting after particular female body parts and garments emerged in this time period, with possession of female fetish symbolizing male power and accomplishment.[1]

For the next hundred years fashion concerned itself with ever new inventions of womanhood, always playing off the original fetish of femininity created in the Victorian period (see Vinken, 2005 for a more complete discussion). Playing with such traditions as the male dandy, designers like Coco Chanel marked the 'modern' woman, by playing with the vocabulary of the fetish female through cancellation of key aspects of the fetish female by removing the corset and flattening the chest. The feminine fetish in different form returned in the 1950s with the New Look, the last strong statement before the emergence of post fashion.

Fashion as performance emerged in the post-fashion era as designers in collaboration with people in the streets deconstructed the original fetish of femininity. It was at this point that fashion became performative and generative, according

---

1. For a discussion of the theoretical basis for the fact that males fetishize female body parts and garments, while this behavior is not common among women, see Valerie Steele (1996: 12-13).

to Vinken (2005). Unleashed from the design establishment, no longer tied to either marking or canceling the fetish of femininity, fashion came to life as the embodiment of discourse on gender and the contemporary condition:

> In the West, fashion becomes 'carnivalistic': it cancels the divisions of classes and genders, and, more than this, it exposes the function of costume and disguise at work in categories of class and gender. (2005: 64)

Vinken (2005) provided a number of good case studies of post-fashion Zeitgeist performance; our case study will focus on one of the earliest versions of post fashion: the English female punk street fashion, as influenced by British designer Vivienne Westwood.

Essential to Vinken's concept of post fashion is the denial of the 'natural' categories of gender, and the refusal to accept the social principles of class. Sub-cultural punk style, as analyzed by Evans and Thornton (1989), deconstructed both class and gender, creating a street performance that in its popular manifestation created broader fashion change. In terms of Vinken's concept of post-fashion emanating out of the street, it is important to point out that sub-cultural punk style's meanings were embedded within the female fetishized 'bad woman of the streets,' contrasted with the good virtuous woman at home. The Victorian dichotomy between good domesticated women, and street prostitutes was thus deconstructed by punk women as they defied accepted-class and gender-based categorization systems by the way they decked themselves and performed in the public arena.

In terms of female gender punk women deconstructed multiple other aspects of the female fetish as first presented in the fashionable Victorian world. Firstly, the notion that a woman constructs herself as a sexual object to be desired by men is turned on end by punk women. As analyzed by Evans and Thornton:

> Punk women . . . jettisoned conventional prettiness and sought instead to look tough, menacing and threatening. In doing so they pinpointed the masquerade of femininity, the unholy alliance of femininity, naturalness, good taste and good behavior. (1989: 18)

Class distinctions are also deconstructed in punk looks, with punk women defying class-based rules instructing women to dress tastefully, as an expression of social background and accomplishment:

> Punk fashion for women was an alternative to the perfect gloss of high fashion orthodoxy, with its notions of good taste, naturalness and wholesomeness, and its insistence on conventional beauty, slenderness and flawless skin. By contrast punk seized on the flashy, cheap, and tacky: fluorescent colours, fake leopard-skin,

fishnet stockings, plastic stilettos, pancake make-up and obviously dyed hair. These accoutrements together signified an interaction of sexuality and class that was resolutely unsoftened by tastefulness. (Evans and Thornton 1989: 20)

The popularization of punk and its integration into broader Western culture, spreading (as personally documented) as far as rural college campuses in the Midwestern United States, involved what Hebdige (1979) termed the 'conversion' of the sub-cultural style into mass-produced and marketed fashion objects. These fashion products, while carrying references of the original subcultural look, are void of the style's original nonconformist meanings. An example of this conversion process is the Zandra Rhodes couture version punk on display at the Victoria and Albert Museum which Evans and Thornton describe as 'a meticulously torn, beaded . . . safety-pinned and zip-riddled black evening dress', designed to apply 'taste to the wound', creating a pleasing and conventionally attractive appearance style (1989: 31). Appearing in 1979, this dress signaled the conceptual end of the authentic punk movement with the adoption of the punk trend by upper-class women, and the linking of the punk look to beauty culture.

Sub-Cultural Style as Performance: Punk Violation of the Codes of Masculinity

Dick Hebdidge's analysis of male punk style, centered more on issues of class than gender, focused on the meaning of sub-cultural style within the consumer-dominated late twentieth century. Viewing punk styles as a form of disturbing conspicuous consumption, Hebidge viewed sub-cultural style as a reflection of 'the tensions between dominant and subordinate groups' (1979: 2). Hebdige argued that punk street performance challenged accepted class and gender norms by creating what he termed 'noise,' 'interference in the orderly sequence' of normal life, through disturbing use of consumer products to create violations of accepted codes of behavior (1979: 91).

Similar to others in this chapter, Hebdige interpreted male punk styles as performance, as a drama that focuses and forces an audience to see surrounding reality in a different way:

the punks were not only directly responding to increasing joblessness, changing moral standards, the rediscovery of poverty, the Depression, etc., they were dramatizing what have come to be called 'Britain's decline' . . . The punks appropriated the rhetoric of crisis which had filled the air waves and editorials throughout the period and translated it into tangible (and visible) terms. (1979: 87)

The drama presented by punks was in part the visible display of objects displaced from the trashy world of late twentieth-century Britain and worn on the body as an emblem of Refusal, the unwillingness to accept the status quo:

> Objects borrowed from the most sordid of contexts found a place in the punks' ensembles: lavatory chains were draped in graceful arcs across chests encased in plastic bin-liners. Safety pins were taken out of their domestic 'utility' context and worn as gruesome ornaments through the cheek, ear or lip. 'Cheap' trashy fabrics . . . in vulgar designs . . . and 'nasty' colours . . . were salvaged by the punks and turned into garments which offered self-conscious commentaries on the notions of modernity and taste. (1979: 107)

The public behavior of punks completed the performance, by matching the visible display of outrage with blatant disregard for social codes and normative expectations:

> The punks wore clothes which were the sartorial equivalent of swear words, and they swore as they dress—with calculated effect . . . clothed in chaos, they produced Noise in the calmly orchestrated Crisis of everyday life in the late 1970s. (1979: 114)

In the disturbance created by punk street performance, as enacted through dress and behavior, fashion change occurs as perceptions are altered by the challenge created by sub-cultural discourse.

The ultimate impact of punk on mainstream fashion is captured in this quote from a 1977 fashion editorial in *GQ*, counseling readers on how to wear punk:

> Punk, if treated with extreme delicacy and sensibility, can be made to work with the season's overall fashion direction. Take the torn T-shirt. Carefully slashed to ribbons, it can work perfectly with freshly minted blue jeans and a wool over-shirt. Worn as part of the overall Punk statement, however, it is unsubtle. (quoted in Jones 1987: 133)

With this fashion column in *Gentleman's Quarterly*, men's punk styles, like their female counterparts, are absorbed into trends supporting accepted forms of gendered identity – serving no longer to challenge but to reinforce hegemonic masculinity.

Stage Performances: Tickets Required

The formal stages on which fashion change is initiated include rock perform-ances, runway shows, sports events, and film. The ability of mass media to broadcast such performances to a much broader audience than those seated at the live show, has increased the power of these staged events to create broadly based and widely accepted fashion change. The second half of this chapter introduces you to a range of staged and ticketed performances and discusses how they initiate fashion change.

Runway Shows as Performance

Runway fashion shows emerged at the turn of the twentieth century staged in couture houses, department stores, and at charity events throughout the United States and Europe. Related to the democratization of fashion made possible through mass production and mass dissemination of fashion-trend information, fashion shows became the arena of fashion performance, with the spectacle helping to create the names and labels sold throughout the twentieth and twenty-first century. With the movement in the late twentieth century toward experimentations with identity, fashion shows became performances with diverse intentions, launching ideas as well as products.

Caroline Evans viewed the runway as 'space of artifice that offers a particularly modern platform for the performance of gender as image and idea' (2001: 273). Citing the long association between cultural construction of femininity and fashion, Evans saw runways as the performing zone for enacting gender, with changes visibly brought to the fore by fashion products, teamed with special effects and spectacle. As an example, Vivienne Westwood's introduction of the mini-crini, worn with a blazer and platform shoes on runway shows in 1985, is apt. A knocked-off favorite of the mid 1980s, Westwood's original design drew together meanings of female dress from the Victorian and the 1960s to create a modern interpretation of femininity:

> The mini-crini re-presents a consideration of the history of sexuality and of fashion's changing definition of the female body. The hooped crinoline is an invention of the nineteenth century, associated with empire, while the mini is a product of the 1960s and swinging London. It is a cultural hybrid that is required to be read in terms of both its antecedents. If the crinoline stands in for a mythology of restriction and encumbrance in women's dress, in the mini-crini that mythology is juxtaposed with an equally dubious mythology of liberation associated with the mini-skirt. In it two sets of ideas about female desirability are conflated: one about covering, the other about uncovering the female body. (Evans and Thornton 1989: 148)

Imitations, according to Evans and Thornton (1989), were often knocked off void of the concept originally put on the runway by Westwood. This draining of the conceptual meaning of fashion objects through the mass-production process is common, as meaning laden performance is translated into popularized trend.

111

Duggan (2001, see also Khan, 2000) usefully categorized fashion shows into distinct categories,[2] and then went on to link the different types of shows to performance art. In all cases the runway show becomes a visible means of performing style for an audience, affecting them through spectacle, concept and/or form, process, or socio-political statement. Fashion changes initiated by such shows expand beyond simple dictation of sleeve length or skirt shape, to selling ambiance, ideas, and attitudes.

The spectacle show focuses on production and dramatic effects, captivating audiences through venue, model selection, lights, and music. Audiences are encouraged to adopt fashion change through the seduction of the production, in combination with the looks which are presented on the runway. The 1964 Courreges 'space age' show in Paris, is often cited as one of the first spectacle shows that sold an audience a new look through model choice, venue, music, and production ambiance:

In January 1964, the journalists filing into the Courreges salon in Paris were astonished to find themselves in a stark modern room with white vinyl walls and white boxes to sit on. Loud beat music was playing and when the show started, giant girls with close cropped hair, freckles, suntans and wide, white grins came pounding out wearing skirts inches above the knees and flat white boots. Courreges was launching his 'space age' clothes and he was shrewd enough to know that it would be useless to show such revolutionary ideas unless you did it on a new kind of girl in a new kind of salon. (Keenan, 1977, quoted in Evans, 2001: 297)

In contrast to spectacle shows, conceptual approaches to runway show production focus on concept, process, or form with a designer or design house presenting an idea to the audience. Individual designs and models in this type of show, are secondary to the abstract concept. Duggan (2001) provided the example of the 1999 Viktor & Rolf haute couture show, which explored the concept of a designer dressing a static and passive female fashion figure:

An example of this emphasis [a substance approach] can be seen in Viktor & Rolf's Fall 1999 haute couture show, which featured a single model standing on a circular rotating platform. At the start of the show she is wearing only a burlap slip and undergarments. As the show progresses, the designers clothe her in successive layers of burlap and Swarovski crystals, Russian-doll style, until her head is barely visible. The intimacy of the act, as well as the designer involvement in the process, focuses on the action of clothing the body, allowing process to overshadow product. (2001: 251)

---

2. Duggan's categories and category names have been slightly modified in order to clarify the meaning for the reader. For original discussion see Duggan (2001).

Designers interested in sculptural form sometimes devote an entire show to exploring new shapes on the body. For example Yomamoto's 1992 show experimented with Madeleine Vionnet's innovative use of bias cut:

> If one follows up on the experiments of Yomamoto . . . sooner or later one is led to Madeleine Vionnet, whose cutting technique created a body that was no longer divided into a two-dimensional plane . . . but rather self-moving, and three-dimensional, its form constantly changing space. The fabric modeled the body in different ways, depending on whether it was cut with, against or diagonal to the wave of the thread; . . . Behind Vionnet's clothes stood the femininity of the classical statue. Yomamoto appropriates Vionnet's technique for his own purposes—not in order to establish a normativized beauty in a static space, but rather to reveal the beauty of the incomplete and the imperfect: a transitory beauty, beauty in transit. (Vinken, 2005: 112–13)

Fashion change was thus initiated by Yomamoto's show through altering the audience's concept of ideals of feminine beauty as expressed through the sculptural form of the dressed body. Women were moved to adopt new looks, through appreciation for new concepts of beauty.

Designers interested in process focus on technological or structural innovation, exposing the audience to the creative or inventive process. Duggan cites Miyake's 1999 show as an example:

> In his Spring and Fall 1999 shows, Miyake featured a team of assistants dressed in black, who participated in the production by reshaping a garment while it was on the model, or cutting out a new shape on the floor of the stage. These mini-performances reinforce Miyake's interest in manipulation and transformation by making the process of garment design and construction the focal point of the show. (2001: 255).

Similarly, novel applications of traditional fabrications, or newly emergent textile products are sold to an audience through emphasis on function and fiber performance.

Designers interested in social and political commentary stage fashion shows that focus on communicating a message. For example, Miguel Adrover has staged shows in which he has turned products produced by luxury labels such as Burberry and Louis Vuitton inside out, reconstructing them into anti-fashion commentaries on the trend toward conspicuous consumption as expressed through established luxury logo merchandise (Duggan 2001: 265). In some cases the message is carried not by the design, as much as the production itself. Duggan describes a 1999 statement show focused on highlighting fashions damaging endorsement of narrowly defined body ideals:

Red or Dead, a label based in London, have repeatedly defied ideal body types in their shows. The Fall 1999 collection featured an obese male model who lifted his shirt to reveal the word 'unique' on his chest. The label also featured atypical models such as albinos and dwarfs to reinforce their message (2001: 267).

While the fashion change impact on these shows may seem indirect, they have the power to create changing attitudes, and in so doing changing fashion trends.

Film as Performance

Stardom demonstrates the extension of commodification even to the most intimate, personal realms: all aspects of the star personality—from clothing, hairstyles, and makeup, to biographical details, tastes and fantasies—are grist to the commodity's mill, and can be sold as part of the star products. (Suarez 1996: 221)

Film, with its ability to link fantasy, fashion, and identity has historically played a strong role in the display and spread of fashion trends. Silk evening wear from 1930s depression era American films was knocked off in less expensive mass-produced rayon, and worn in living rooms throughout the United States. Similarly, the menswear-inspired fashion looks designed by Ralph Lauren and worn by Diane Keaton in Annie Hall, were immediately found in fashion magazines in 1977 (Bruzzi, 1997). Andy Warhol's underground films, featuring marginal social characters dressed in cutting-edge street versions of high fashion, have been credited with helping to move fashion from the couture houses to the streets (Suarez, 1996).

While certainly 'stardom' sells fashion, the role of film performance in creating fashion change is larger than individual celebrities – with costume sometimes standing independent of character and plot line, and influencing the audience toward new looks and new identities (Bruzzi and Church Gibson 2000; Bruzzi 1997). These films successfully captured the spirit of the times through fashion imagery, causing audiences to look past plot lines, actual celebrity lives, and character, and focus on their own desires, needs, and fantasies as expressed in fashion objects. The following case study researched by Jacqueline Reich (2000) demonstrates the power of film to communicate and create desire for a fashion trend, with costume leading the way, rather than character and plot.

In 1959 Federico Fellini released *La Dolce Vita* staring Marcello Mastroianni as Marcella Rubini, an Italian gossip journalist. Dressed in the latest Italian men's fashions, Rubini made his way through seven days in the film, fumbling ineptly through a series of humiliating circumstances, victimized by a number of women who take advantage of his provincialism. Ironically, given his role in the film, Mastroianni emerged from this film labeled by the public as 'The Latin Lover' – a term indicating sexual prowess and svelte style:

> Yes, from La dolce vita on, this label of the Latin Lover, which doesn't fit me, stuck to me. At first I played chauffeurs, ingenuous workers modest but very nice young men. After this film new proposals for more intellectually committed roles started to arrive, but there was always some story in the middle involving the Latin Lover, with which I had nothing to do because I have never been one. In fact, I was always busy saying: 'Excuse me, but in La dolce vita this protagonist is not a lady-killer – he doesn't conquer anyone. If anything he is the one conquered. It's women who use him and he, being provincial, innocently falls for it every time! The foreign actress uses him; his mistress uses him, even though she may be the only one over whom he has the least bit of authority; the woman in the castle of aristocrats uses him – he is only the victim!' So, I'm not exactly sure what this idiotic term palmed off on me means. People have labeled me as such evidently because I wore a blue blazer in the film and moved in a circle with a lot of women. (Faldini and Fofi 1981: 17, quoted in Reich, 2000: 217)

What in fact audiences caught hold of and remembered was the image of Mastroianni as a style symbol for post-war Italian affluence. The meaning of his character, and later his 'stardom,' was wrapped up in the audience's desire for Italian style, as captured in an individual male actor in this particular film, in this particular time period:

> Both the genesis and the success of La dolce vita arose in part out of the post-war cultural climate of Rome as it evolved from 'open city' to the hot spot of the rich, famous, and beautiful. It became a haven for the international jet set, the cultural elite, and the Italian and American film communities. As a result of this world-wide exposure, by the late 1950s Italy emerged as a cosmopolitan style-maker and trendsetter with the success of Vespa, the Fiat 500, and, last but not least, Italian fashion. (Reich, 2000: 210)

Mastroianni as a star thus served as a catalyst for his audience's blossoming identification with all that was Italian. He is remembered not for the character he played, or the plot of the film, but rather for the fashionable figure he cut, and what that image of male identity symbolized for the audiences of the late 1950s:

> The Latin Lover is above all a product, a consumer icon, a cultural commodity offered up for consumption to the international public. Mastroianni was a

symbol for Italian style, for a style of life that resonated with a national public experiencing greater prosperity after years of struggle and with an international consumer market hungry for all things Italian. (Reich, 2000: 210)

Fashionable dress in *La Dolce Vita* thus stood independent of plot, character, and identity of the actor, to create a visible embodiment of a new look, which was captured in the short-hand commodity term 'Latin Lover.' The term 'stuck,' not just to Mastroianni, but to a whole series of fashion objects which were then marketed internationally carrying the aura and meaning first planted by the Italian fashions worn in this film.

Music as Performance

Nike, then the number-two company in the shoe business, was in a bruising but losing battle with Reebok . . . In 1986, they fired their ad agency and hired Wieden and Kennedy . . . One night, two W & K admen saw 'She's Gotta Have It' [hip-hop video], in which Spike Lee's oddball character Mars Blackman stomped around in Air Jordans. A light bulb went off. They called Lee and told him they wanted to pair him with Jordan. In 1988, when Spike [Lee] and Mike [Jordan] began filming a series of spots that would shock the advertising world, Reebok was a $1.8 billion dollar company, and Nike trailed at $1.2 billion. A year later, Spike and Mike's ads helped propel Nike past Reebok, and the company never looked back. Not only did Nike's success confirm that niches were the future, it also confirmed that a massive shift in tastes was occurring— from baby boomer to youth, from suburb to city, from whiteness to Blackness. (Chang, 2005: 415)

Strong feelings of identification and collective identity are experienced through musical performance (McLaughlin, 2004; Frith, 1996). The connection of the body – through movement, stance, and dress, to the meaning of the music – draws the audience into a physical and emotional relationship with performers, as they experience the music as sound, energy, and visual spectacle. Audiences are bonded through this experience, as commonly they live through the performance and react to its impact in their everyday lives. Hiphop, initially a musical form that helped construct inner-city youth identity, spread in the 1980s beyond those borders into the suburbs, with white youth wanting Air Jordans to get to Blackness, drawn to the message and energy of hip-hop music, and the attraction of a high-performance sports figure, Michael Jordan.

As a popular music performance scholar, Frith spoke to this as he commented 'music is especially important for our sense of ourselves because of its unique emotional intensity—we absorb songs into our own lives and rhythm into our own bodies' (1996: 273). Further, in discussing the impact of music on formation of identity, Frith commented that 'identity comes from the outside, not the inside; it is something we try on, not something we reveal or discover' (1996: 273). This tendency to feel that we as an audience can 'try on' a musical identity, translates into well-documented examples of audiences using dress to mark connection and identification with popular musical performers such as David Bowie and Grateful Dead.

Hip-hop initially 'was tried on' as an urban style, when the music of 'Niggaz with Attitude,' a group from Compton, an urban underclass neighborhood in LA, released an album that opened up the floodgates to youth across the nation to do it themselves:

> After the album was officially released on January 25, 1989, it went gold in six weeks. It had been recorded for under $10,000 . . . Like a hurricane that had gathered energy over hot open waters before heading inland, Straight Outta Compton hit American popular culture . . . Hip-hop critic Bill Jam says 'Niggaz With Attitude' (NWA) made it look easy inspiring a Do-It-Yourself movement for anyone from the streets to crank out gangstra rap tapes.' All one had to have was a pen and pad of paper, a mic, a mixer and a sampler. Thousands of kids labored over their raps in their dark bedrooms, then stepped onto the streets. (Chang, 2005: 320)

The powerful sound and timely release of 'Straight Outta Compton', a hip-hop anthem that celebrated the power of local narratives springing out of deindustrialized inner city street neighborhoods, made African-American, Chicano and Latina youth spring alive with their own stories. Listening to NWA rapping 'We're born and raised in Compton!' made youth denied access to jobs and the American dream who were 'increasingly uninterested in whitewashed hand-me-downs' (Chang, 2005: 320), feel empowered to create their own culture and values. Chang pointed out the powerful impact of the local to identity construction during this time period, going as far as to link Clinton's 1992 Democratic Convention video-biography to the NWA release:

> After Straight Outta Compton, it really was all about where you were from. NWA conflated myth and place, made the narratives root themselves on the corner of every [neighbor] 'hood. And now every 'hood could be Compton, everyone had a story to tell. Even Bill Clinton's sepia-toned videobio, aired at the 1992 Democratic Convention, could have been titled Straight Outta Hope. (2005: 321)

At the same time that 'Straight Outta Compton' rooted rap in the local neighborhood, it also called for an embrace of what hip-hop critics came to call 'The Real,' unapologetic rapping that forced a reaction, often by using lyrics that were blatantly violent, misogynistic, and homophobic. Claiming to be the only artists 'speaking for the brother on the corner' (Chang, 2005: 328), musicians like NWA and Ice Cube unapologetically used violence to raise the power of their music to a riveting intensity, working to broaden its appeal out of their own neighborhoods and into affluent white suburbs. The music became an anthem for a generation that included youth from a cross section of neighborhoods and circumstances:

> rappers had to represent—to scream for the unheard and otherwise speak the unspeakable. Life on the hair-trigger margin—with all of its unpredictability, contradiction, instability, menace, tragedy and irony, with its daily death and resistance—needed to be described in its passionate complexity . . . A generation needed to assassinate its demons. (Chang, 2005: 328)

The look of rap became a fashion movement capturing the meaning and mood of the music, popular well beyond the neighborhoods giving rise to the musical style. Advertisers and product-development teams 'discovered that urban youth of color—until then an ignored niche—were a more brand-conscious, indeed brand-leading, demographic than they had ever realized' (Chang, 2005: 417). The term 'urban' became linked in young consumers' minds with being hip, and being powerful, and multi-racial youth were both initiating and spreading hip-hop style. Companies like Nike, as captured in the quote opening this case study, cashed in and led this trend.

Judith Butler: Undoing Gender on Stage

> And while he has been no stranger to theatrical, gender-twisting finery onstage, and while his earliest work was presented in the queer mecca of the East Village's Pyramid Club in the early 90's, it would be wrong to call him a drag act. The makeup and silk slips he has worn onstage have never seemed to be an imitation of womanliness but more a pursuit of a kind of inclusive idea of beauty that he is still in the midst of defining. He has also appeared in handsome suits and, once, with a sack over his head. (Hodgman, 2005: 26)

This description of Antony, of Antony and the Johnsons, captures Judith Butler's concept of gender as performance, with the role of the repeated act as a means of altering or challenging the accepted male/female binary gender system in the West. The essentialist position that femininity and masculinity are 'natural' categories is challenged by Butler (2004a, 1999), who argued that gender is constituted through what she called a 'series of acts which are renewed, revised, and consolidated through time' (2004b: 157). Focusing attention on stylization of the body through gestures, movements, and appearance, Butler argued that the body 'becomes its gender' (2004b: 157) through a series of performances. Transformation of gender occurs (and we as authors add, style change occurs) as individuals alter the performance, subvert the normative by ignoring or purposefully violating the unstated rules of gendered identity.

Using Butler's ideas, Antony's series of performances in which he altered dress and hair styles, pushing audiences to transcend normative categories of gender, forced novel considerations of gendered identity and style. For example, in 1995, Antony staged a play in New York in which a businessman gets pregnant and gives birth to Anne Frank. The manipulation of gender expectations unsettled the audience, both in terms of how he appeared and the subject matter he presented in text and performance. This type of unsettling experience can act as a catalyst, giving rise to newly formulated concepts of male, female, and transgendered identity.

At the same time that Antony was on stage manipulating gender in theatre and music, the designer Gaultier was performing a series of challenging gender acts on the men's runways in Paris. Leaving behind the normative definitions of male gender performance focused on unmarked sexuality and sober competence, Vinken points out the exuberant embrace of fetishized sex that Gaultier put on the runway during this time period:

> In Gaultier designs, it is evident that the age of renunciation has been left behind. Men's fashion no longer appears in the name of unmarked sexuality, but is instead unscrupulously marked, covered with all the sex symbols available on the market. Like women, Gaultier's men wear furs, bright colors, funky cuts, skin tight leggings; every form of uniform fetish is indulged. In his winter 1997 fashion show, one could even catch a glimpse of the codpiece. (2005: 32)

Gaultier did not just confine his gender experimentation to men. During this same time period, Gaultier performed femininity on the runway, challenging the concept of 'natural' female sexuality, by putting bustles, bras and corsets on the outside rather than hidden on the inside of designer garments (Vinken, 2005: 32).

The unleashing of gender from nature, and the notion that gender isn't real until it is performed, while perhaps most articulately stated by Butler, is visually embodied by fashion of the 1990s and early new millennium, with its insistent challenging of the binary system of gender. Popularized trends, such as the wearing of innerwear as outerwear for women, and padded briefs for men, emerged out of this continual renegotiation of gender performed on runways by a range of innovative designers. While it can easily be argued that the overstated codpiece presented by Gaultier on the runway was not adopted widely, the presence of underwear advertisements in the *New York Times* nine years later featuring understated, padded, codpiece-style underwear, illustrated how the subversive becomes the trend in the twenty-first century.

Performing Fashion in the New Millennium

The theories presented in this chapter focused on understanding fashion change as instigated by performances, both those performed to a ticketed audience, and those enacted as a part of popular culture. While the range of performances reviewed is wide, including everything from runway shows, to street fashion, to film, there are several key common theoretical elements. These elements are summarized briefly followed by a set of case studies exploring the performance of masculinity in the twenty-first century.

Summarization of Key Elements of Performance Theories

Element 1: Fashion is Performed both on Stage and as a Part of Everyday Life

Schechner (1985) discerns a useful distinction between performances of everyday life, which we witness without buying tickets, and those performances which are staged for an audience. Fashion is performed in both arenas and both types of performances instigate fashion change and related cultural transformation.

Element 2: Fashion Plays a Role in Formulating the Spirit of the Times, or Zeitgeist

The tracing of changing styles through Western costume history is often accompanied by explanations for the new looks focusing on changing world views and changing times. The simple argument is that as the so-called 'spirit of the times' or Zeitgeist changes, styles in fashion, architecture, music, and other arts also change to express the new mood of the age. Barbara Vinken (2005) has revitalized the term 'Zeitgeist,' focusing on the performance aspect of fashion, with the dressed body performing and therefore playing a role in formulating the spirit of the times. Rather than being a reflection or expression of the times, within the scholarship of Vinken, fashion becomes the very embodiment of the every changing moment.

Element 3: Fashions Allow Us to Embody our Desire and Purchase our Identity

Fashion is the most visible and fluid form of 'commodity fetish.' Living in the age of the consumer, fashion allows us to embody our desire, buy our identity, in the most intimate sense and the most linked to the performance of everyday life.

Performing Masculinity: Emergent Consumer Identities on Stage

From a performance perspective, predicting emergent cultural identities and linked fashion products involves watching for cultural performances with momentum and possible market niche or wide appeal. Scholars interested in cultural studies as well as fashion professionals interested in forecasting trends both depend for direction on sensitivity and submersion in popular culture. The following four case studies focus on new-millennium versions of masculinity. The first case study focuses on a performance that has the potential to recharge a fashion trend of the past. The second case study explores the possible establishing of a new look through the emergence of a new and influential version of male identity. Case study three is an examination of the runway as an arena of gender redefinition and trend development. Finally the chapter ends in West Africa examining the role of a new male masking tradition in revising the look, the relationships, and the attitude of young Central Pende males. Unlike the case studies used earlier within the chapter, the impact of these performances is untested, but the potential for their market niche or more broadly based acceptance is explored and discussed.

Bull Marketing: Cowboy Culture Rides into the New Millennium

On an early November Sunday, the crowd at the Gator—in the Orleans Hotel and Casino just across the street from the strip—was made up of bull men, ranch hands and stock contractors, just as it had been all week. They were here for the annual Professional Bull Riding finals—a 10-day pageant of smokeless tobacco and Western wear and strange contradictions, not to speak of the central spectacle of seven evenings of men trying to stay on the backs of enormous bucking bulls. The event is held every fall in America's No. 1 city of sin, filling Las Vegas with cowboys of all stripes—from working ranchers spitting in cups to C.E.O.'s who carry Palm Pilots in their holsters and make Armani and Stetson look as if they go together. (Halpern, 2006)

The Western shirt is an emblem of American identity with a power to recur as a trend on a regular basis, carrying varying meaning linked to particular cultural time periods. The first adoption of the shirt as a popular trend was in response to the wearing of extremely ornate western wear as costume by early rodeo and Wild West show performers and by actors in early Western movies. Tamed versions of the shirts became associated with the lifestyle of a working rancher, thus moving from stage to real life. In tracing the movement of the shirt from the stage to the ranch owner, Weil and DeWeese also gave credit to the popular dime novels of the period, that attracted not only working ranchers and ranch hands to the apparel, but a more general American audience enthralled with the lifestyle messages of Western wear:

> In order to understand how Western fashion became popular, it should be put in the context of popular culture. The West was first popularized by dime novels. Billions of them were published during a fifty-year period beginning in 1860, according to the Buffalo Bill Museum in Golden, Colorado. This was the first, mass-produced entertainment industry, something like the television of its day. Dime novels fed the myth of the West to the hero-starved East. The Wild West shows of Buffalo Bill and the Miller Brothers' 101 Ranch took the West on the road, thrilling audiences across the United States of America and Europe. Silent films, and later 'talkies', took off where the Wild West shows had left off, perpetuating the romance and excitement of the West (2004: 19).

Predicting and understanding the cultural meaning of an emergent Western-wear trend involves not only comprehending the performance-based spread of the fashion, but also the spirited appeal of the Western myth to the American imagination and sense of identity. The concept of the frontier, not only within the United States but worldwide, is a recurring and retold myth conjured at key points in history to construct and reconstruct American male identity. The integral role of the conquering of the Western frontier to American economic growth pointed out by Slotkin (1992), served to embed Western mythology in notions of individual success and national identity. The predictable recurrence of men's Western wear on both American and European runways and the closets of American men is living testimony to the continuing power of this myth.

The emergence of bull riding as a men's spectator sport, compared by Halpern (2006) to the popular culture phenomenon of Nascar, has the potential to once again revive the Western shirt and cowboy boots as widely worn emblems of male identity. Obvious symbols of wealth and accomplishment in the form of fashion products are displayed at bull-riding events as the wealthier audience members flash Western wear worn with Rolexes. Mixed into the crowd of working cowboys, these high-end fashionable versions of Western identity help to perform a uniquely American version of masculinity. Evidence of the spread of the trend to American college campuses is emerging as mechanical bull contests and Western line dancing are being offered as weekend entertainment for students.

Performing Masculinity: The Neanderthal TV Hero

> According to research conducted by the upstart male oriented network Spike TV men responded not only to brave and extremely competent male leads but to a menagerie of characters with strikingly antisocial tendencies . . . The code of

such characters, said Brent Hoff, 36, a fan of 'Lost,' is: 'Life is hard. Men gotta do what men gotta do, and if some people have to die in the process, so be it.' (St. John, 2005: 2)

Television offers ongoing performances that play fundamental roles in formulating a range of popular cultural identities, including gender. Consumer research provides helpful analysis of the popularity of particular television programs among demographic populations that can help to alert the cultural observer to trends in how masculinity and femininity are being performed on the television stage and their broad or market niche appeal to distinct groups of consumers. In this particular case study covered by the *New York Times* in 2005, Spike TV, a cutting-edge network focused on young male viewers between eighteen and forty-nine, conducted research revealing the emergence of a new male anti-hero tough guy, with broadly based appeal to young American men.

Examination of the behavioral trends of these popular male television leads reveals an edgy, flawed-personality type often drawn to resolving conflict through violence and direct action, and openly sexist in attitudes toward women. Revenge behaviors are often condoned within the plot lines, with male audiences drawn in and identifying with a flawed and typically violent protagonist. Related trends contributing to this 'I am not ashamed about it' bad-boy look is a series of best-selling books by self-declared sexist males, with such book titles as *I Hope They Serve Beer in Hell, The Modern Drunkard,* and *The Alphabet of Manliness.* An editor for one of the books summarized their appeal: 'I think all these books are about men searching for a model other than what they're being told to do, something more rebellious, less cautious and less concerned with external approval.' (St. John, 2006: 8)

Styles of dress worn by these television anti-heroes are in dramatic contrast to the super-clean good guys of earlier television history, typically expressing the bad good boy, with emphasis on dark edgy looks dominating in black. Similarly the authors of the bad-boy books present themselves in public appearances as sloppy frat boys holding drinks and/or cigarette-toting lounge lizards in bad suits. The question then becomes, for the fashion trend analyst, how this set of related male performances will be embodied in new fashion looks.

'Fred and Fred' Ballroom Dance as Runway Activism

Caroline Evans's concept of the runway as a performance arena wherein gender is manipulated and redefined through a complex mixture of special effects, ambiance, and design was brought to life in a underground theatre below the Louvre in the presentation of the collection of Viktor & Rolf in Fall 2006. This runway show, falling into the classification of a concept show according to Duggan's (2001) categorization system, was intended by Viktor

& Rolf to challenge gender rules and expectations. This challenge was linked to the show's commercial intent of launching Victor & Rolf's new cologne for men, Antidote. With backing from L'Oreal, the cosmetic giant, this cologne is primarily marketed within Europe to a gay audience and has been purposefully named and promoted to carry 'its own tantalizing wiff of AIDS-era politics' (Trebay, 2006e: E8).

The ambiance of the show, with its intended linkage to formal ballroom dancing, was introduced to the audience by the set-up of the theatre which included chandeliers and small tables with gilded chairs. Guy Trebay (2006e) in particular noted the serving of champagne at this afternoon show, as mood altering for the audience, moving them into a mood of formal anticipation. The show opened with a male and female couple ballroom dancing down the runway, followed by the presentation of models accompanied by a live rather campy performance by Rufus Wainwright of Judy Garland classics. The clear linkage to the classic music of Judy Garland and the ballroom dancing of Fred Astaire and Ginger Rogers is accomplished in these two sections of the show.

The choice of Rufus Wainwright to perform as a part of this fashion show production made a pointed and significant link between the person who Trebay refers to as 'the first postliberation era gay pop star' (2006d, E1) and the launch of Antitode cologne. Wainwright's own camp-inspired tribute concert to Judy Garland in New York at Carnegie Hall in June 2006 set the stage for the campy link of this fashion show to the classic ballroom dance of Ginger Rogers and Fred Astaire. Not coincidently Mr Wainwright was dressed by Viktor & Rolf for this heavily publicized concert.

The conceptual challenge to the audience, and the political content of the show, was expressed on the runway just before the final presentation of models that ended the show. Harkening back to the opening of the show, the classic ballroom male-female runway dance, this pivotal section of the show reinterpreted the Ginger Rogers and Fred Astaire moment in the presentation of a set of six all-male dancers in formal ballroom attire. The significance is captured by Guy Trebay in his review of the show:

> It was just before the final parade of models appeared, however, that what could have been another canned fashion spectacle turned into something else. Pumped from the ceiling, a bank of artificial fog rolled onto the runway. Suddenly, through the mist, appeared eight men in tailcoats and with patent-leather hair. Filing on to the catwalk as the orchestra struck up a song, each turned crisply to one another, partnered and began to dance. Fred and Ginger became Fred and Fred. (Trebay, 2006e: E8)

Similar to Rufus Wainwright's accomplishment of moving classic Judy Garland music into the lexicon of male gay culture, this fashion production staged by two male gay Dutch designers effectively claimed an important element of popular culture history for a gay audience, by changing the rules of its presentation.

The political nature of the show and its conceptual link to the activism of the two Dutch designers is made evident in the comments from Viktor Horsting, captured by Guy Trebay in his fashion review:

> 'We really felt like the show was about making your own rules,' said Viktor Horsting, who is surely one of the few people so committed to his beliefs that he revoked his baptism in the Roman Catholic Church last year to protest the Vatican's stance on homosexuality. 'It was using the very unnatural form,' or ballroom dancing, Mr. Horsting said, 'to question what is natural.' (Trebay, 2006e: E8)

Thus in an intricately designed production these two male designers effectively integrated the launch of a cologne for a cosmetics multi-national leader with a political message of gender redefinition in the new millennium. Again, the role of the trend analyst is to predict the impact of this runway redefinition of gender on up-and-coming fashions.

Masculinity Danced in West African: The Fashionable Young Man

The Central Pende of Zaire have a vibrant masking tradition with a history of invention and reinvention of tradition. The traditional masquerades were danced for religious purposes as well as a form of popular entertainment. Currently the masks are performed almost exclusively as entertainment, most often appearing at festivals, on television, and sometimes in traveling troupes in other countries. This responsive tradition, with its openness to the invention of new characters with changing social circumstances, has proven more resilient than other neighboring traditions. For example, the related Eastern Pende, who have more rigidly held to the traditional role of the masks in religious rituals, have devolved over time to only include a small number of masks which are rarely performed to an audience of primarily older community members (Strother, 1995).

The mask in the traditional arts of West Africa included not only a carved wood face piece but an overall costume, as well as a mode of dance associated with distinct traditional and emerging characters. Among the Western Pende a new mask is carved in response to an idea or a character that emerges as important within the community. In the case of the invention of the mask embodying a fashionable young man, the idea originated with a young male villager named Gambetshi. According to his story, he was up in mango tree trying to pick a ripe mango for himself when a middle-aged woman called up to him to fetch her a good mango. After picking her mango and throwing it down, he again tried to pick himself a piece of fruit, but was interrupted once more by an older woman insisting he serve her interests, and so the afternoon progressed. Finally out of patience he cried out protesting the assumption that the young are always expected to serve the old within his community. Out of this experience grew the desire to dance the modern young man character at a community masquerade, in part as a protest against traditional patterns of power between older and young members of his community.

The first time Gambetshi danced the character his movements were well defined as the modern fashionable young man, but the costume and mask were improvised. Encouraged by the audience response to his mask he sought out a sculptor to carve the wooden portion of the mask. Strother captures the collaboration between this young man and the sculptor as the new version of West Pende masculine is embodied in sculptural form:

> In Gambetshi's mind, modernity was associated with naturalism. He had to insist most emphatically on abandoning the visual codes for which Central Pende masks are known, such as downcast eyes and a continuous brow. [The sculptor] wished to sculpt the facepiece with sharply chiseled features conveying a young man's taut muscularity, with bulging forehead and disproportionate large eyes and nose. Despite the dispute, the sculptor finally had to bow to the custom of meeting a client's wishes. He then created a work unique in Pende masquerading for its soft modeling, naturalistic proportions, fleshy mouth, and painted rather than carved eyes. (Strother, 1995: 27–8)

Most significantly for this case study was Gambetshi's insistence on the newly fashionable retro hairstyle associated with 'young men devoted to up-to-the-minute fashion' (Strother, 1995: 28). The use of fashion trends to embody new masculinity thus became an element of this particular masking tradition and its challenge to historical gerontocracy.

This case study illustrates the applicability of Zeitgeist (or spirit of the times) concepts of fashion-change theory even in diverse settings such as West Africa. In this case the exposure of young men to urban life in West African cities had begun to alter their notions of masculinity, giving rise to a new kind of man with an evolving relationship with others in the community. By going through the process of creating dance movements, a costume, and finally a carved mask to express this modern notion of a man, Gambetshi captured the spirit of this distinct moment in time among the Central Pende. With the dancing of the costume with its fashionable hairstyle and other trend accessories the mask has the potential to instigate transformation of gender and also fashion trends.

7

Fashion as Cycle

And the seasons they go round and round . . . We're captive on the carousel of
time.

Joni Mitchell, *The Circle Game*

It is said that the only consistent behavior regarding fashion is that it continuously changes from season to season. Nevertheless, there are a plethora of
theorists and researchers who have attempted to create models and theories
which lend better understanding or predictability to the timely flow of fashion
modification. The theories of fashion flow or diffusion of fashion into the
population, the rate and extent to which fashions are accepted by the
consuming public, and the duration of, or interest in; a fashion frequently fall
within the subject matter often referred to as the fashion cycle. Those who have
considered the phenomenon of fashion cycles come from a wide array of disciplines including economics, anthropology, business, and textiles and apparel.
Theories and models of fashion cycles typically fall into either short-term or
long-term contexts (Sproles, 1981). Short-term fashion cycles exist during the
life of a product and can last from months to perhaps a year or two. On the
other hand, longer-term fashion cycles follow evolutionary style movement and
have been traced to periods as long as a century, exceeding the life span of most
humans. The emphasis of the remainder of this chapter will be to discuss, in
some detail, the structure of fashion-change theory within short- and long-term
cyclic periods.

Short-Term Fashion Cycles

Style-based Short-term Cycles

To Paul Nystrom (1928) a fashion style and the frequency of its acceptance
among the consuming public was the key to understanding fashion's cyclical
behavior. Style can be defined as a 'characteristic or distinctive mode or
method of expression, presentation or conception in the field of some art'
(1928: 3). In the case of dress, style can be seen as a combination of features
that distinguish a garment in general form from others. For example, a
men's blazer has a combination of stylistic features such as the body shape,
fabric structure, lapel form, location of pockets and vents etc. that distinguish it from other men's apparel, such as a bush jacket. Why style is impor-

tant, in Nystrom's view, is because fashion is defined by the prevalence of a style in the marketplace. In fact, fashion can be defined as the prevailing style at any given time. Said differently, what is fashionable is the style that a significant number of people are wearing. Coming from a business and marketing tradition, Nystrom suggested that fashion should not be defined by opinion, which is too subjective, but instead should be documented quantitatively by actually counting populations of people wearing particular styles.

A major contribution of Nystrom's was to demonstrate graphically the relationship of time's passing to the changing level of consumer acceptance for varying styles. Using a statistical data arrangement, referred to as a frequency distribution, Nystrom plotted time on the horizontal axis and frequency of consumer acceptance on the vertical axis, thus depicting, by his definition, the lifetime of a particular fashion item. The data curve depicting time versus acceptance was almost always in bell-shaped form, which suggested Nystrom's basic understanding of a fashion cycle. Specifically, fashions, for the most part, have a beginning, middle and an end to their life cycle. At time zero, or the point of a style initiation, consumer acceptance is very low; however, if the style possesses the attributes that attract consumer interest, more and more consumers will eventually purchase and wear the product. Depending upon the rapidity of acceptance, the early acceptance portion of the curve slope varies but, nevertheless, rises as consumption among the population increases, creating the rise portion of the belled curve. When the curve reaches a high level of consumer acceptance, the style has, in fact, become a fashion by Nystrom's definition, because of its widespread usage. Eventually, and of course this depends upon the style and its staying power, popularity of the style sooner or later wanes, with consumer acceptance dropping off. When consumer involvement with the style drops to a minimum of usage the curve tails off and this completes the back-end of the bell-shaped curve signifying the end of the fashion's life cycle.

Though all fashion life cycles are typically bell shaped, the true character of the curve can vary in slope steepness at both the inception and completion of the life cycle, depending upon rate of acceptance and rapidity with which consumers jettison the style at its end stage. The curve height can also vary as a function of how many consumers adopt the style at its peak of popularity. Finally the duration at which the style is popular among consumers affects the curve shape too. A fad, for example, will typically rise sharply and fall off almost as quickly, leaving a sharp-peaked, shaped curve. On the other hand, a classic fashion, which is a style favored by consumers for a long, long time will be indicated by a broad and lengthy positioned center portion of the bell curve. Sproles and Burns (1994) do a nice job of illustrating various versions of Nystrom's fashion life cycles. Comparisons, side by side of a fad, classic, and

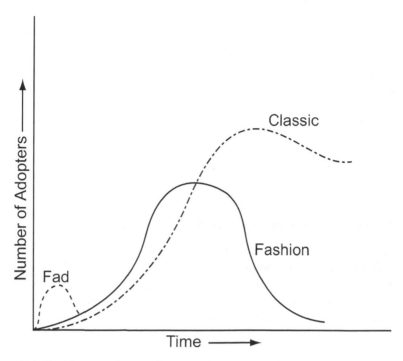

Figure 7.1 Fashion Life Cycles (Source: Sproles and Burns, 1994).

normal fashion life cycle (see Figure 7.1) illustrate the varying sizes and shapes that can be exhibited by distribution curves of time versus frequency of adoption. Sproles and Burns also suggest that life-cycle curves can be parsed to yield more information than just the overall life of a fashion product. For example, they show fashion life cycles that extend over multiple sales seasons, with the individual sub-seasons superimposed within.

While Nystrom (1928) speculated that fashion life cycles could be quantitatively documented, he did not present any concrete, research-developed, fashion life cycles in his work. Instead, his fashion life cycle curves were general in form and almost entirely conjectured. He did however speculate about the lifetimes of various fashion products. For example, he thought that the lifetime of a typical accessory was one season, the color or fabric structural aspects of a fashion item would extend a year, while silhouettes or garment shapes might last several years. Speculations aside, Nystrom gave to fashion professionals a theoretical shape from which to consider the lifetime of a fashion article. The shapes of his fashion lifetime curves were also useful for defining fashion as the prevailing style, and for distinguishing fashion subsets, such as fads and classics.

The means by which fashions spread and diffuse into the population affect the shape and longevity of fashion cycles, thus the way in which people respond to the myriad of style choices available to them is an integral aspect of fashion-change theory. We saw in the earlier chapter on collective behavior of fashion that social motivations such as assigning oneself to group membership or claiming status through appearance can affect the adoption of fashion. In line with the sociologists, Nystrom believed that imitation was the primary motivation that drove fashion diffusion across the population; however, he also cited a number of external macro environmental factors that impact the rate of fashion adoption, including relative prosperity, availability of leisure time, consumer education levels, and technical innovations.

Diffusion of Innovation: The Impact of the Consumer

Fashion analysts have also sought to understand and predict short-term cycles, focusing on variations among consumers, rather than style differences. This approach examined the impact of human receptiveness on the adoption and spread of a fashion trend. Some of our best understanding of the relationship between people and the fashion diffusion process is built upon a foundation of research on the spread of innovation by Everett Rogers (2003), who began his career studying innovation diffusion in agriculture. He later expanded his findings to many arenas of innovation diffusion, including fashion. The concept most pertinent to the study of fashion was Rogers' identification of the varying degrees of human receptiveness to embracing innovation. If receptiveness to innovation is synonymous with openness to new fashion, than Rogers' work is directly applicable to deepening our understanding of fashion-change theory.

What Rogers observed was that people do not all adopt innovations at the same rate. Some adopt innovations earlier than others, and conversely, some people are more resistant to innovations. Rogers concluded that the tendency of people to adopt or resist innovations is a continuous variable that can be plotted as a frequency distribution over time, yielding the familiar bell-shaped curve. He observed that many human behaviors, including the inclination to adopt innovation, are normally distributed. In the case of innovation diffusion, the bell curve commences with a small number of people who are the very earliest to adopt an innovation. As time progresses, more and more people embrace the innovation at an increasing rate, in what Rogers refers to as a binomial expansion. This continues until adoption peaks out at some point in time, and then begins to subside and slope downwards as adoption rate falls off. Rogers suggested that a normal distribution for innovation or fashion diffusion should be expected because as people begin to adopt the innovation there is a cumulative increase in influence upon others who have not yet adopted. In other words, as knowledge about an innovation increases with more people adopting, there is also a rising level of communication and information exchange, which further expands the rate of adoption until the innovation is so well placed in the population it reaches a maximum rate of diffusion. Subsequently, the number of people who have not yet adopted begins to dwindle and thus the normal curve begins to dip downwards, completing the path of a normal distribution.

A very important conclusion here is that people adopt innovations, or in our case fashions, at different rates. More importantly, adoption rate can be used to group people into different categories and the people within those categories, according to Rogers, demonstrate common behaviors and predilections. Rogers found that adoption rate is a linear function, so it could be examined using standard statistics. Using two key statistics based on normal distributions – the mean, which represents the average proclivity for innovation adoption, and second, the standard deviation, which is the average variability of innovation adoption – Rogers segmented innovation adopters into five fundamental categories:

Innovators – these individuals are located on the 'pointy end of the stick.' They are the first to experiment, perhaps even create new innovations. Located two standard deviations beyond the mean, they account for only 2.5 percent of the population. Described by Rogers as venturesome and located on the left extreme of the normal curve, innovators are 'the rash, the daring, and the risky' who play an exceptionally important role in the diffusion process by launching new ideas (Rogers, 2003: 283). In sum, the fashion life cycle begins when the innovators choose to be the first to exhibit a new look. Not all fashions launched by the innovators reach maturity, but enough do to consider this group an important gatekeeper to the inception of fashion ideas.

Early Adopters – following behind the innovators in the adoption hierarchy, holding the highest degree of trust among all those who consider innovation adoption, the early adopters represent 13.5 percent of the population and are located between one and two standard deviations from the mean. Not as rash as the innovators, the consideration given to adoption of innovation by early adopters makes them 'the individuals to check with' (Rogers: 283) before the larger majority steps up to adopt an innovation.

Early Majority – choosing to adopt an innovation a little quicker then the average member of a population, the early majority show more deliberate caution than the previous category, early adopters and are located between the mean and one standard deviation. A large 34 percent portion of the population, the early majority do not resist innovation; however, they exhibit initial caution which prohibits them from being considered leaders in the adoption process.

Late Majority – also representing a considerable 34 percent portion of the population, the late majority are located between the mean and a standard deviation away towards the later adoption direction. These individuals will adopt innovation mostly because they feel they have to. By the time the late majority adopter has made a move, half the population has preceded them, resulting in peer and marketplace pressure that will be considerable, which often pushes them to adopt a fashion innovation despite their skeptical natures.

Laggards – comprising 16 percent of the population and located beyond one standard deviation from the mean in the right-hand portion of the normal curve, laggards are the very last to adopt a new innovation. By Rogers' description, 'laggards tend to be suspicious of innovations' and those who precede them in the adoption process (Rogers: 284).

Non-adoptors – these individuals are outside Rogers' statistical analysis because they do not ever adopt the innovation in question, consequently they are not evident in the diffusion curve or its statistics. In sum, there are those individuals that for social, psychological or economic reasons will not adapt to innovations.

Rogers used the term 'social system' to describe the context within which individuals choose to adopt innovations. Clearly, as a result of his findings, individuals adapt to innovations at different rates, they fall into definable categories and they can be distinguished by their inclinations. Rogers explored the varying individual inclinations of different adoptor categories and found general characteristics that distinguished earlier from later adoptors. These would be the same categories that would distinguish early fashion adopters too. The defining characteristics he found clustered around socioeconomic status, personality values and communications behavior. These were very important findings because they illuminate the characteristics of individuals who from within the social system drive fashion change.

In the area of socioeconomic characteristics, Rogers found earlier adoptors functioning at a higher social level, being more literate, higher positioned socially, and upwardly mobile from an economic standpoint. The notion that higher socio/ economically positioned adopters who influence later adopters certainly sounds reminiscent of the trickle-down fashion-change theories explored elsewhere in this book. In fact, Rogers suggested that apparel fashion adoption was, to a great extent, a status- seeking activity and that early adopters have higher social aspirations.

Rogers found personality issues too that affected the propensity for innovation adoption. For example, early adopters are less rigid and more open to change. They are intellectually brighter, more rational and can deal with uncertainty and abstract concepts more effectively than later adopters. Finally, from a communication standpoint, early adopters were found to be more in tune with mass media and consequently more aware of current events and potentially new innovations.

In sum, through Rogers' work, we witness innovations, or in our case fashion flowing through a temporal life cycle, which as Nystrom described has a beginning, middle and end. The beginning is characterized by a small number of individuals who either instigate fashion change or adapt very early to it. Furthermore, Rogers described their characteristics from a social and personality standpoint. The influential early adopters are later followed by the mass majority of individuals in the social system, who either cautiously or perhaps reluctantly follow along. Completing the cycle are the laggards who are very change averse, but are somehow pulled into the system and though late in the process eventually adopt the change.

In fact, a number of researchers have applied Rogers' concepts to the study of fashion diffusion. For instance, Behling (1992) did a thorough job of summarizing twenty early studies of fashion diffusion that applied Rogers' concepts. Though Behling's conclusions indicated some problems with direct application of Rogers' work to fashion studies, the community of fashion scholars continues to accept Rogers' work unabashedly as an excellent framework for understanding fashion diffusion, so it merited exploration in some depth within this chapter.

Status-driven Models of Fashion Cycles

While Nystrom focused on the cyclical spread of fashion items throughout the population, and Rogers considered the nature of people and the rate at which they adopted fashion items, both theorists suggested that imitation from within the social system contributed to the spread of fashion change. Collective behavior theories based on the principle that people use consumer products to express and maintain status have also been used as a foundation for examining fashion cycles. During the past two decades there have been several publications from economists (Coelho and McClure, 1993; Fritjers, 1998; Pesendorfer, 1995) who have developed mathematical models to account for fashion-change behavior, built firmly upon sociologically based assumptions regarding status acquisition. Three related models drawing on three different sets of assumptions are presented: (1) Pesendorfer's (1995, 2004, 2005) status-signaling theory; (2) Coelho and McClure's (1993) fashion as a positional status-marker theory; and (3) Paul Fritjers' (1998) high-status, purchaser theory.

Wolfgang Pesendorfer (1995, 2004, 2005) worked with fashion cycles by developing a theoretical economic model that encompassed collective behavior, but also included product design, its relative availability, and pricing structure all as interacting variables. Two key fashion concepts were elucidated by Pesendorfer's model. First, fashion items serve as a signaling device to establish social status, and second, fashion items typically have a finite lifetime, being replaced cyclically by other fashion items.

Pesendorfer's economic model considered the fashion cycle in both equilibrium and dynamic contexts. In the equilibrium situation, Pesendorfer defined two basic types of people who participated in the fashion process, whom he referred to as either high or low types. High types were located in the upper social strata and distinguished from low type's status by indicators such as wealth, family, or education. Pesendorfer's model is built on the assumption that high types wish to commune or match with other high types and avoid social involvement with 'less than' low types. He further assumed social status was unobservable without the benefit of dress. Thus without fashion as a tool, high and low types could not distinguish each other on a scale of status hierarchy which would inevitably lead to unfortunate social chaos. To avoid chaos, it is dress, expensive, fashionable dress that high types use to signal who they are and to identify each other in some form of grand matching game.

Pesendorfer could not fathom why anyone would pay a premium for an expensive fashionable item when a less costly, less fashionable item would serve a similar functional purpose unless there was an overriding social demand to do so, which was his primary supporting argument for the pricey fashion items exhibited by high types. In Pesendorfer's theoretical construct, fashion items have no intrinsic value other than to serve as status signals. In economic terms, there is a demand among high types for fashions for which they are willing to pay a high price if the design facilitates matching with other high types. Demand will fall off if the design is not suitable for matching. With the aid of their signaling fashions, high types match with high types, and low types with each other, reaching an equilibrium state with everyone finding a match. Nevertheless, equilibrium is temporary and can be disrupted particularly when a fashion item suffers degradation in its ability to clearly signal type. This may happen if too many low types begin wearing high-type fashions. The demand will fall off for high types, if too many low types adopt the fashion, reminiscent of trickle-down theory as discussed in Chapter 4.

What causes fashion to cycle lies in the second feature of Pesendorfer's model, the dynamic aspect, which invokes the influence of the fashion item producer. According to the model, fashion producers play their role by offering the marketplace an expensive fashionable item that high types consume for the purpose of social-status signaling. Low types are not interested in purchasing the fashionable items because of prohibitive costs. The model suggests that if a fashion maintains its signaling integrity, the price will remain high and high types will continue to wear and purchase it, creating a relatively long fashion cycle. From this point, a fashion producer has a number of different directions to take. Anticipating that high types may eventually tire of an existing fashion, the fashion producer may see economic advantage to lowering the cost of the product so that more people purchase it, including low types. This action is possible if the fashion items have a low production cost, which most fashion items do. Of course, when low types begin to wear the same fashion as high types, it becomes increasingly difficult to distinguish between high and low types. Pesendorfer referred to this circumstance as status-signaling degradation. So here we see the end of a fashion cycle because the marketplace is saturated and the item's capacity to designate status has diminished. The process of diminishing a product's signaling properties through market saturation may be viewed as a form of planned obsolescence. At this point, a new fashion cycle may be initiated with the introduction of a new, status-conferring design for high types to purchase.

Even if the producer does not lower the cost of a fashion, the item is likely to suffer status-signaling degradation because high types also seek novelty as a way of conferring social position. In this case, the producer may restart the fashion cycle by offering a competitive fashion to the marketplace, anticipating high-type boredom with existing styles. In sum, Pesendorfer's model is built on the concept that goods cycle in and out of fashion depending upon the strength of their social-status signaling quality, and fashion producers take advantage of this circumstance by manipulating pricing of existing fashion products or by producing new and novel 'high end' fashion products.

Coelho and McClure (1993)[1] developed their economic model by defining the purpose of a fashion product as being a positional good, which conferred upon the wearer a high degree of social status. Invoking evolutionary theory, they believed the pursuit of elevated social status was a socio-biological drive that humans have as well as other animals, motivated largely by the biological urge to pass on genetic material or DNA. The higher the social status, the greater will be the probability of genetic propagation. Wearing fashionable dress is an important means of constructing social status. Consequently, Coelho and McClure's fashion cycle begins with the seeking of status as a primary ingredient. At this inception point, fashion products are high priced, with limited demand. Status seekers will pay high prices for a limited demand

1. Phillip Coelho and James McClure (1993) also developed an economic model for fashion cycles. In addition, Coelho and McClure (1993) were quite critical of Pesendorfer's work. Among a long list of criticisms, Coelho et al. seemed particularly perturbed with Pesendorfer's notion that fashion was expressly concerned with matching individuals of similar social status. Coelho and McClure (1993) structure their economic model on social status too; however, matching of high and low types is not a central premise. For the full details of their critique of Pesendorfer, please refer to Coelho, Klein, and McClure (2004, 2005).

product because of the social distinction the item will confer on the wearer. This is referred to as the 'snob effect' (Leibenstein, 1950). Taking advantage of these circumstances, fashion producers offer high-priced products to the marketplace to attract status seekers. This practice is referred to as prestige pricing, which creates snob effect through arbitrarily high pricing. Inevitably, positional goods, such as fashions, lose their snob effect or capacity to confer social distinction when they become more commonly seen in the population. This may be because many people are willing to pay prestige pricing, or perhaps the supplier reduces the product costs thus allowing more people to afford it. When the social distinction a product carries diminishes, so does its price, and though demand may increase for a time, eventually it will dwindle when the product becomes too commonplace, thus the fashion cycle reaches it termination point.

Paul Fritjers' (1998) analysis of fashion cycles is another illustration of an economic model based upon assumptions drawn from collective behavior-status theories. Contrary to Coelho and McClure (1993) and Pesendorfer (1995) who assumed that the purchase of a high-priced fashion item was the primary means of acquiring status for the purchaser, Fritjers suggested that the status of a fashion item was actually created when a high-status individual purchased it. His model was built on the proposition that early adopters were wealthy, high-status individuals who were willing to pay a lofty price for a fashion product and thus confer status on the purchased object, thereby making the item desirous to those seeking status. Not all pricey fashion items attracted wealthy buyers in Fritjers' model – only those items that had a high probability of maintaining high price levels out into the future. Fritjers' model demonstrated that the high-status buyer viewed a fashion purchase as an investment into the future, and what they sought to avoid was too quickly witnessing their fashion selections proliferating among the 'unwashed masses,' which would reduce the fashion item's intrinsic value and terminate the cycle. For the fashion producer seeking the business of elevated-status consumers, Fritjers' model suggested that maintaining product selectivity can be achieved through stable high pricing.

Fashion Cycles Driven by Purposeful Obsolescence

George Sproles (1981) suggested that constant introduction of new styles is the lifeblood of the fashion industry, although altering fashion life cycles is more complex than simply creating and marketing new styles. The rejection of midi dresses (Reynolds and Darden, 1972) in the late 1970s was a classic case study of consumer rejection of an industry offering. Despite the occasional rejections of new product styles, the industry continues to churn out new products in the hope of capturing broad-scale consumer interest. To that end, Paul Gregory (1947a, 1947b), an economist, explored the rate of introduction of new fashions into the marketplace, and concluded that the industry introduced more fashion changes than could possibly be justified. He criticized the fashion industry for creating economic waste and inefficiencies by artificially increasing the rate of fashion change. Hastened product turnover with concomitant sales increases were the motivations Gregory assigned to the fashion industry for artificially hyped fashion change.

'Purposeful obsolescence' is the term Gregory used to describe the behavior when a manufacturer conspired to shorten the lifetime of a product. He cited deliberately shortened life cycles for a variety of products including automobiles, razor blades, pharmaceuticals, and fashion items, particularly women's fashions. There were two specific forms of purposeful obsolescence that Gregory defined. They included the deliberate under-engineering of a product so that it would wear out and fail faster than expected, given the current production technologies and manufacturing costs. Weighting of silks with metallic salts was an example given by the author. Weighted silks are artificially enhanced to appear heavier and more luxurious; however, the weighting caused the silk to prematurely 'shatter' and fail more quickly than would be expected. The other form of purposeful obsolescence was the calculated destruction of the psychological utility of a product. Though the product is still functionally useable, the user is made to feel that the product is not of value any more. Fashion items are the best example of products that can be diminished in value long before they are actually worn out and no longer functional as clothing. This is done via the accelerated replacement by industry of existing fashions with newer ones, which as we saw earlier reignites the fashion life cycle.

Long-term Fashion Cycles

As we have seen in earlier sections of this chapter, the basic foundations of fashion- cycle theory were done by professionals outside the textile and apparel discipline. Economists dominated the theoretical landscape, though communication diffusion theorist Rogers (2003) also made important contributions. The other branch of fashion theory regarding cyclic behavior focuses on long-term cycles, which would be fashion cycles extending decades, perhaps even centuries in wavelength. It was Alfred Kroeber (1919, 1940), an anthropologist, who first uncovered the very long-term cycles of fashion. As an anthropologist Kroeber was interested in documenting the life cycles of civilizations. His original work was published in 1919 and he produced a follow-up analysis with Jane Richardson, a graduate student, in 1940. Together, the two publications comprised the foundation of long-duration analysis of fashion cycles and have become lore in the scholarly community of textile and apparel professionals (Carter, 2003).

At the outset of his research, Kroeber observed that there was a plethora of anecdotal evidence demonstrating that nations, empires, arts, and culture originate then cyclically rise and fall over time. What anthropology at that time was lacking, in his judgment, was a scientific approach to study the time flow of civilization. He reasoned that the solution lay in the objective analysis of cultural artifacts. After evaluating the various measurable attributes of human activity that could be studied to understand cyclic developments in history, Kroeber chose to focus on manufactured objects since they were direct reflections of civilization and because of their ease and accuracy of measurement.

Because of sample size, accuracy of dating, and relative ease of accessibility in fashion magazines, Kroeber eventually settled on dress as his object of measurement. Having determined that it would be best to use a focused, single-purpose form of apparel, Kroeber selected women's evening dress as his vehicle for analysis. He also decided not to measure the more superficial, rapidly changing aspects of dress, which he referred to as the mode, and included features such as details, color, and trim. Instead, he decided on precisely measuring the dimensions of six basic elements of form, which he referred to as style. These included skirt length and width, waist length and width, and finally depth and width of décolletage. The original study spanned seventy-five years, with a sampling of ten dresses per year. His follow-up research with Richardson sought a broader and deeper understanding of the long-term cyclic phenomenon and was thus expanded to 150 years, with a greater sampling per year.

What Kroeber found was an almost steady change over time in the dimensions of the dress form elements he measured. From what he described as a basic average dimension, the form, such as dress width, either continuously increased or decreased in size, although with some interim variations, for a very lengthy period of time until some end point was reached, and then the trend would reverse itself and return to the basic average dimension, but continue to pass through until a reverse end point was reached. This procession of increasing or decreasing dimensional change took many years, and he referred to the duration from one extreme to another as a periodicity. Some periodicities extended well beyond a century in length, however, the duration depended on which dress form element was being measured.

Kroeber was astonished by his findings (Carter, 2003). Beneath the chaos of rapidly altering changes in superficial surface effects such as trim and color, there existed a slow, inexorable, and in his words 'majestic' procession of change in basic dress form, 'often exceeding the duration of human life with the even regularity of the swing of an enormous pendulum.' Kroeber conjectured the existence of a hidden scheme or natural law 'on a scale not without a certain grandeur' that seemed to propel forward the changes he observed (1919: 258). In what must have been astounding to other fashion theorists, Kroeber suggested that the long duration of fashion periodicities, which often exceeded a human life span, minimized the impact that an individual such as a designer might have on fashion. Instead, fashion change must be the product of some other unknown, unidentified, and complex social force at work and outside human perception. This 'super-organic' force, a form of civilizational determinism, overrode the influence of the individual.

In his later work (1940), Kroeber attributed short-term variations that occur within the longer-term 'majestic procession' to unsettled times resulting from political conflict or social upheaval. To our regret he never clearly identified the hidden force behind long-term fashion cycles other than to suggest some unconscious force at work. Nevertheless, his identification of long-term periodicities established a small cottage industry of other researchers (Barber, 1999; Belleau, 1987; Curran, 1999; Lowe and Lowe, 1982; Robinson, 1976; Weeden, 1977; Young, 1966) who identified and/or analyzed long-duration patterns in other forms of dress. Much of the research on long-term fashion cycles that followed in Kroeber's footsteps used methodologies similar to his, in which fashion illustrations were examined for dimensions of form and changes plotted over time. Long-term cycles of varying periodicities were found among apparel fashions, for example in women's daywear (Young, 1966; Belleau, 1987). Other work replicated Kroeber's original analysis of women's evening wear (Weeden, 1977). While the follow-up research studies continued to indicate long-term periodicities they did not contribute substantively to our understanding of the underlying causes of fashion cycles beyond some educated speculation.

Out of the number of studies that followed Kroeber's original work, there were three that deserve focused discussion as they added substantively to our understanding of long-term fashion cycles: the work of Dwight Robinson (1958), John and Elizabeth Lowe (1982), and Nigel Barber (1999). Robinson (1958) wrote that fashion fluctuated cyclically over long periods in the form of pendulum movement. As did Kroeber, he used the fashion behavior of women's apparel to build his argument, and, borrowing a concept from the early twentieth-century couturier, Paul Poiret, Robinson indicated that the basic trend flow of fashion was to typically swing outwards back and forth, ending in some form of design excess on either end of the pendulum swing. In other words, fashions tended to pendulum back and forth from extreme to extreme. He suggested that a never-ending human requirement for novelty drove fashion changes from season to season. Later, Robinson (1961) refined his concept of novelty and motivation driving fashion to be expressed more accurately as the pursuit of the rarity of new designs which are consequently perceived as novel and desirable. Whether or not new designs are rare or novel, Robinson observed fashion as moving towards extremes in design before swinging back into an opposite direction. The relative design restraint of women's French Regency gowns in the early 1700s, sandwiched between two periods of design extreme, including the earlier ornate dresses of the Baroque and the later extravagant look of the Rococo periods, served as excellent examples cited by Robinson.

Robinson noted too that when an extreme in dress design was reached, the fashion suddenly collapsed under its own oppressive weight and almost instantly reverted back to a center point between the outer possibilities of extravagance, or as he refers to it, a 'golden mean.' Examples of this phenomenon include the disintegration of overstated crinoline hoop skirts into a variety of designs such as trains, loops, and bustles. An even better example was the exaggerated bustle and leg of mutton sleeves of the Victorian period degenerating to be displaced by the shirt waist, hobble skirt, or the relative sparseness of flapper designs.

Some years later, Robinson (1975) refined his view on fashion cycles by adding a time element to his consideration. As a result of his research on men's facial hair (1976), combined with that of Kroeber's (1919, 1940) earlier work on long-term cycles in women's fashions, he concluded that fashion cycles were predictable, consistent, and exceptionally long term in character. He speculated that the periodic cycle of fashion movement spanned and repeated itself over the course of a century, beginning when Europeans exited the dark ages. He also believed that this cyclical movement was inevitable and relentless, as well as independent from external forces, including social change, technological advancement, or the impact of individual designers.

Congruent with Kroeber's findings, Robinson spoke of a master force that pushed fashion forward through its century long cycles. Here again he referred to the notion of novelty compelling people to seek and adopt new looks, whether it was in apparel, housing, appliances, or automotives. From a business and product development standpoint, the predictability and relentless forward movement of fashion change could be ignored only at one's peril. In sum, Robinson followed in Kroeber's footsteps by using long-term fashion cycles as his frame of reference. His contribution included emphasizing the end points of Kroeber's periodicities as being points of excess. Furthermore, he expanded the concept of long-term flow of fashion to include products other than apparel. Finally, like Kroeber, his work was limited to identifying long-term fashion cycles, without determining the underlying force that caused cycles to occur. He speculated but did not prove that the primary cause of fashion-change cycles was the psychological need for novelty.

Lowe and Lowe (1982) reexamined the Richardson and Kroeber (1940) work using multivariate statistics to analyze the original results. Richardson and Kroeber had basically used only a metric analysis for the original study. In other words, they measured dimensions of dress form change and plotted them over time. Smoothing out variations of their periodicity curve with a five-year moving average was as sophisticated as their analysis got. Essentially they used a visual analysis of their curves to draw conclusions. In their defense, high-speed computing was not available when they did their research, so sophisticated statistical analysis was not within their analytical tool set. Lowe and Lowe anticipated that a more sophisticated mathematical analysis might lead to a deeper understanding of the complexities of the long-term periodicities that Kroeber had found.

Based upon their analysis, Lowe and Lowe drew conclusions that they considered to be indisputable. Their statistical analysis confirmed that the long-term periodicities Kroeber found were to a large extent statistically significant, although included within the wave-like periodicities were random variations. A portion of the long-term periodicities were considered by Lowe and Lowe to be deterministic, which means that future fashion movement could be predicted with reasonable confidence based on past occurrences. On the other hand, the random variations found in the periodicities caused the relationship of fashion change over time to be stochastic, which meant that accurate prediction of the future diminishes the farther out in time one attempts to predict what the future fashion will hold.

Based on their statistical analysis, Lowe and Lowe defined which factors were associated with the predictable (structural) and unpredictable (random) portions of the long-term periodicities originally uncovered by Kroeber. The structural aspects of the long-term cycles consisted of a subtle force which pushed stylistic change in a slow and continuous direction, which they referred to as inertia. Countering the force of inertia was a form of gravity or a damping factor that resisted and slowed change, and this they referred to as cultural continuity. Finally, another constraint on the system was the 'rule of esthetic proportions' (1982: 540) that biased change toward the directions determined by our expectations for the fundamental dress form. These three factors combined caused the slow fundamental oscillations of fashion change that Kroeber found spanning the decades. Contrary to Kroeber, Lowe and Lowe believed that an individual could impact the long-term fashion cycle. They concluded that the random, non-predictable, previously unaccountable variations in the long-term cycles that Kroeber found were, in fact, the influence of 'individual innovation and initiative' as well as 'happenings elsewhere in the sociocultural system' (1982: 540).

Lowe and Lowe also commented upon the equilibrium point of the long-term fashion cycle. The equilibrium point, which Robinson (1961) called the golden mean, was the point from which the cyclic fashion changes emanated away from and eventually returned to. They believed that the equilibrium point represented the 'intersection of esthetic constraints' (1982: 540). Furthermore, they believed that two forms of stylistic change occurred. First there were random perturbations around the equilibrium point, which would cause the long cyclic drifts away from and back to the golden mean. They also believed that structural change could occur, where a form or style was altered so much that a permanent new equilibrium point was established. This was a saltational or step-like leap to a new form that resulted from large and sustained variations away from the equilibrium point. The example they used was the shift from traditional gowns to new forms of evening wear that included pants. This, they believe, was caused by the incessant style variations emanating from the 'changing attitudes toward women's roles in the family, production system, and society' (1982: 541).

Nigel Barber's (1999) research stands out as being one of the only follow-up studies using Kroeber's original work that directly correlated changes in social and economic circumstances to long-term fashion changes, so it is fitting to end this discussion with a brief summary of his findings. In sum, he recognized changes in women's conditions as a major cause of long-term fashion cycles. Using Kroeber's original data, subsequent analysis of the same data by Lowe and Lowe (1982), and an extended analysis of that same data by Weeden (1977), Barber concluded that the long-term fluctuations of women's evening dress around its central equilibrium point were directly attributable to women's reproductive strategies. He noted fashion fluctuations congruent with variations in factors such as economic independence and marital opportunities which varied as a function of population sex ratios.

To summarize Barber's findings briefly, his results suggested that as women became more accomplished financially, their dress changed to reflect less dependence on marriage. His findings indicated that when marriage was an economic necessity, women's dress styles became more modest, making women seem less sexually accessible. In other words, when the marital union was the primary vehicle for financial security, dress was modest to make women appear less easily accessible. Conversely, when marriage was not viewed as an institution of economic survival, dress became more revealing because the appearance of chastity was not correlated to financial necessity. Barber's findings were not entirely surprising as some years earlier, Lowe and Lowe (1985) also suggested that cultural construction of women's sexuality might underpin long-term fashion cycles, by pointing out that Flügel's (1930) shifting erogenous zones correlated with the peaks and valleys of Kroeber's periodicities. Flügel, who is discussed in more detail in Chapter 2, believed that fashion change was driven largely by sexual competition.

Cyclical Theory in the New Millennium

Long-term and short-term cyclical explanations for fashion change have their place in analyzing millennium fashion, with attention being paid to differences that come into play when globalization, Internet communication, and other twenty-first-century trends are considered. In particular, cyclical theories focused on transmission of status through consumer products resonate with the growing divide between rich and poor nations, and people living in extreme wealth and poverty in this century. In the final section of this chapter the seven cyclical theories are summarized, followed by a series of twenty-first-century case studies.

Summarization of Cyclical Theory

Theory 1: Style-based Fashion Cycle Theory

According to style-based fashion cycle theory, characteristics of a fashion product impact its rate and level of acceptance over time. Fads, classics, and trends are classified as different types of styles, resulting in different adoption patterns and different graphic representations of level of adoption over time.

Theory 2: Diffusion of Innovation Theory

This theory as articulated by Rogers (2003) argued that people adopt innovations, or in our case fashions, at different rates. More importantly, adoption rate can be used to group people into different categories and the people within those categories demonstrate common behaviors and predilections.

Theory 3: Status Signaling Theory

According to Pesendorfer's cyclical theory fashion items serve as signaling devices to establish and announce social status for both what he refers to as high- and low-type consumers, who are distinguishable as a result of observable, status-laden, fashionable apparel. Fashion change is explained by this theory as a cyclical response to the loss of status that occurs when a trend is picked up by a low-type consumer, which then causes the high-type consumer to move on to another status-signaling fashion.

Theory 4: Fashion as a Positional Status-marker Theory

Coelho and McClure (1993) defined the purpose of a fashion product as being a positional good that confers status upon the wearer. This theory utilized evolutionary theory to argue that human beings seek positional goods like fashion as a result of a socio-biological drive for status. According to this theory the fashion cycle begins with the seeking of status through high-priced fashion products. When the social distinction a product carries diminishes, so does its price, resulting in an increase in demand that dwindles when the product becomes too commonplace and no longer confers status.

Theory 5: Status Conferred by the Purchaser Theory

Fritjers' (1998) status-based economic theory argued that the status of a fashion item is created by virtue of its purchase by a high-status individual. His model is built on the proposition that early adopters are wealthy, high-status individuals who were willing to pay a lofty price for a fashion product and thus confer status on the purchased object, thus making the item attractive to others seeking status-marking fashions.

Theory 6: Artificial Obsolescence Theory

The economist Paul Gregory (1947a, 1947b) argued that fashion changes were in large part the result of planned and purposeful obsolescence imposed on the consumer by the textile and apparel industry to increase the rate of product turnover and thus increase profit.

There were two specific forms of purposeful obsolescence that Gregory defined. They included the deliberate under-engineering of an apparel product so that it will wear out and fail faster than expected. The other form of purposeful obsolescence was the calculated destruction of the psychological utility of a fashion item through the rapid introduction of a newer trendier version.

Theory 7: 'Super Organic' Long-term Fashion Cycle Theory

The anthropologist Alfred Kroeber's research uncovered predictable long-term cyclical changes in the dimensions of women's dress styles. Arguing that the cycle of these changes frequently exceeded a human life span, he concluded that fashion change is the product of some other unknown, unidentified, and complex 'super organic' force outside the range of human perception. Robinson (1958) further refined Kroeber's theory by adding that fashion cycles tend to move in a pendulum movement transitioning back and forth between extremes. Lowe and Lowe (1985) also elaborated on the theory, concluding that random, non-predictable variations in the long-term cycles were the result of individual, social and cultural influences, which were not recognized as influential in the original theory.

Theory 8: Women's Dress Fashions as a Function of Reproductive Strategy

Barber's theory argues that long-term fluctuations of women's evening dress were directly influenced by changes in women's reproductive strategies. He noted fashion fluctuations congruent with variations in factors such as economic independence and marital opportunities which varied as a function of population sex ratios. His findings indicated that when women consider marriage an economic necessity their dress styles are modest, making them appear less sexually available. In contrast, during time periods when women are more independent, and not locked into seeking marriage for financial security, dress became more revealing because the appearance of chastity is not correlated to financial necessity.

New Millennium Fashion Cycles

Paris Hilton Invents 'Doggie Bags'

Is a small dog the most fashionable accessory a girl can have these days? Oh, definitely . . . the current trend is credited to Paris Hilton and her Chihuahua, Tinkerbell. (Wadler, 2004, archives)

In a three-bedroom colonial house in New Jersey, Jessica Alpert-Goldman runs a small handbag business that caters to the famous including Sarah Jessica Parker, Gwyneth Paltrow, Janet Jackson, and Paris Hilton. The style writer Jonathan Miller, quoting *Lucky* magazine, described her handbag design this way: 'Original, whimsical, and functional, these bags are an "Excuse me, where did you get that?" eye-catcher' (*New York Times*, February 6, 2005). It is this perfect 'eye-catcher' designer that put together the doggie bag for Paris Hilton's famous Chihuahua Tinkerbell that became a signal status symbol leading to a short-lived new millennium cycle in pricey dog handbags.

The cycle caught on throughout the New York City accessory scene with young cutting-edge designers catching the fashion moment as well, with an accessory with both functional and status-signaling properties:

Charo, Jane August's Chihuahua, wears pearls and makes her home away from home a capacious leather satchel. 'I wanted that dog to go with me everywhere,' said Ms. August, who designed her carryall at least partly to accommodate that desire. She fashions luxuriously scaled handbags, some roomy enough to double as flight bags – out of pliant leather, patterned suede and tapestry cloth – and sells them at stores including Bergdorf Goodman, Saks Fifth Avenue and Susan of Burlingame near San Francisco. (Miller, 2005, archives)

By November 2005, over a year after Paris Hilton made a fashion statement carrying Tinkerbell in a custom-designed handbag, stores like PawPalace in

New Jersey were offering Puppypurses, selling for $55 in denim, and $200 in leather (*New York Times*, November 27, 2005). As early as April 2005 fashion leaders had already started carrying something new in their 'eye catching' handbags:

> The really smart [fashion forward] thing and, perhaps frighteningly prophetic thing came from Ellen Carey, who runs Seedhouse, a fashion showroom in Chelsea. Poking out of Ms. Carey's purse, just about where a Chihuahua's head should be, was a plastic Edna Mode, the little Edith Head-inspired fashion designer character from the 'Incredibles'. (Miller, 2005, archives)

This doggie handbag trend, initiated by Paris Hilton, aptly illustrates Fritjers' (1998) concept that the status of a fashion item is created by virtue of its purchase by a high- status individual. His model, built on the idea that early adopters are wealthy, high-status individuals who were willing to pay a lofty price for a fashion product, is played out in this fashion story, in which Paris Hilton's presentation of her dog as a fashion statement is identified as a short-term trend, not only in small dogs, but in handbags as well.

Sinful Ideals of Femininity in the New Millennium

Barber's (1999) long-term cycle theory holds that women's fashions change as a reflection of their dependence on men for financial security. Related to fashion changes are the ideals of femininity espoused in different time periods. In the 1950s, with high numbers of women staying home and dependent on men's income, ideals of femininity and dress styles stressed a proper, modest appearance. Women in the twenty-first century are confronted with a wealth of popular culture models of femininity who are financially independent, and often notorious in terms of scant dress styles and notoriously unseemly behavior.

The headline on Guy Trebay's article on the supermodel Kate Moss's fall and redemption on a public cocaine charge read 'Being Bad: The Career Move,' with the text of the column arguing that being bad gets press, and that women who dress naughty and act accordingly, are put on pedestals in the current cultural system:

> What seems evident is that public humiliation has lost its barb. There might have been a time when being caught on camera in flagrante delicto or hoovering up lines of coke would have ended a career. But as Paris Hilton proved, being video-taped by one's boyfriend in a zonked-out state and naked on all fours does not put a hitch in one's five-year plan. (Trebay, 2006, archives)

Trebay goes on to document the press and attention that Kate Moss racked in just as she emerged from her detoxification drug program:

> even before the model had checked out of the drying out clinic, she was inundated in attention and work. W magazine ran a cover story on Kate Moss in November 2005. Vanity Fair made her its cover subject the following month. An issue of the influential fashion magazine French Vogue was dedicated to Ms. Moss, who also served as guest editor. If her notoriety was bad for the brand, it is hard to see how. (Trebay, 2006, archives)

The dress behavior associated with Kate Moss, as well as other related celebrity figures like Paris Hilton, is one of a scantily clad image, with Hilton, for example, famous for celebrity endorsement of the widely adopted 'thong that shows' trend of the late 1990s and early twenty-first century. Not surprisingly it was Kate Moss that Nikon choose to model nude with its product as it was attempting 'to shed its fussy image and seduce the notoriously fickle imaginations of young consumers' (*New York Times,* April 20, 2006).

Supporting Barber's long-term cycle theory is the clear message that both Kate Moss and Paris Hilton send to the public that they are financially secure and on their own, without need for the financial support of a man, and fully at home with their sexuality and free lifestyle. The relationship Barber conceived between the presentation of a moral and modest look, and dependence on a male partner's income, is aptly illustrated in this case study example where financial independence is pared with flagrantly sexual demeanor and dress by these two new millennium celebrity role models.

'Shop Your Closet': Vintage Styles Make a Rapid Comeback

As we have seen, fashions have been documented to run in short-term cycles with a definable beginning, middle, and an end. In the past, a fashion cycle for a garment may have lasted several buying seasons; however, because of some of the recent fashion-related cultural trends examined in the opening chapter of this book, fashion cycles have been truncated time-wise rather dramatically. Trends such as the all-pervasive Internet exposure of fashions and new looks to the public, as well as the industry's quick response strategy to consistently push a plethora of new fashions out into the marketplace during a single buying season, have all contributed to a more rapid turnover of fashion styles and a shortening of the fashion life cycle as we progress into the twenty-first century.

Consistent with these aforementioned trends, Mark Jacobs documents the surprising, contemporary practice of 'shopping your closet,' for vintage clothing items. He has observed the creation of a 'new to vintage [apparel market occurring] within a ridiculously short time frame . . . [which] is the product of a shrinking fashion cycle' (Jacobs, 2005, archives). According to Jacobs, fashion followers were now reintroducing as vintage remakes items that were still in their closets, due to the extremely high rate of style change.

This trend reflects the changing way we must now interpret style-based cyclical theories of fashion change. The notion of a recently set-aside fashion item being resurrected to fit a new look has the potential to change the standard introduction, peak and decline fashion curve on trended items – with reintroduction in some way tied to the ability of the older item to correlate and express the new style.

The Mechanical Watch: The Visible Status Marker

> For many years now, the 'in' thing to do when first achieving success is to purchase a Rolex. A Mercedes, Porsche of Ferrari comes in second, and house comes in a lowly third. It's not just a watch first, it's a Rolex. And why a Rolex before a car or a house? Well, it's quite simple. That watch will be on your wrist up to 24 hours a day for everyone to see, and that includes your own admiring glances, to appreciate and to illustrate that yes, you've arrived, you've made it, you're of the elite. (Lakin, 2006: 30)

The quartz battery operated watch was introduced in the 1970s as the modern-age, impeccably accurate, battery driven, carefree method of keeping time. The quartz watch's rapid diffusion into the marketplace left many watchmakers prognosticating that the old-fashioned mechanical version was on its way out. As predicted, mechanical watch manufacturers were dramatically impacted by the new technology, with many shutting down or cutting back operations, particularly in Switzerland (Strandberg, 2006a: 21). While this was a logical response by the manufacturers to the onslaught of quartz movements, they unfortunately lost sight of the remaining status conferred by a mechanical watch. For men in particular, the mechanical watch remained a subtle style statement, as well as a constantly worn status marker embodied best by the perpetually popular Rolex. Thirty-five years after the introduction of quartz movements, the mechanical watch has been reborn in a huge way both as a major fashion statement and widely accepted status marker. It is now impossible to pick up a popular magazine or major metropolitan newspaper without being assaulted with numerous advertisements for highly pricey and complicated mechanical wristwatches. Quoted from a recent *New York Times* magazine spread on watches, 'You could be wearing the latest complicated watch on the beach, wearing only your Speedo, and instantly those in the know, know' (Strandberg, 2006a: 21) – in other words other men of status will immediately recognize your watch and confer position to you automatically.

The implied old-world craft associated with the mechanical watch distinguishes it from the mass-production quartz watch alternative. The renaissance of the complicated mechanical watch is driven to some extant by new computer manufacturing techniques that make the new mechanical watches wonders of precision. Ironically, the quartz watch is still by far the more accurate time piece for the wrist. The quartz watch may drift for seconds over a year, while even the best mechanical watch will drift seconds daily. Nevertheless, for the individual of financial means who seeks a status marker, the mechanical watch provides an aesthetic that accuracy in timekeeping cannot compete with:

> There is something special about a mechanical watch on your wrist. A quartz watch is just a circuit board with a battery, a gadget that tells time, while a mechanical watch is something that has to be created, crafted and has had life breathed into it by a skilled watchmaker. Mechanical watches cannot be made on an assembly line, they have to, at one point or another, regardless of how much they cost, be attended to by a watchmaker. Once the watch is purchased, it is kept alive by its owner, wearing and winding it every day (Strandberg, 2006a: 21).

In sum, this special intangible appeal has led to a revival of the mechanical watch, with sales and popularity at the beginning of the new millennium at an all time high (Strandberg, 2006a).

Watch companies have taken note of this trend and many are now producing what they consider entry level mechanicals with starting prices ranging from $300 to $1,000. Focused on consumers who are anxious about abandoning their quartz watches for a more complicated mechanical, these entry level prices are intended to minimize the risk for a new purchaser who is interested in the status conferred by a mechanical watch but intimidated by the technology (Strandberg, 2006a). The goal of the watch companies is to move that entry consumer into appreciation for the technical craft of a mechanical watch hoping to move them up into more complicated watches featuring day/date display, dual time zones, minute repeaters, and perpetual calendars.

The status conferred by a high-quality mechanical watch is most appreciated by those who themselves own and covet the object. Men recognize other men's watches because they have taken the time to understand the technology and appreciate the value of a highly crafted watch. Celebrity endorsements affect watch trends for men as well as women and watch advertising often features well-known people of accomplishment within their field wearing the latest high-end version of a mechanical watch. Product placement within popular films has also had a dramatic impact on the popularity of some mechanical watches. For example:

> Hamilton Watch has had several movie tie-ins, the most successful and visible being their involvement with 'Men in Black'—where they took a classic

Hamilton design and put it on the wrists of the most forward thinking, technically advanced characters in the film, Tommy Lee Jones and Will Smith. The result? The watch became a sales leader (Strandberg, 2006b).

Thus advertising and celebrity endorsements instigate changes, moving the high-status watch from one brand to another, and from one style to another within the same brand – thereby illustrating Coelho and McClure's theory that the fashion cycle begins with the seeking of a high-status object, with a different style emerging to replace the old style as it loses value when it becomes more commonly worn. The emergence of the entry level styles into the mechanical watch product category has the potential to accelerate fashion changes in this product category, as the investment on an individual watch is diminished.

8
Millennium Dress History: Artifacts as Harbingers of Change

The multi-disciplinary interest in understanding, interpreting, and forecasting fashion change in the late twentieth and early twenty-first century has been both influenced by innovative approaches to the study of dress history and impacted the way dress history is currently practiced. This chapter examines the work of dress historians who expanded the disciplinary standard of concentration on physical documentation and description of dress artifacts by turning their focus to a deeper understanding of the role dress and appearance plays in cultural and social transformation. Unlike the previous chapters, contemporary case studies will not be included in this chapter, as the attention is directed toward scholars who documented dress history with a focus on interpreting its role in cultural and social change.

Lou Taylor, in her text on dress history (2002) articulated what she referred to as 'the great divide' (p. 65) between academic historical/cultural analysis and object-based dress history. Taylor argued that academy based researchers working in base disciplines such as economics and history often dismissed the value of concrete dress artifacts, focusing instead entirely on the abstract role of textiles and dress in social and cultural transformation. Conversely, dress historians, often working in museum-based jobs, tended to focus primarily on documenting and dating the artifact and did not concentrate the same degree of effort in understanding the role of the artifact in charting new cultural direction and social change.

The drawing together of these two sides of the dress history debate began to happen when both social and economic historians and museum-based costume curators began to call informally and formally for scholars crossing over the great divide (Taylor, 2002: 67–9). Citing the social/economic historian Negley Harte as a 'determined agent provocateur,' Lou Taylor (2002: 67) credited Harte with an early challenge to fellow historians to regard textiles and dress seriously. Referring to a 1976 public address, Harte is credited by Taylor for arguing for the fundamental role of textiles in the social and economic development of Europe. Taylor also noted that Harte challenged dress historians by stating that costume scholarship was undeveloped, arguing that the field of 'clothing [scholarship] is quite inadequately related to wide matters of concern to the historian of social change' (Harte as cited in Taylor, 2002: 67). Dress historians and curators joined forces with Harte calling for building a conceptual bridge between concrete artifact study and analytical historical analysis. Lou Taylor also cited Jane Tozer's 1984 appeal to Costume Society members to 'seek to relate dress to its historical, artistic, social and economic context'(2002: 68).

Since these pivotal key discussions many dress historians have moved toward a multi-disciplinary approach to interpret the role of dress artifacts and appearance in understanding social and cultural change. The following examples of the new fashion-change approach to dress history provide an overview of the contributions of scholars primarily focused on dress artifacts of the past as a means of constructing fashion change-theory.

Material Culture Approaches to Dress History

Material culture studies emerged in the 1970s and 1980s as art historians, archeologists, and folklorists sought methodologies to embed artifact analysis into a cultural analysis approach. First developed as a means of interpreting artifacts commonly studied by art historians and archaeologists, such as pottery, architectural elements, and furniture, the methodology was quickly adapted to the study of textiles and dress in part due to its primary reliance on systematic analysis of artifacts. Jules David Prown's 1982 article introducing material culture theory and method was influential in the dissemination of the approach which had been gaining momentum among art historians at Yale. In the introduction to an edited volume featuring the work of his students, Prown articulated the goals and approach of material culture and analysis:

> For purposes of material culture study, any artifact can usefully be subjected to the kind of visual analysis we have traditionally applied to works of art. The goal of such analysis is to discover the patterns of mind underlying fabrication of the artifact. These patterns are often, indeed are usually, metaphorical in character. Artifacts can embody metaphors for aspects of the human condition—states of being, activities, relationships, needs, fears, hopes. The metaphors articulate patterns of mind most usefully when they reflect beliefs of which the makers, individually or collectively (as a society), were unaware or, if aware, unwilling to express openly, to verbalize. (Prown and Haltman, 2000: x)

DeLong and Hegland (2002) provided a helpful definition of the material culture approach as interpreted by those working within dress history: 'Material culture is a means of cultural investigation where objects are used as primary data. The underlying premise is that objects reflect those who made and used them and, by extension, the beliefs of the larger society to which they belonged' (2002: 1). The material culture approach is systematic moving from a concrete description of the artifact through cultural analysis and interpretation. Prown's art historical model (1982) included three steps: description, deduction and speculation. DeLong's (1987, 1998) model specifically developed for apparel and textile research included four steps: observation, analysis, interpretation, and evaluation. In both models there is a commitment to a systematic approach vesting great value in initial careful examination of the artifact, followed by a stage of analysis and deduction, leading to interpretation, and in the case of DeLong a final evaluation stage.

Both Marilyn DeLong and Jules Prown stressed that metaphoric meaning is often embedded in the expression of visual polarities such as smooth/rough (Prown and Haltman, 2000: 3) or, as an example, the more dress-related polarity identified by DeLong (1987, 1998) open/closed silhouettes. Thus searching out artifacts that contain what Haltman refers to as 'analytic hooks' (2000: 3) in the form of visual polarities helps move the material culture analysis forward toward meaning.

Both Marilyn DeLong at the University of Minnesota and Jules David Prown at Yale University taught graduate level seminars in which students engaged in material culture analysis leading to a body of research in which dress artifacts were keys to understanding belief structures and ideals of past time periods. Not all students engaged in material culture analysis focused on understanding change. For example, Leslie Miller's material culture analysis of a late-nineteenth-century corset led to a description of women's role in this time period:

> Because the corset emphasized roles in which women were not only related to others but also dependent on them in everything from earning a living to lifting heavy objects, to getting dressed in the morning, the woman who chose to wear one signaled her acceptance of a position within a defined social framework in which she was not the primary actor. (2000: 145)

Dress historians committed to using material culture analysis to understanding dress as an emblem of change and transformation are represented well by textile and apparel academic Linda Welters. Welters (1981) used a systematic detailed worksheet approach to document the physical features of Greek women's chemises in American collections, which she then linked to political and social change. In her words, 'Through analysis and interpretation of fibers, fabrics, cut, construction, and embellishment, the chemises revealed the tumultuous history of Greece' (Welters, 2002: 1). Thus material culture analysis can be used effectively to understand historical social and cultural upheaval, with the artifact leading the researcher into an understanding of change and transformation.

Cultural Authentication: A Dress Historical Mode of Analysis

The separation of traditional – often called folk – styles of dress from fashionable impulses was also challenged by dress historians working on nonWestern cultures and later Euro-American culture in the late twentieth century. Focusing on the impact of cultural interchange on traditional dress patterns in nonWestern settings, theories of dress change were developed incorporating dress styles from throughout the world. One of the most notable and influential theories emerging from this body of scholarship was the concept of cultural authentication, first introduced by Tonye Erekosima (1979), then further developed by Tonye Erekosima and Joanne B. Eicher (1981) working in Nigeria on Kalabari textiles.

The concept of cultural authentication focused on analyzing the process by which an outside aesthetic influence is integrated into and becomes a part of an existing style tradition. The focus of Erekosima and Eicher's (1981) research was on ceremonial textiles created by Kalabari women from imported gingham and multicolored madras. Stress is placed within the theory of cultural authentication on the importance of the creative transformation of borrowed artifacts by the accepting culture as a means of internalizing the outside influence. In this case the imported textiles were creatively transformed by Kalabari women through the use of cut-thread and pulled-thread design techniques thus becoming a unique Kalabari art form which was then used within ceremonial contexts.

Erekosima and Eicher (1981) presented four stages of the cultural authentication process, with each progressive stage leading to a higher level of value assigned to the borrowed artifact. Level one of cultural authentication was the selection stage, which included the acquisition of the chosen cloth and use of the cloth in its current form. Characterization, level two of the process, involved giving the cloth a particular name, thus investing it with linguistic significance. Level three, incorporation, within the Kalabari was exclusive use and ownership of a particular cloth by a particular group or family. Finally transformation, the highest level of the process, involved creative manipulation of the textile turning into a distinctly Kalabari art object.

As dress scholars turned their attention to dress changes that occurred as a result of cultural interchange, the four-stage cultural authentication model proved to be very useful. Rachel Pannebecker (1988) applied the model to the study of European-produced silk ribbon absorbed into Native American textile traditions during the mid-eighteenth and mid-nineteenth century. Pannebecker affirmed the value of the concept to understanding dress change within the Native American culture. She also noted the absence of the third characterization stage in her research which suggested a need to reconsider this stage and how it is manifested cross-culturally.

Linda Arthur (1997) applied the same conceptual model in her investigation of a style shift toward Euro-American female appearance by indigenous

Hawaiian women in the early nineteenth century. Attributing the change to the arrival of missionary women in 1820, Arthur traced the replacement of the traditional bare-breasted style with a breast-covering garment being first adopted by Hawaiian royal women, then followed by wider adoption among more common women. Similar to Pannabecker, Arthur encountered problems applying cultural authentication as a progressive model ending in transformation. In the case of Hawaiian assimilation of Euro-American influences the transformation of the garment happened immediately following the selection stage, as women manipulated the apparel item to fit their own needs. The naming stage in this case study occurred as the final stage – which Arthur argued is logical given that language is 'the highest, and most symbolic level of communication' (1997: 137). Arthur ended her manuscript by affirming the value of the identification of the stages of cultural authentication as a means of understanding dress history, but questioning whether the stages need to be seen as progressive.

The concept has also been used in examining the assimilation of outside influences into Western dress styles. Hae Joen Kim and Marilyn DeLong (1992) investigated the integration of Sino-Japanism into fashion dress illustrated in *Harper's Bazaar* magazines published between 1890 and 1927. In their systematic examination of fashion changes influenced by oriental dress styles, Kim and DeLong illustrated the four stages of the cultural authentication process moving Sino-Japanism into the mainstream of fashionable dress of their study period.

Function to Fashion in Dress History

The transformation of functional apparel into fashion was a theme in the twentieth century, for example with bib overalls converted in fashion in the 1970s, blue jeans emerging as a multi-decade ever-changing trend, and the adoption of working men's apparel by 1960s folk musicians such as Bob Dylan. Dress historian Laurel Wilson (2001) has provided some of the most substantive contributions in this area with her investigations of the emergence of fashion from functional cowboy apparel and accessories. Wilson attributed the shift from functional to fashionable in cowboy apparel, gear, and accessories to both changes in cowboy culture and the introduction of new technologies during the late nineteenth and early twentieth centuries.

The golden years of cowboy culture, as referred to by Laurel Wilson, were the years of the working cowboy, who dressed in functional apparel designed for a specific work environment. While the impact of the cowboy era on international culture and fashion has been considerable, the period of the working cowboy in the Great Plains was relatively brief. According to Wilson, being a cowboy in 1880 was the dominant male occupation of these Great Plains states. However, in only twenty short years open-range ranching was replaced by the fencing system that brought to an end the classic cattle round-up culture of western cowboy myth. Early working cowboy dress styles, according to Wilson, were limited in decorative effects both by the low working salaries of the cowboys and the utilitarian requirements of their occupation. Embellishments during this early period tended to grow out of function. For example, Wilson pointed out that the decorative fringes of chaps 'helped to wick the water away' and the sometimes decorated ties 'connected the outer leg of the chap' (2001: 41).

Wilson attributed the trend toward more fashionable cowboy apparel of the late nineteenth and early twentieth centuries primarily to changes in cowboy culture. As ranching practices became more efficient, fewer cowboys were needed to run the enterprise. During this same time period the myth of the Wild West cowboy took root in the American soul. Wild West shows, staged rodeos, singing cowboys, film stars, and dude ranches emerged as a way of capturing the vanishing lifestyle and widening the experience to include pretend as well as working cowboys. Fashionable cowboy apparel, focused more on capturing the look rather than functioning within a work environment, became an integral part of American culture. Cowboy hats once designed to protect from sun, wind and rain, now had overly large crowns and brims, to capture the attention of the audience at Wild West performances and on film. Other aspects of cowboy dress were impacted, such as rodeo cowboys competing before judges and audiences:

> It was important that cowboys and cow girls displayed both skill and style . . . Style soon included appearance, resulting in gear that became even more flamboyant to catch the eye of audiences and rodeo judges. To capitalize on this trend, manufacturers of cowboy gear began selling their goods by touting appearance rather than function. (Wilson, 2001: 46)

Technological advances worked in tandem with the need for more showy styles to prompt manufacturers to offer a wider range of affordable fashion styles. Wilson (2001), in particular, focused her analysis on the introduction of silver or nickel metal embellishments referred to as 'spots' and the perfecting of chrome tanning, both introduced around the turn of the twentieth century. Chrome tanning created a softer less dark leather finish allowing for a wider range of dye possibilities and also permitting heavier concentrations of decorative metal spots than the more brittle and dark oak-tanned leather.

Jeans and denim have also been focused on by popular culture analysts as a means of exploring American identity and cultural change through examination of the evolution of a functional apparel item to a fashion. James Sullivan, a pop culture newspaper and magazine critic, opened his book

Jeans by making the link between the blue jean and the experience of freedom:

> There is an old proverb: He who has pants, has freedom. The bifurcated, tube-legged, full-length trouser, a European peasant garment embraced by settlers in the untamed New World, has always suggested many kinds of freedom, including convenience, mobility—and suggestiveness. Pants drew attention to body parts that other garments were designed to conceal. The Mormon leader Brigham Young was appalled when men's trousers were first outfitted with front buttons in America in the 1830s. He called them 'fornification pants' (2006: 9).

Sullivan then goes on to chart chronologically the fashion change history of this garment which he argued was 'originally designed as utterly unremarkable workwear' from its American origins in mid-nineteenth-century San Francisco to what is referred to now as the 'rear-view peep show' (Sullivan, 2006: 9).

Key moments in denim fashion change highlighted by Sullivan (2006) were correlated to the continual reinvention of the jean as brand by a wide range of designers and companies. In his cultural history Sullivan noted a range of technological breakthroughs that led to new fashion trends including the original invention of the riveted pocket in the 1870s, and stonewashing in the 1970s. He also discussed the impact of pop-culture performances on stage and on the screen to the meaning of jeans as a cultural symbol. As an example of the international impact of jeans he cited the 1989 fall of the Berlin Wall and the simultaneous opening of Rifle jean store on Red Square. In this discussion Sullivan neatly tied together dramatic political and social upheaval with the heavily symbolic jean – which at that time period expressed the ideals of Western-style democracy.

Role/Status Ambivalence and Fashion Change

Notable dress historians have utilized the theoretical contributions of Fred Davis (1992) as well as Kaiser, Nagasawa, and Hutton (1995) in their analysis of nineteenth- and twentieth-century fashions. Close scrutiny of dress artifacts has illustrated that fashion change can emerge out of the stress related to shifting identities linked to role or status ambivalence.

Focused on investigating the relationship of the broadening of women's roles during the late Victorian and Edwardian eras with dress changes, Cosbey, Damhorst and Farrell-Beck conducted a visual analysis study of fashion illustrations published in *Harper's Bazaar* and *The Delineator* from 1873 to 1912. Role ambivalence in this study was defined as 'conflicting notions about or expectations of how individuals occupying the role should behave' (Cosbey, Damhorst and Farrell-Beck, 2003: 105). The central hypothesis of the study was that they would find a 'positive association between women's role ambivalence and heterogeneity in women's clothing fashions' during the same time period (Cosbey, Damhorst, and Farrell-Beck, 2003: 105). Thus fashion change would be a reflection of shifting notions of the female role during the time period.

Using a statistical approach with women's social role ambivalence serving as the independent variable and with feature diversity and feature frequency of dress as dependent variables, the researchers concluded that there was a positive association between increases in women's gender role ambivalence and style diversity from 1873 to 1912. Accordingly, the authors concluded that 'Results supported the proposed positive relationship between ambivalence and heterogeneity in dress; specifically, fabrics in general and several bodice features showed increasing stylistic diversity as ambivalence about women's roles increased' (Cosbey, Damhorst, and Farrell-Beck, 2003: 101).

In a different study, historians Shane and Graham White (1998) traced the changing styles of African Americans from the slavery era to the present using the idea that status ambivalence functioned as a fuel for fashion change. Using terminology directly linked to the fashion change theory of Fred Davis, White and White stressed that the relationship between African American and hegemonic white dominant culture was fraught with 'ambiguities and ambivalences' (White and White, 1998: 16) that often resulted in creative and novel fashion presentations of the male and female body. The researchers stressed that black appropriation of elements of mainstream Caucasian dress 'disturbed the nuanced social order that clothing was supposed to display' (White and White, 1998: 16). As a result multiple examples of style changes emerged from status ambiguity and ambivalence.

In their chapter focused on the post-Civil War period, White and White argued that the ambiguity of the newly emerging social order gave rise to a heightened expression of style by the newly freed slaves. For example, White and White cited an instance in which 'one group of [newly freed] Charleston slaves disported themselves on a major city thoroughfare "arrayed in silks and satins of all colors of the rainbow"'(1998: 127). White reaction to the flamboyant styles of African Americans during this period was often outrage. White members of the middle and upper class quickly labeled African American style as caricatured versions of white style, dismissing the ability of blacks to make reasoned and tasteful decisions regarding personal style. For example, a white Charlotte, North Carolina hotel owner regarding a young black women's fondness for parasols quipped: '[They] must have a parasol when they ha'n't got no shoes' (1998: 127).

As a third and final example, in a study of the fashions of Jacqueline Kennedy, dress historians Monica McMurry and Laurel Wilson argued that the then First Lady 'used her sense of style to negotiate social change under the direction of Oleg Cassini' (2003: 1). Using a sample of 296 pictures of

Jacqueline Kennedy and other prominent women, the two researchers defined style characteristics of 'the Jackie look.' This look was then compared to what the researchers defined as the style characteristics of the 'Old Guard.' The results indicated that Jackie used fashion as a means of challenging existing gender roles, with style emerging out of the ambivalent gender definitions of the late 1950s.

Ethnohistorical Approaches to Dress History

Ethnohistory, an interdisciplinary approach utilizing qualitative research techniques from both anthropology and history, has been used by dress historians to reconstruct the cultural and historical underpinnings of fashion change in a diverse range of societies. While based on close analysis of artifacts, the methodology also includes anthropological approaches such as participant observation and interviewing techniques, as well as the study of historical documents (Pannabecker, 1986, 1996; Welters, 1992).

A pioneer of and strong advocate for the method, Rachel Pannebecker (1996) utilized period manuscripts and print materials to reconstruct the integration of European-produced silk ribbon into the dress styles of Great Lakes Indians during the years 1735 to 1839. Pannabecker's contribution to understanding dress changes within traditional dress styles was significant. Discussing others who had written about the dress styles of Great Lakes Indians during this period Pannabecker commented that they were 'apparently oblivious to the process of cultural change' and had thus written 'as if the garments they described were timeless' (1996: 272). Attributing the rise and diffusion of ribbon-trimmed dress styles among the Great Lakes Indians to the development of a trade and diplomatic relationship with Euro-Americans, Pannabecker went on to argue that the style of dress created by Great Lakes Indians was a unique and non-European look that marked Indian from non-Indian within the region.

Welters (1992), in a series of research projects dating from 1983 to 1995, applied ethnohistorical methodology to women's folk dress in Greece. Using historical sources, interviews with elderly women who had worn the dress styles, photographs from museum collections, and examination of family photographs and dowry chests, Welters amassed a wealth of data which she then used to piece together the effects of social and political change on women's traditional dress styles. For example, in a 1986 investigation of *zonari,* a fringed women's belt believed to protect women of child-bearing age, Welters described her methodology as:

The methodology combined documentary research with fieldwork. I read traveler's accounts and studied notes from previous field research . . . In museums I examined extant belts and gathered pictorial images. In the villages . . . I conducted interviews with the aid of a Greek-speaking assistant over a two-month period. Together we asked a series of questions regarding clothing and the traditions associated with them. (Welters, 1999)

In addition, Welters (1999) carefully studied the impact of geographical and historical variations on the rate of and receptivity to changes to traditional Greek dress styles. She was thus able to piece together the process of fashion change in the more urban areas, which adopted Western styles beginning in the 1830s, in contrast to some of the more conservative villages in the mountains, where she found women who still owned the belts of their younger days, and remembered how to make them.

Similarly, Oakes and Riewe (1992) used participant observation techniques coupled with historical approach in their study of dress changes among the Polar Inuhuit of North Greenland. Fieldwork was used to build substantive case studies including information on how individual Inuhuit artisans prepared skins, created and manipulated patterns, and constructed garments. These data were then combined with the study of personal and public historical documents and third-party reports to examine the impact of cultural, religious, environmental, and political changes on style features and assembly techniques. While Oakes and Riewe found that some style features and techniques had been and continued to be passed down as traditional dress, they also found that new technology, lifestyle changes, and exposure to European belief systems had instigated dress change.

Dress History Surveys: A Focus on Change

Dress historians writing survey texts have also taken note of the movement toward focusing on fashion change. Late-twentieth-century and early millennium editions of classic costume history texts typically discuss fashion change in their introductory comments. For example in the 1992 edition of Blanche Payne's *History of Costume* the introduction stresses the linkage between historical changes and dress noting that:

> Analysis usually reveals that basic, lasting costume changes occur in conjunction with fundamental social, economic, and political changes. Furthermore, costume styles can change without obvious cause. (Payne, Winakor and Farrell-Beck, 1992: 7)

Similarly, Douglas Russell's introduction to his survey text stresses that 'dress is not just a passive reflection of the self but an active, changing, unspoken means of expression' (1983: xii).

More focused dress histories have also been impacted by fashion change theoretical approaches. Lois Banner's (1983) book on the history of American female ideals of beauty as expressed through fashionable dress in the nine-teenth and twentieth centuries linked changing ideals to social and cultural trends. For example, she linked the emergence of the voluptuous ideal of the Victorian period to changing notions of female role, in particular the emphasis in this period on fecundity and domesticity.

The emerging field of gender studies, particularly scholarship focused on changing gender roles for women, also linked fashion changes to historical reinterpretations of male and female gender roles. For example, Kidwell and Steele (1989) systematically traced the relationship between dress styles and changing cultural constructions of masculinity and femininity in a costume exhibit catalogue. In the catalogue Steele traced the relationship between gendered work identities and dress styles, while Kidwell focused on the gender symbolism of fashion, arguing that 'The language of clothes is not static. The only constant seems to be that distinctions will always be made between men and women, though significant gender symbols change' (Kidwell and Steele: 126).

Similarly Valerie Steele's (1997) history of the last half of the twentieth century probed the relationship between shifting gender roles, social and polit-ical change, and fashionable dress for both men and women. A fundamental contribution of both this volume and the earlier Steele and Kidwell catalogue was the even-handed approach to analyzing male and female fashions. While acknowledging that men's dress styles often change more slowly, Steele insisted that a true analysis of the dress of a period must not only include women's wear but the fashions of men as well:

The idea that men wear functional clothing, while women wear frivolous fashion, is simply wrong. Clothing is the general and inclusive term for all the various coverings and articles of dress designed to be worn on the human body. Fashion is a particular kind of clothing that is 'in style' at a given time. The concept of fashion thus implies a process of style change. It is true that men's clothing fashions change more slowly and less dramatically than women's, but they do change. (1997: 3)

As an example of this even-handed gender approach, Steele traced the devel-opment of mod style in the 1960s, linking it to the lifestyle of British male musicians of the era. As support for her argument she quoted Pete Townsend of The Who: 'To be a mod, you had to have short hair, money enough to buy a real smart suit, good shoes, good shirts, plenty of pills all the time . . . and you had to be able to dance like a madman' (Steele, 1997: 58).

Dress History in the New Millennium

Contemporary dress history has thus become a multi-disciplinary investigation, not only focused on what styles were worn in the past, but also a search for understanding the fashion change process. The early distinction between artifact analysis, practiced by museum professionals, and social/economic history practiced by those working within the academy, has been replaced by a wealth of research exploring the integral role of style and dress in negotiating and sometimes initiating social and cultural transformation. The sampling of methodological and theoretical approaches within this chapter should not be interpreted as exhaustive, but rather as a starting point to consider how to practice dress history in the new century. They are briefly summarized for the reader below.

Summarization of Approaches to Dress History

Approach 1: Material Culture

Material approaches to dress history utilize a systematic approach that begins with careful documentation and study of the dress artifact, followed by an analytical stage in which physical characteristics of the artifact are deductively linked to human thought patterns, and ending with an interpretation of the dress artifact revealing fundamental belief patterns and values of the time period and culture when it was first made and worn. This approach to dress history makes the assumption that the objects human beings make and wear function metaphorically to express conscious and subconscious ways of organizing reality and the world of the imagination.

Approach 2: Cultural Authentication

The concept of cultural authentication provides a systematic approach to understanding how style influences, textiles and trims, and dress artifacts from one culture become absorbed into the aesthetics and dress patterns of another culture. Based originally on a progressive four-stage model developed by Erekosima and Eicher (1981), the model has been tested and reworked resulting in a more flexible model still stressing the fundamental original concept of gradual integration of outside influences into a dress tradition over time, through creative manipulation of both the pre-existing tradition and the new outside influence.

Approach 3: Function to Fashion

Functional apparel designed for specific work or leisure environments often crosses over and becomes fashion. Understanding and predicting these types of trends involves understanding the meaning of the functional apparel to those both practicing the work role or the sport, and those who are an audience to the behavior. The impact is reflexive, in that once the functional apparel becomes fashion, the fashion begins to affect the design of functional apparel, and vice versa. For example, once long basketball shorts became the fashion, regulation basketball shorts for college and professional basket ball teams changed as well. Related to the case study in this chapter, once fashionable cowboy apparel became more flamboyant, working cowboy dress also became more decorative.

Approach 4: Role/Status Ambivalence

This dress history approach is based on the sociological argument put forward by Fred Davis (1992) that fashion change is related to identity ambivalence and feelings of ambiguity regarding appropriate or expected role. In these social situations fashionable expression becomes a means of exploring yet undefined and unresolved role and status, with more rapid changes in dress styles associated with those social identities that are in flux or debate.

Approach 5: Ethnohistory

This approach to dress history is fundamentally methodological in contribution, and stresses the application of both historical and ethnographic research methods. Relying on a multidisciplinary approach including participant observation, examination of historical documents and artifacts, and ethnographic interviews, the approach has been used by dress historians to reconstruct the cultural and historical underpinnings of fashion change in a diverse range of societies.

9

Fashion Change – Binding the Threads Together

It makes sense to remind the reader that fashion is all about change. Without an engine to drive change, fashion would not exist. This book has been focused on analyzing the various theories that account for the engine or momentum that pushes fashion inexorably forward. It is also important to remember that fashion movement surrounds us and sweeps us along from birth to the end of our days. Quotidian activities such as what we do, who we are, and how we present ourselves to each other are all constantly in evolution driven by subtle forces that fashion professionals need to understand. To that end, in this book we have discussed in detail the various theoretical perspectives that are considered most relevant to contemporary scholars and practitioners when analyzing and forecasting fashion change.

Using the diamond gemstone as metaphor, we see that each of the theoretical perspectives considered in this book allows us to view fashion change from the variety of angles that a multi-faceted gem presents to us. When each facet is viewed in isolation we see a finite, logical explanation that accounts for the fashion phenomenon; however, if we step back from the diamond it is possible to see in the flashing spectral lights that threads exist binding the various theoretical explanations together. In essence, many of the theories that make perfect sense when viewed independently from within their respective frameworks borrow from or share key elements with each other. It is not our aim that this chapter should create a unified theory of fashion, as this has been attempted before (Miller, McIntyre and Mantrala, 1993). Instead we delineate the important threads that suggest common ground among the various perspectives presented throughout the book. We conclude this analysis of fashion change theories by discussing the more prominent threads that bind the many theoretical perspectives together: the never-ending search for novelty; identity conflict as instigator of fashion change; the human drive to mark status; and emulation as a key to understanding fashion-driven behavior.

The Never-ending Search for Novelty

In our chapter that focused on the underlying psychological principles that drive fashion change, we were introduced to the Freudian notion that our subconscious sexual energy, which resides in the id and is referred to as the libido, virtually compels us to seek visual novelty as part of our human condition. As you may recall, Steele (1985) referred to this phenomenon as the libido of looking, and it accounts, from a psychological perspective, for why people have a never-ending thirst for new and novel fashionable appearances.

We also see the impact of Freudian psychology in our chapter on fashion and style which focused on fashion evolution as a continuously changing relationship between body form and dress. Steele (1997) suggested that the underlying momentum which drove the changing perceptions of body form, resulting in a subsequent new design problem, was in fact the same libido-driven search for novelty that Freud theorized. In agreement with Steele, Hollander (1975) also viewed sexuality as the engine which drove reinterpretation of the body/dress relationship. It is further possible to link Freudian theory and fashion theory as style to Kroeber's (1919) century long majestic procession of style change that he discovered during his anthropological overview of civilization's evolution. What would cause the slow but steady progression of style change other than the incessant human need for novelty? Though he never stated it explicitly, Kroeber's observation of decades-long movement in style certainly speaks to the continuing alterations of the relationship between body form and design solutions. In addition, we note that many of the short-term cyclic explanations for fashion change such as Robinson's (1975) rely on the drive for novelty as a primary force behind the repetitive inception, growth, and demise of fashion products. Finally we note the relationship between the continuous searching for novelty with one of the key millennial themes addressed in the introduction to this book. As we pointed out, with the world at our fingertips via the ready accessibility of the World Wide Web, we are now inundated at any moment with fresh novel fashion looks which appeal to our libido and accelerate the movement of fashion change.

Where There is Identity Conflict, Fashion Change is not Far Off

Central among all the factors that correlate closely with fashion change is identity conflict. Cutting across almost all of the basic fashion theories the concept of identity in flux is often used to explain and examine the hidden forces that push new fashion forward. As we saw in the introductory chapter, today we exist in an era of negotiable identity which is a major global trend. Our identity is not cast in concrete, but is open to construction and reconstruction, often with fashion as a primary creative component of identity development. All this identity flux and conflict accelerates the rate of transformation and increases the role of changing fashion in construction of contemporary versions of self.

Most often when we see identity conflict, there is a tension that exists between polar opposites. For example, from a psychological viewpoint, Young (1956) suggested two of the key purposes that dress served: on the one hand dress preserved modesty while on the other it was used to generate sexuality and eroticism. What tension is more exquisitely human than our identities as defined in terms of modesty versus our sense of individual sexuality? What direction do we choose at any particular moment and how do we use fashion to express our choice?

As we read in the chapter on anthropological fashion theories, identity ambivalence is common in a world where unstable and shifting cultural categories compel us to redefine ourselves. The corresponding experiments with newly emergent identities that are often constructed to accommodate or respond to external pressures serve as important grist for the fashion mill. This is because fashion change is often used to bridge the gaps created by these anthropologically based conflicts. In a related manner, the historical and performance theorists also spoke of destabilized identities, which they linked to pressures on gender construction, role, and class status leading to fashion change. Finally, fashion theory emanating from the field of collective behavior also drew upon identity conflict as a key explanation for fashion movement. Very important is the tension that exists between maintaining individuality in contrast to an equivalently forceful desire to self-assign ourselves to a desirable group. Fashionable dress and appearance very often straddle the divide between these simultaneous but conflicting desires for union and segregation.

Status Combat Drives Fashion

For centuries in Western culture, a predominantly and consistent behavior among people was competition for status positioning. In other words, we make status claims we feel we deserve or chase after a higher level of status to embellish our sense of position and well-being. Status combat is the conflict that occurs between individuals on either side of a status boundary. The conflict occurs most often when those possessing status respond disagreeably to perceived incursions by 'others' they feel belong elsewhere. Because of tensions occurring between those seeking and those preserving status positions, status combat ensues taking the typical form of upper-class inhabitants rapidly developing alternative symbols, often in the form of new fashion, to distinguish themselves anew from those chasing them.

With the growing economic disparity of 'haves and have-nots' that we identified in this book's introduction, we now observe status combat becoming even more prevalent throughout the world. Introduction of new apparel fashions and other forms of conspicuous consumption such as exorbitantly priced mechanical wristwatches fuel status combat resulting in the phenomenon referred to as 'chase and flight,' which propels fashion change along. Status combat exists primarily but not exclusively on social and economic playing fields. For example, social status conflict is seen to exist between those laboring under a sense of discrimination or 'otherness' when they compare themselves to those in hegemonic positions who will fiercely protect their social status. We saw this in the case of Tulloch's (1992) analysis of West Indian blacks struggling unsuccessfully to break into the all-pervasive white world of England. Collective behavior theorists such as Tulloch have established, on the one hand, that dress and fashion are often weapons used to express social alienation by the discriminated 'others,' while conversely fashion is used to preserve the status quo and social position of hegemons. Similar to the collective behaviorists, performance theorists and anthropologists have also observed evolving identities and shifting cultural categories which lead to status repositioning, subsequent crossing of status boundaries and resultant conflict too.

In the same vein, the short-term cycle theorists almost invariably select status combat as the primary motivation behind the repetitive and cyclic beginning, middle and end of fashion adoption patterns. Pesendorfer's (1995) cyclic theory hinges on people using fashion to signal membership to other individuals who reside in the same social plane, while Coelho and McClure (1993) spoke of fashion as a basic form of status marking. And of course we cannot forget the economist Thorstein Veblen (1899), who wrote in his classic work on the pecuniary behavior of the upper classes that fashion served as a status delineator marking class differences.

Mimetic Behavior: A Basic Instinct that Drives Fashion Forward

Mimetic behavior is a simple concept: people observe and then copy what they see. Fashion spreads largely because of this common human characteristic. Without this behavior fashion would not diffuse and would not have the mass adoption aspect to it that almost, in and of itself, defines fashion. Fashion trends discussed in Chapter 1 such as improved communications through the Internet, the globalization of taste, the increasing proximity of people to each other through urbanization, and the intensified quest to emulate those who vault into fame all drive mimetic behavior to an even more fevered pitch.

The performance theorists saw mimetic behavior pushing the diffusion of fashion and cultural transformation to the larger population. Similarly, the collective behavior theorist viewed the copying that occurs across lines of social status as an elemental human behavior that drove fashion forward. Finally, the short-term cycle theorists frequently relied on the mimetic instincts of humans to explain the diffusion of fashion from its early innovation phase to large-scale mass acceptance.

The Threads That Bind

In conclusion, it is instructive to remember that theoretical explanations of fashion change have emanated from multiple disciplines all with their own internal logic that make perfect sense when examined in isolation. Those interested in the subject matter of fashion change, whether fashion professionals, or from other disparate fields such as sociology, anthropology, psychology, and performance studies will find fashion theories that will work within their own disciplinary frameworks. Nonetheless, it is also instructive to remember the similarities in theoretical underpinnings exist that cut across the various disciplinary perspectives. Some examples of those common underpinnings have been examined in this conclusion section because they are, in fact, the threads that bind us all together when we examine this fascinating subject.

References

Anderson, P.F. (1996), *The Davy Crockett Craze: A Look at the 1950s Phenomenon and Davy Crockett Collectibles*, Hillside, Illinois: R & G Productions.

Arthur, L.B. (1997), 'Cultural Authentication Refined: The Case of the Hawaiian Holoku', *Clothing and Textiles Research Journal* (15)3: 129–39.

Atlas, J. (1984), 'Beyond Demographics', *The Atlantic*, 254: 49–58.

Banner, L. (1983), *American Beauty*, Chicago and London: University of Chicago Press.

Barber, N. (1999), 'Women's Dress Fashions as a Function of Reproductive Strategy', *Sex Roles*, 40(5/6): 459–71.

Barnes, R. and Eicher, J. (1992), *Dress and Gender: Making and Meaning*, Oxford and Providence: Berg.

Bartky, S. (1990), 'Narcissism, Femininity, and Alienation', in S. Bartkey, *Femininity and Domination: Studies in the Phenomenology of Oppression*, New York and London: Routledge.

Behling, D. (1977), 'French Couturiers and Arts/Illustrators: Fashions from 1900 to 1925', Ph.D. Dissertation, Columbus: The Ohio State University.

Behling, D. (1992), 'Three and a Half Decades of Fashion Adoption Research: What Have We Learned?' *Clothing and Textiles Research Journal*, 10(2): 4–41.

Belleau, B. (1987), 'Cyclical Fashion Movement: Women's Day Dresses: 1860–1980', *Clothing and Textiles Research Journal*, 5(2): 15–20.

Belluck, P. (2006). 'Vermont Losing Precious Resource as Young Depart', *New York Times,* March 4, 2006, archives.

Black, S. (2002), *Knitwear in Fashion*, New York: Thames and Hudson.

Bliss, S. (1916), 'The Significance of Clothes', *American Journal of Psychology*, 10(2): 217–66.

Blumer, H. (1968), 'Fashion', in D. Sills (ed.), *International Encyclopedia of the Social Sciences*, 5: 341–5, New York: Macmillan.

Blumer, H. (1969), 'Fashion: From Class Differentiation to Collective Selection', *Sociological Quarterly*, 10: 275–91.

Blumer, H. (2003[1939]), 'Fashion Movements', in Johnson, K., Torntore, S. and Eicher, J. (2003), *Fashion Foundations – Early Writings on Fashion and Dress*, Oxford: Berg.

Bradshear, K. (2005), 'Starbucks Aims to Alter China's Taste in Caffeine', *New York Times*, May 21, 2005, B1.

Brooks, G. (1997), 'The Centerfold Syndrome', in R. Lavant and G. Brooks (eds), *Men and Sex*, 28–60, New York: John Wiley & Sons.

Browne, D. (2004). 'Footwear Darwinism: Doc Martens Evolve', *New York Times*, November 7, 2004, archives.

Bruni, F. (2006). 'Critics Notebook: Life in the Fast Food Lane', *New York Times*, May 24, 2006, ST 1.

Bruzzi, S. (1997), *Undressing Cinema: Clothing and Identity in the Movies*, New York and London: Routledge.

Bruzzi, S. and Church Gibson, P. (2000), *Fashion Cultures: Theories, Explorations and Analysis*, London and New York: Routledge.

Butler, J. (1999), *Gender Trouble: Feminism and the Subversion of Identity*, New York and London: Routledge.

Butler, J. (2004a), *Undoing Gender*, New York and London: Routledge.

Butler, J. (2004b), 'Performative Acts and Gender Constitution', in H. Bial (ed.), *The Performance Studies Reader*, New York and London: Routledge.

Calogero, R.M. (2004), 'A Test of Objectification Theory: The Effect of the Male Gaze on Appearance Concerns in College Women', *Psychology of Women Quarterly*, 28: 16–21.

Carter, M. (2003), *Fashion Classics from Carlyle to Barthes*, Oxford: Berg.

Changing Minds (2006), http://changingminds.org/explanations/behaviors/coping/displacement.htm

Chang, J. (2005), *Can't Stop Won't Stop: A History of the Hip-Hop Generation*, New York: St Martin's Press.

Church Gibson, P. (1998), 'Film Costume', in J. Hill and P. Church Gibson (eds), *The Oxford Guide to Film Studies*, Oxford: Oxford University Press.

Coelho, P. and McClure, J. (1993), 'Toward an Economic Theory of Fashion', *Economic Inquiry*, 31: 595–608.

Coelho, P., Klein, D. and McClure, J. (2004), 'Fashion Cycles in Economics', *Econ Journal Watch*, 1(3): 437–54.

Coelho, P., Klein, D. and McClure, J. (2005), 'Rejoinder to Pesendorfer', *Econ Journal Watch*, 2(1): 32–41.

Cosbey, S., Damhorst, M.L. and Farrell-Beck, J. (2003), 'Diversity of Daytime Clothing Styles as a Reflection of Women's Social Role Ambivalence from 1873 through 1912', *Clothing and Textiles Research Journal*, 21(3): 101–19.

Curran, L. (1999), 'An Analysis of Cycles in Skirt Lengths and Widths in the UK and German, 1954–1990', *Clothing and Textiles Research Journal*, 17(2): 65–72.

Curtis, A. (2002), *The Century of the Self*, London: British Broadcasting Corporation.

Damase, J. (1991), *Sonia Delaunay: Fashion and Fabrics*, New York: Harry N. Abrams, Inc.

Davis, F. (1985), 'Clothing and Fashion as Communication', in M. Solomon (ed.), *The Psychology of Fashion*, Lexington, MA: Lexington Books.

Davis, F. (1992), *Fashion, Culture, and Identity*, Chicago: University of Chicago Press.

DeLong, M.R. (1987), *The Way We Look: A Framework for Visual Analysis of*

Dress, Ames: Iowa State University Press.

DeLong, M.R. (1998), *The Way We Look: Dress and Aesthetics* (2nd Edition), New York: Fairchild.

DeLong, M.R. and Hegland J.E. (2002), 'Common Goals, Diverse Perspectives: Learning Through Material Culture Analysis', *International Textile and Apparel Proceedings*, #59.

DeLong, M.R. (2005), 'Theories of Fashion', in V. Steele (ed.), *Encyclopedia of Clothing and Fashion*, Detroit: Thomson/Gale.

DeLoria, P. (1998), *Playing Indian*, New Haven and London: Yale University Press.

Dichter, E. (1985), 'Why We Dress the Way We Do', in M. Solomon (ed.), *The Psychology of Fashion*, Lexington, MA: Lexington Books.

Douglas, M. (1966), *Purity and Danger: An Analysis of Concepts of Pollution and Taboo*, London, Boston and Henley: Routledge and Kegan Paul.

Duggan, G.G. (2001), 'The Greatest Show on Earth: A Look at Contemporary Fashion Shows and Their Relationship to Performance Art', *Fashion Theory: The Journal of Dress, Body, and Culture*, 5(3): 241–2.

Durkheim, E. (1915), *The Elementary Forms of Religious Life: A Study in Religious Sociology*, translated by Joseph Ward Swain, New York: Macmillan.

Dylan, B. (1965), 'Maggie's Farm', Sony Music Entertainment, Inc., New York: Columbia Records.

Dylan, B. (2004), *Chronicles, Volume One*, New York: Simon & Schuster.

Eicher, J.B. and Roach Higgens, S.E. (1992), 'Definitions and Classifications of Dress', in R. Barnes and J.B. Eicher (eds), *Dress and Gender: Making and Meaning*, Oxford: Berg.

Ellis, B.J. and Symons, D. (1990), 'Sex Differences in Sexual Fantasy: An Evolutionary Psychological Approach', *Journal of Sex Research*, 27: 527–55.

Erekosima, T.V. (1979), 'The "Tartans" of Buguma Women: Cultural Authentication', *The Proceedings of the Association of College Professors of Textiles and Clothing*: 83–4.

Erekosima, T.V. and Eicher, J.B. (1981), 'Kalabari Cut-Thread and Pulled-Thread Cloth', *African Arts* 14(2): 48–51.

Evans, C. (2001), 'The Enchanted Spectacle', *Fashion Theory: The Journal of Dress, Body, and Culture*, 5(3): 271–310.

Evans, C. and Thornton, M. (1989), *Women and Fashion: A New Look*, London and New York: Quartet Books.

Faldini, F. and Fofi, G. (1981), *L'avventurosa storia del cinema italiano raccontato dai suoi protagonista 1960–1969*, Milan: Feltinelli.

Field, G.A. (1970), 'The Status Float Phenomenon: The Upward Diffusion of Innovation', *Business Horizons* 13(4): 45–52.

Finch, M. (1974), *Style in Art History: An Introduction to Theories of Style and Sequence*, Metuchen, NJ: The Scarecrow Press.

Flügel, J.C. (1930), *The Psychology of Clothes*, London: Hogarth.

Fredrickson, B.L. and Roberts, T. (1997), 'Objectification Theory: Toward

Understanding Women's Lived Experiences and Mental Health Risks', *Psychology of Women Quarterly*, 21: 173–206.

Freidman, T. (2005), *The World is Flat*, New York: Farrar, Straus and Giroux.

Frith, S. (1996), *Performing Rites: On the Value of Popular Music*, Cambridge: Harvard University Press.

Fritjers, P. (1998), 'A Model of Fashions and Status,' *Economic Modeling*, 15: 501–17.

Gallup, G. and Bezilla, R. (1992), *The Religious Life of Young Americans*, Princeton: George H. Gallup International Institute.

Geertz, C. (1973), *The Interpretation of Cultures*, New York: Basic Book Publishers.

Gilligan, S. (2000), 'Gwyneth Paltrow', in S. Bruzzi and P. Church Gibson (eds), *Fashion Cultures: Theories, Explorations and Analysis*, London and New York: Routledge.

Gombrich, E.H. (1979), *The Sense of Order: A Study in the Psychology of Decorative Art*, Ithaca, New York: Cornell University Press.

Greenburg, J. (2002), 'Mideast Turmoil: THE DEAD; 2 Girls Divided by War, Joined in Carnage', *New York Times*, April 5, 2002, archives.

Gregory, P. (1947a), 'A Theory of Purposeful Obsolescence', *Southern Economic Journal*, 14(1): 24–45.

Gregory, P. (1947b), 'An Economic Interpretation of Women's Fashions', *Southern Economic Journal*, 14(2): 148–62.

Grossman, J. (2006), 'IN BUSINESS: A Simple Little Party, That's so Last Year', *New York Times* Magazine, October 15, 2006, 26.

Hall, G.S. (1898), 'Some Aspects of the Early Sense of Self', *American Journal of Psychology*, 9(3): 351–95.

Halpern, D. (2006), 'Bull Marketing', *New York Times* Magazine, February 12, 2006, archives.

Halter, M. (2000), *Shopping for Identity: The Marketing of Ethnicity*, New York: Schocken Books.

Hebdige, D. (1979), *Subculture: The Meaning of Style*, London and New York: Routledge.

Hitt, J. (2005). 'The Newest Indians', *New York Times* Magazine, August 21, 2005, archives.

Hodgman, J. (2005), 'Antony Finds His Voice: How an Androgynous Nina Simone-Loving Downtown Cult Artist Became This Year's Alt-Music Discovery', *New York Times* Magazine, September 4, 2005, 24–9.

Hollander, A. (1975), *Seeing Through Clothes*, Berkeley: University of California Press.

Hollander, A. (1995), *Sex and Suits*, New York: Alfred A. Knopf.

Holson, L. (2005), 'Gothic Lolita: Demure vs. Dominatrix', *New York Times*, March 13, 2005, S1.

Horyrn, C. (2006). 'Galliano Plays His Hand Smartly', *New York Times*, May 21, 2006, ST1 and 11.

Jacobs, M. (2005), 'The Remix: Vintage Point', *New York Times*, February 20, 2005, archives.

Johnson, K., Torntore, S. and Eicher, J. (2003), *Fashion Foundations – Early Writings on Fashion and Dress*, Oxford: Berg.

Johnston, J.E. (1997), 'Appearance Obsession: Women's Reactions to Men's Objectification of Their Bodies', in R.F. Lavant and G.R. Brooks (eds), *Men and Sex*, 61–83, NewYork: John Wiley & Sons.

Jones, M. (1987), *Getting it On: The Clothing of Rock and Roll*, New York: Abbeville Press Publishers.

Joseph, J. (1992), *Selected Poems*, Tarset, England: Bloodaxe.

Kaiser, S. B., (1997), *The Social Psychology of Clothing: Symbolic Appearances in Context*, New York: Fairchild Publications.

Kaiser, S.B., Nagasawa, R.H. and Hutton, S.S. (1995), 'Construction of an SI theory of Fashion: Part I. Ambivalence and Change', *Clothing and Textiles Research Journal*, 13(3): 172–83.

Keenan, B. (1977), *The Women We Wanted to Look Like*, London: Macmillan.

Khan, N. (1992), 'Asian Women's Dress: From Burqah to Bloggs – Changing Clothes for Changing Times', 61–74, in J. Ash and E. Wilson (eds), *Chic Thrills: A Fashion Reader*, Berkeley and Los Angeles, California: University of California Press.

Khan, N. (2000), 'Catwalk Politics', in S. Bruzzi and P. Church Gibson (eds), *Fashion Cultures: Theories, Explorations and Analysis*, London and New York: Routledge.

Kidwell, C.B. (1989), 'Gender Symbols or Fashionable Details?' in C.B. Kidwell and V. Steele (eds), *Men and Women: Dressing the Part*, 124–43, Washington DC: Smithsonian Institution.

Kidwell, C.B. and Steele, V. (1989), *Men and Women: Dressing the Part*, Washington DC: Smithsonian Institution.

Kim, H.J. and DeLong, M.R. (1992), 'Sino-Japanism in Western Women's Fashionable Dress in *Harper's Bazaar*, 1890–1927', *Clothing and Textiles Research Journal* (11)1: 24–30.

King, C.W. (1963), 'Fashion Adoption: A Rebuttal to the "Trickle Down" Theory', in S.A. Greyser (ed.), *Toward Scientific Marketing*, 108–25, Chicago: American Marketing Association.

König, R. (1973), *A La Mode*, New York: Seabury Press.

Kroeber, A. (1919), 'On the Principle of Order in Civilization as Exemplified by Changes in Fashion', *American Anthropologist*, New Series, 21(3): 235–63.

Krugman, P. (2002), 'The Class Wars: The End of Middle-Class America (and the Triumph of the Plutocrats)', *New York Times* Magazine, October 20, 2002, 62–7, 76–7, 141.

Kuczynski, A. (2004a), 'Peter Pan Collars in a Vintage Never-Never Land', *New York Times*, June 1, 2006, E4.

Kuczynski, A. (2004b), 'Now You See It, Now You Don't', *New York Times*, September 4, 2004, archives.

La Ferla, R. (2005), 'Over the Shoulder, Over the Top', *New York Times*, October 6, 2005, E1, 9.

Lakin, D.M. (2006), 'It Costs HOW Much?' *Watch Your Time: Special Watch Edition, New York Times* (Special Advertising Supplement), October 15, 2006, 30–2.

Lehman, U. (2000), *Tigersprung: Fashion and Modernity*, Cambridge, Massachusetts and London: The MIT Press.

Leibenstein, H. (1950), 'Bandwagon, Snob, and Veblen Effects in the Theory of Consumers' Demand', *Quarterly Journal of Economics*, 64(2): 183–207.

Leland, J. (2006a), 'Rebels With a Cross', *New York Times*, March 2, 2006, E1–2.

Leland, J. (2006b), 'A Spirit of Belonging, Inside and Out', *New York Times*, October 8, 2006, archives.

Levy, A. (2005), *Female Chauvinist Pig: Women and the Rise of Raunch Culture*, New York, London, Toronto, and Sydney: Freepress.

Litewka, J. (1974), 'The Socialized Penis', *Liberation*, 18(7): 61–69.

Lowe, J. and Lowe, E. (1982), 'Cultural Pattern and Process: A Study of Stylistic Change in Women's Dress', *American Anthropologist*, New Series, 84(3): 521–44.

Lowe, J. and Lowe, E. (1985), 'Quantitative Analysis of Women's Dress', in M. Solomon (ed.), *The Psychology of Fashion*, Lexington, MA: Lexington Books.

Lynch, A., Stalp, M.B. and Radina, E. (2007), 'Growing Old and Dressing (dis)Gracefully', in D.C. Johnson and H. Foster (eds), *Senses of Dress*, London: Berg.

Maslow, A. (1943), 'A Theory of Human Motivation', *Psychological Review*, 50: 370–96.

McCracken, G. (1985), 'The Trickle Down Theory Rehabilitated', in M. Solomon (ed.), *The Psychology of Fashion*, Lexington, MA: Lexington Books.

McCracken, G. (1988), *Culture and Consumption: New Approaches to the Symbolic Character of Consumer Goods and Activities*, Bloomington: Indiana University Press.

McLaughlin, N. (2004), 'Rock, Fashion and Performativity', in S. Bruzzi and P. Church Gibson (eds), *Fashion Cultures: Theories, Explorations and Analysis*, London and New York: Routledge.

McMurry, M.P. and Wilson, L. (2003), 'Jackie: Gateway to Style, Taste and Social Change', *International Textile and Apparel Proceedings #60*.

Miller, C.M., McIntyre, S.H. and Mantrala, K.M. (1993), 'Toward Formalizing Fashion Theory', *Journal of Marketing Research*, 30(May): 142–57.

Miller, J. (2005), 'In PERSON: A Bag Lady with Panache', *New York Times*, February 6, 2005, archives.

Miller, L. (2000), 'The Many Figures of Eve: Styles of Womanhood Embodied in a Late-Nineteenth-Century Corset', in J.D. Prown and K. Haltman (eds), *American Artifacts: Essays in Material Culture*, East Lansing, Michigan: Michigan University Press.

References

Mitchell, J. (1966), *The Circle Game*, Siquomb Publishing Co. BMI.

Munro, T. (1970), *Form and Style in the Visual Arts: An Introduction to Aesthetic Morphology*, Cleveland: The Press of Case Western Reserve University.

Navarro, M. (2004), 'The Most Private of Makeovers', *New York Times*, November 28, 2004, S1.

Nystrom, P. (1928), *Economics of Fashion*, New York: Ronald Press Company.

Oakes, J. and Riewe, R. (1992), 'A Comparison of Historical and Contemporary Skin Clothing Used in North Greenland: An Ethnohistorical Approach', *Clothing and Textiles Research Journal* (10)3: 76–85.

Pannabecker, R.K. (1986), 'Ribbonwork of the Great Lakes Indians: The material of acculturation' (Doctoral dissertation, Ohio State University, 1986), *Dissertations Abstracts International*, 47, 961A-962A.

Pannabecker, R.K. (1988), 'The Cultural Authentication of Ribbon: Use and Test of a Concept', *Clothing and Textiles Research Journal* (7)1: 55–6.

Pannabecker, R.K. (1996), '"Tastily Bound with Ribands": Ribbon-bordered Dress of the Great Lakes Indians, 1735–1839', *Clothing and Textiles Research Journal* (14):4, 267–75.

Pareles, J. (2006), 'Korean Superstar Who Smiles and Says, "I'm Lonely"', *New York Times*, February 4, 2006, archives.

Pareles, J. (2006), 'Korean Superstar Who Smiles and Says, "I'm Lonely"', *New York Times*, February 4, 2006, archives.

Payne, B., Winakor, G. and Farrell-Beck, J. (1992), *The History of Costume*, New York: HarperCollins Publishers.

Pesendorfer, W. (1995), 'Design Innovation and Fashion Cycles', *American Economic Review*, 85(4): 771–92.

Pesendorfer, W. (2004), 'Response to "Fashion Cycles in Economics"', *Econ Journal Watch*, 1(3): 455–64.

Pesendorfer, W. (2005), 'Second Reply to Coelho, Klein, and McClure', *Econ Journal Watch*, 2(1): 42–6.

Poiret, P. (1931) *King of Fashion: The Autobiography of Paul Poiret*, translated by S.H. Grasset, Philadelphia and London: J.B. Lippincott Co.

Polhemus, T. (1978), *Fashion and Anti-Fashion: Anthropology of Clothing and Adornment*, London: Thames and Hudson.

Prown, J.D. (1982), 'Mind in Matter: An Introduction to Material Culture Theory and Method', *Winterthur Portfolio* (17): 1–19.

Prown, J.D. and Haltman, K. (2000), *American Artifacts: Essays in Material Culture*, East Lansing, Michigan: Michigan University Press.

Regnerus, M., Smith, C. and Fritsch, M. (2003), *Religion in the Lives of American Adolescents: A Review of Literature*, National Study of Youth and Religion, Report #3.

Reich, J. (2000), 'Undressing the Latin Lover: Marcello Mastroianni, Fashion and "La dolce vita"', in S. Bruzzi and P. Church Gibson (eds), *Fashion Cultures: Theories, Explorations and Analysis*, London and New York: Routledge.

Reisman, D. (1965), *The Lonely Crowd*, New Haven: Yale University Press.

Reynolds, F. and Darden, W. (1972), 'Why the Midi Failed', *Journal of Advertising Research*, 12: 39–44.

Rich, F. (2006), 'The Rove Da Vinci Code', *New York Times*, May 21, 2006, archives.

Richardson, J. and Kroeber, A. (1973 [1940]), 'Three Centuries of Women's Dress Fashions: A Quantitative Analysis', in G. Willis and D. Midgley (eds), *Fashion Marketing* (1973), 47–105, London: Allen and Unwin.

Robertson, C. (2005), 'BOLDFACE', *New York Times*, April 5, 2005, archives.

Robinson, D. (1958), 'Fashion Theory and Product Design', *Harvard Business Review*, 36(6): 126–38.

Robinson, D. (1961), 'The Economics of Fashion Demand', *Quarterly Journal of Economics*, 75(3): 376–98.

Robinson, D. (1975), 'Style Changes: Cyclical, Inexorable, and Foreseeable', *Harvard Business Review*, 53: 121–31.

Robinson, D. (1976), 'Fashions in Shaving and Trimming of the Beard: The Men of the Illustrated London News', *American Journal of Sociology*, 81(5): 1133–9.

Rogers, E. (2003), *Diffusion of Innovations*, New York: The Free Press.

Rubin, R. (2006), 'Not Far From Forsaken', *New York Times* Magazine, April 9, 2006, archives.

Russell, D. (1983), *Costume History and Style*, Englewood Cliffs, New Jersey: Prentice Hall.

Santelli, R. and Dylan, B. (2005), *Bob Dylan Scrapbook, 1956–1966*, New York: Simon & Schuster.

Schechner, R. (1977), *Essays on Performance Theory, 1970–1976*, New York: Drama Books Specialists.

Schechner, R. (1985), *Between Theatre and Anthropology*, Philadelphia: University of Pennsylvania Press.

Schwichtenberg, C. (1993), *The Madonna Connection*, Boulder, San Francisco and Oxford: Westview Press.

Sciolino, D. (2003), 'Ban Religious Attire in School, French Panel Says', *New York Times,* December 12, 2003, archives.

Simmel, G. (1904), 'Fashion', *International Quarterly*, 10: 130–55.

Slotkin, R. (1992), *Gunfighter Nation: The Myth of the Frontier in Twentieth Century America*, Norman: University of Oklahoma Press.

Solomon, M. (1985), *The Psychology of Fashion*, Lexington, MA: Lexington Books.

Solomon, M. and Englis, B. (2000), 'Consumer Preferences for Apparel and Textile Products as a Function of Lifestyle Imagery', *National Textile Center Research Briefs*.

Spencer, H. (1924), *The Principles of Sociology*, New York and London: Appleton.

Sproles, G. (1981), 'Analyzing Fashion Life Cycles – Principles and Perspective', *Journal of Marketing*, 45: 116–24.

Sproles, G. and Burns, L. (1994), *Changing Appearances: Understanding Dress in Contemporary Society*, New York: Fairchild Publications.

St. John, Warren (2005), 'What Men Want: Neanderthal TV', *New York Times*, December 11, 2005, archives.

St. John, Warren (2006), 'Dude, Here's My Book', *New York Times*, April 16, 2006, archives.

Steele, V. (1985), *Fashion and Eroticism: Ideals of Feminine Beauty from the Victorian Era to the Jazz Age*, New York and Oxford: Oxford University Press.

Steele, V. (1988), *Paris Fashion: A Cultural History*, New York and Oxford: Oxford University Press.

Steele, V. (1989), 'Dressing for Work', in C.B. Kidwell and V. Steele, *Men and Women: Dressing the Part*, 64–91,Washington DC: Smithsonian Institution.

Steele, V. (1996), *Fetish: Fashion, Sex and Power*, New York and Oxford: Oxford University Press.

Steele, V. (1997), *Fifty Years of Fashion: New Look to Now*, New Haven and London: Yale University Press.

Stone, G.P. (1965), 'Appearance and the Self', in M.E. Roach and J.B. Eicher (eds), *Dress, Adornment and the Social Order*, 216–45, New York: John Wiley and Sons.

Strandberg, K.W. (2006a), 'Like a Phoenix: The Stunning Rebirth of the Mechanical Watch', *Watch Your Time: Special Watch Edition*, *New York Times* (Special Advertising Supplement), October 15, 2006, 21–8.

Strandberg, K.W. (2006b), 'Lights, Camera . . . Watches?' *Watch Your Time: Special Watch Edition*, *New York Times* (Special Advertising Supplement), October 15, 2006, 52–4.

Strother, Z.S. (1995), 'Invention and Reinvention in the Traditional Arts', *African Arts*, Spring 1995, 24–33.

Suarez, J.A. (1996), *Bike Boys, Drag Queens, and Superstars: Avant-Garde, Mass Culture, and Gay Identities in the 1960s Underground Cinema*, Bloomington and Indianapolis: Indiana University Press.

Sullivan, J. (2006), *Jeans: A Cultural History of an American Icon*, New York: Gotham Books.

Taylor, L. (2002), *The Study of Dress History*, Manchester and New York: Manchester University Press.

Thurman, J. (2003), 'Broad Stripe, Bright Stars: The Spring-Summer Men's Fashion Shows in Milan and Paris', *The New Yorker*, July 28.

Trebay, G. (2006a), 'A Tremor of Rebellion', *New York Times*, February 9, 2006, E1 and E7.

Trebay, G. (2006b), 'Being Bad: The Career Move', *New York Times*, April 20, 2006, E1, E9.

Trebay, G. (2006c), 'Back to the Beach', *New York Times*, June 1, 2006, E1, E5.

Trebay, G. (2006d), 'A Judy is Born', *New York Times*, June 4, 2006, E1.

Trebay, G. (2006e), 'Radical Chic: Two Designers Use a Paris Show to Demonstrate that Fashion and Politics Can Mix', *New York Times*, October 6, 2006, E1, E8.

Troy, N. (2003), *Couture Culture: A Study in Modern Art and Fashion*, Cambridge and London: The MIT Press.

Tulloch, C. (1992), 'Rebel Without a Pause: Black Street Style & Black Designers', in J. Ash and E. Wilson (eds), *Chic Thrills: A Fashion Reader*, Berkeley: University of California Press.

Turner, T.S. (1980), 'The Social Skin', in J. Cherfas and R. Lewin (eds), *Not Work Alone: A Cross-Cultural View of Activities Superfluous to Survival*, 112–40, Beverly Hills: Sage Publications.

Turner, V. (1988), *The Anthropology of Performance*, New York: PAJ Publications.

Uzanne, L. (1898), *Fashion in Paris: The Various Phases of Feminine Taste and Aesthetics from 1797 to 1897*, London: William Heinemann.

VALS™ (2006), http://www.sric-bi.com/VALS/types.shtml (accessed May 24, 2006).

Veblen, T. (1894), 'The Economic Theory of Women's Dress', *Popular Science Monthly*, 46: 198–205.

Veblen, T. (1899), *The Theory of the Leisure Class*, New York: The Modern Library.

Vinken, B. (2005), *Fashion Zeitgeist: Trends and Cycles in the Fashion System*, Oxford and New York: Berg.

Von Boehn, M. (1933), translated by Joan Joshua, *Modes and Manners: Volume III*, Philadelphia: J.B. Lippincott Company.

Von Drehle, D. (2003), *Triangle: The Fire that Changed America*, New York: Grove Press.

Wadler, J. (2004), 'Boldface Names', *New York Times*, August 12, 2004, archives.

Walker, R. (2005a), 'Middle-age, Bring it On', *New York Times* Magazine, January 30, 2005.

Walker, R. (2005b), 'Girls Just Want to Belong', *New York Times* Magazine, August 21, 2005.

Walker, R. (2006a), 'Faux Logo: A Brand That Appeals to the Toughest Consumers—The Ones Who are Sick of Brands', *New York Times* Magazine, May 14, 2006, 24.

Walker, R. (2006b), 'The Princess Buy', *New York Times* Magazine, October 15, 2006, 26.

Weeden, P. (1977), 'Study Patterned on Kroeber's Investigation of Style', *Dress*, 3: 9–19.

Weil, St E. and DeWeese, G.D. (2004), *Western Shirts: A Classic American Fashion*, Salt Lake City, Utah: Gibbs Smith, Publisher.

Welters, L. (1981), 'Greek chemises in American collections', unpublished doctoral dissertation, University of Minnesota.

Welters, L. (1992), 'Greek Folk Dress: Application of the Ethnohistorical Method', *Clothing and Textiles Research Journal* (10)3: 29–35.

Welters, L. (1999), 'The Peloponnesian "Zonari": A Twentieth-century String Skirt', in L. Welters (ed.), *Folk Dress in Europe and Anatolia: Beliefs About Protection and Fertility*, 53–70, Oxford and New York: Berg.

Welters, L. (2002), 'Material Culture: Textiles in Women's Lives', *International Textile and Apparel Proceedings*, #59.

White, S. and White, G. (1998), *Stylin: African American Expressive Culture from its Beginnings to the Zoot Suit*, Ithaca and London: Cornell University Press.

Williams, A. (2006), 'Here I Am Taking My Own Picture', *New York Times*, February 19, 2006, ST1 and ST12.

Williams, W.L. (1986), *The Spirit and the Flesh: Sexual Diversity in American Indian Culture*, Boston: Beacon Press.

Wilson, E. (2003 [1985]), *Adorned in Dreams: Fashion and Modernity*, New Brunswick, New Jersey: Rutgers University Press.

Wilson, E. (2005a), 'Fashion Refigured', *New York Times*, May 12, 2005, S1.

Wilson, E. (2005b), 'The Mohawk Becomes, Well, Cute', *New York Times*, September 1, 2005, archives.

Wilson, L. (2001), 'American Cowboy Dress: Function to Fashion', *Dress* 28: 40–52.

Wolf, J. (2006), 'And You Thought Abercrombie and Fitch Were Pushing It', *New York Times* Magazine, April 23, 2006, archives.

Young, A.B. (1966), *Recurring Cycles in Fashion, 1760–1937*, New York: Cooper Square Publishers.

Young, K. (1956), *Social Psychology* (Third Edition), New York: Appleton-Century-Crofts.

Zeitz, J. (2006), *Flapper: A Madcap Story of Sex, Style, Celebrity, and the Women Who Who Made America Modern*, New York: Crown Publishers.

Index

2601718164